Flyrodding Florida Salt-

How and Where to Catch Saltwater Fish on Flies in the Sunshine State

by Captain John A. Kumiski

<u>High Praise for the First Edition of Flyrodding Florida Salt</u>:

"What a great number of gifts you have given me through your great book... it was loaded with everything that I could possibly want" -Terry Baird, Portland, OR

"You did a fine job. Some guides are going to be horrified."
-Bernard "Lefty" Kreh, Cockeysville, MD

"Flyrodding Florida Salt is a darn fine book. I wouldn't be without it in my travels around Florida." -Charlie Richter, Miami, FL

"With the information gleaned from your book we were able to find a piscatorial gold mine. Thank you for your help and insight." -John Madert, Gaithersburg, MD

"This book contains an unbelievable amount of information for light tackle anglers. I would recommend this book to anyone." -Mike Ware, Panama City, FL

"This book is a wealth of information. If it was Kumiski's intent to write the definitive book about fly fishing in Florida, he succeeded admirably." -David Lambert, Jacksonville, FL

"For any saltwater fly rodder living in Florida or going there sometime, this book is a must read." -C. Boyd Pfeiffer, Phoenix, MD

"This book is a must for the angler who wants to fish Florida without a guide."
-Lou Tabory, Ridgefield, CT

"A practical, easy-to-follow guide for anyone who wants to explore the rich saltwater fly fishing opportunities Florida has to offer." -Ed Jaworowski, Chester Springs, PA

Argonaut Publishing Company
Chuluota, FL

Cover design by Barry Kent, Kent Advertising, 352.751.0966.

Flyrodding Florida Salt- How and Where to Catch Saltwater Fish on Flies in the Sunshine State– Revised Edition

BY CAPTAIN JOHN A. KUMISKI

Published by:
 Argonaut Publishing Company
 284 Clearview Road
 Chuluota, FL 32766
 U.S.A.

Publisher's Cataloging in Publication Data
Kumiski, John A., 1952-
Flyrodding Florida Salt: how to find and catch saltwater fish on flies in the Sunshine State
/ by John A. Kumiski.
  p. cm.
  Includes bibliographical references and index.
  Preassigned LCCN:
  ISBN 0-9635118-5-8

  1. Saltwater fly fishing--Florida--Guidebooks. 2.
Florida-- Guidebooks. I. Title.

WARNING-DISCLAIMER

This book is designed to provide information in regard to the subject matter covered. It is not, and was never intended to be, a substitute for good judgment or common sense. The reader ventures into or onto the water at his or her own risk.

Every effort has been made to make this book as complete and as accurate as possible. However, there may be mistakes both typographical and in content. Therefore, this book should be used only as a general guide and not as the ultimate source of boating or fly fishing information.

The purpose of this book is to educate and entertain. The author and Argonaut Publishing Company shall have neither liability nor responsibility to any person with any loss or damage caused, or alleged to be caused, directly or indirectly by the information contained in this book. If the reader does not wish to be bound by the above, he may return this book to Argonaut Publishing Company for a complete refund.

Table of Contents

Section Two, Where-to, continued

Section 3- Flies for Florida Salt

Acknowledgements

This book would never have happened without the cooperation and help of literally dozens of people. Steve Baker and Ron Rebeck took me under their "wings" when I got to Florida over 20 years ago, and showed me much that I didn't know about saltwater fishing here. I will always be in their debt.

During fifteen years of writing for magazines I have had the pleasure of fishing with many of the guides interviewed in this book. I learned a lot from every single one of them.

I have to thank the incredibly talented Barry Kent for once again designing the covers, and the people at Stren Fishing Lines for allowing me to use some of their knot illustrations.

Suggestions for improvements in the original edition came from some of the best known and most respected names in saltwater fly fishing: Ed Jaworowski, Lefty Kreh, Boyd Pfeiffer, and Lou Tabory. Thank you, gentlemen.

My proof reader for this edition was Scott Radloff. Thank you, sir!

But the folks who really made the book were the interviewees, mostly guides but others who are simply extremely knowledgeable saltwater fly fishers. They are: Russell Tharin, John Bottko, Larry Miniard, Steve Moore, Kent Gibbens, Mike Hakala, Ron Rebeck, Rodney Smith, Terry Parsons, Eric Davis, Marcia Foosaner, George LaBonte, Steve Kantner, Carl Ball, Jim Weber, Bob Branham, Lee Baker, Ben Taylor, Steve Huff, Tim Borski, Nat Ragland, Jose Wejebe, Dexter Simmons, Jeffrey Cardenas, Rick Murphy, Flip Pallot, Joe McNichols, Al Keller, Todd Geroy, Steve Bailey, Zeke Sieglaff, Phil O'Bannon, Pete Greenan, Tommy Locke, Rick Grassett, Paul Hawkins, Dan Malzone, Mike Locklear, Jim Dupre, Tommy Thompson, Sam LaNeave, Dave Lear, Trey Landry, the late Mike Ware, Buddy Dortch, James Pic, Paul Darby, Gordie Hinds, Bob Gray, and Hugh Smith.

You all have my most sincere thanks. I am grateful and deeply indebted to each and every one of you, for without your cooperation and information this project would never have reached fruition.

Introduction

Dear Reader,

You're holding the newly revised edition of Flyrodding Florida Salt. You've picked up this book because you need information about fly fishing in Florida's saltwater. You need to know what tackle to use, and how to rig that tackle. You need to know what techniques work, and which ones do not. You need to know some fly patterns that are effective, and how to tie them. You need to know, probably more than anything else, where to go to find Florida's great saltwater gamefish.

This book contains all that information, and _more_!

Since the original edition of <u>Flyrodding Florida Salt</u> was printed in 1995, many things have changed in Florida's fishing scene. New guides have appeared, while others have vanished. It seems like every area code in the state has changed. New techniques and flies have been developed. And it should come as no surprise that I have learned a whole lot more about fishing opportunities here, which I pass on to you in the pages of this book.

Like the original, this book is divided into three sections. The first section has three chapters, which discuss tackle, techniques, and describes most of the species you are likely to encounter while fishing in Florida salt.

The second section contains the results of interviews with dozens of top fly fishing guides from all sections of the Florida coast. New sections have been added– Amelia Island, Jupiter, Marco Island, Steinhatchee, and Apalachicola. In these interviews the guides, both the ones originally included and a bunch of new (to this book at least) ones share information on access, types of fishing available, best times of the year, favorite spots and flies, and a great deal of little known how-to information.

The third section discusses fly selection and contains detailed descriptions on tying locally important fly patterns. What you will find are some of the classic saltwater patterns like the Deceiver and the Seaducer, and some more modern patterns like the Merkin Crab, or my own SexyFlies.

The appendix includes information on getting licensed to fish, an index, and a Resource Catalog for those wanting even more information.

The Florida coastline is more than 2000 miles long. No one individual could possibly 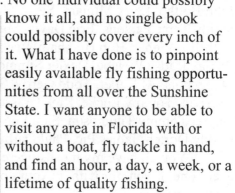 know it all, and no single book could possibly cover every inch of it. What I have done is to pinpoint easily available fly fishing opportunities from all over the Sunshine State. I want anyone to be able to visit any area in Florida with or without a boat, fly tackle in hand, and find an hour, a day, a week, or a lifetime of quality fishing.

Try the book on for size, and let me know how it helps you. I welcome your corrections, comments, criticism, and of course praise, too! I love good news, especially when I helped make it happen! I'm available at 407.977.5207, or at spotted-tail@spottedtail.com.

Good luck fly fishing in Florida's great saltwaters!

Captain John A. Kumiski

The author during simpler times, circa 1956, at Monponsett Pond in Halifax, Massachusetts. Photo by John Kumiski (my father).

6

Chapter 1   Get Ready!

A young angler faces a school of tarpon on a Gulfside flat.

Shaking with excitement, a lone angler sat on the boat's deck and forced himself to calm down. Surrounding his boat in the crystalline water swam the cause of his excitement, hundreds of big tarpon looking like small submarines as they cruised and rolled.

Composure regained, he stood up and presented his fly to one of the giants. The tarpon obliged, and the biggest fish of his life shot into the air, attached to his hand by means of a graphite wand and a gossamer leader.

Florida rightly owns a heady reputation as a fly fishing destination. The "glamour" species (bonefish, permit, and tarpon) get a lot of press, but there are so many other opportunities for saltwater fly rodders. Redfish may keep more guides working than any other species in the state. They hit flies readily and exceed thirty pounds in the Indian River Lagoon system. While casting a popping bug in most parts of the state a five pound and sometimes larger seatrout is always a possibility.

Snook make an exceptional fly rod target, and commonly reach double digit weights. Cobia, black drum, ladyfish, jack crevalle, Spanish mackerel, bluefish, sharks, and even flounder, all these fish will take flies.

Offshore aficionados find plenty of fly fishing opportunities, too. Exciting fisheries for blackfin and yellowfin tuna exist in the Keys and elsewhere. Little tunny, called bonito along both Florida coasts, present awesome fly rod opportunities and are a formidable adversary at the end of a leader. Revered as false albacore by fly fishers in the northeast, Florida bonito are the same fish! They are available a good part of the year. Kingfish, pelagic species of sharks, and of course the (almost) always cooperative dolphin are all taken regularly by fly fishers.

A fishing trip to Florida, like any fishing trip, requires planning in order to maximize the chances for success. Unlike fishing trips to wilderness or overseas destinations, Florida anglers can readily find and purchase overlooked tackle needs. Information on fish and fishing spots is easily obtained. Fine fly shops can be found all over the state.

This chapter takes a look at various aspects of planning a trip to Florida, or within Florida for those who are Florida residents. Topics covered in this section include tackle and accessories; boats and boating; finding and hiring guides; and hazards and safety concerns for Florida's saltwater angler.

What Tackle?

Rods

Rod choice for any fishing depends on what flies you prefer using and what you hope to catch. Someone casting small glass minnow patterns for seatrout in a Panhandle creek would not need the same gear as a potential tarpon tamer on a Homosassa flat. You must also consider your own skills as a caster and a fish fighter.

For day-in, day-out fishing for redfish, snook, bonefish, and seatrout the best choice for most folks would be a nine foot, eight-weight rod. This stick has plenty of power to push large flies into the wind, be they streamers or surface baits like poppers or hair bugs. Unfortunately it overpowers most of the seatrout we find, but it has the strength to stop a tarpon up to fifty pounds (or larger, in skilled hands).

Good casters might appreciably increase their sport by dropping to a smaller rod, depending on fly size and the anticipated fish. You really don't need an eight-weight to subdue your average eight pound redfish. But always remember that in Florida's saltwater a fish much larger than anticipated could show up at any time.

I won't recommend specific brands or manufacturers, but almost any rod costing more than $150.00 performs well. Before running off to purchase the latest high-tech wonder from the trendy rod companies, remember those famous words from Lefty Kreh: "Most rods cast a lot better than the people using them."

Having gone through all of the above, should a different rod besides the basic 7-8-9-weight be needed for any specific type of fishing or fish, that point will be made in the specific section that deals with that particular fishery.

Reels

The "old standby" for years for saltwater use was the Pfleuger Medalist 1498. It had adequate line capacity, would not immediately self-destruct in saltwater, had a rudimentary drag system, balanced well on an eight-or nine-weight rod, and was inexpensive enough (about fifty dollars) to be considered a starter reel. Sadly these reels are now made overseas and the quality of the product has decreased markedly.

The past few years have seen the market for saltwater fly reels simply explode. Redington, Teton, Valentine, Ross, Scientific Anglers, Lamson, Orvis, and STH all manufacture reels in the $150-250 price range. These reels are quality pieces of equipment with good drag systems, and provide as much reel as most anglers ever need.

For the person who wants the best, get out the wallet and take a look at reels like the

A selection of saltwater fly reels. From left: Medalist 1798, Valentine, Scientific Anglers, Fin-Nor.

Tibor, Islander, Bauer, or Abel. There are several manufacturers of premium fly reels, all of whom ask plenty for their products. These reels are made for those who take pleasure in owning the finest, and will last for several lifetimes with a modicum of care. Regardless of the reel you get, make sure it balances properly with the rod!

Lines
"Oh, what a tangled web we weave..." -Sir Walter Scott, <u>The Lay of the Last Minstrel</u>

The number of specialty fly line types on the market rapidly approaches mind boggling proportions. Most anglers fishing Florida need to purchase a weight-forward, floating line first. A saltwater or bass bug taper works well for general use.

While some manufacturers want you to believe that without a bonefish taper you can't catch a bonefish, the fish don't care what type of taper you use. If you spend the majority of your fishing time bonefishing, the bonefish tapers work wonderfully. However, an angler throwing hairbugs at seatrout near St. Augustine in November will likely find that the bonefish tapers simply become too stiff to work well in those cooler temperatures .

Not all Florida fly fishing occurs in shallow water. Certain circumstances require lines other than floating types. Surf casting offers a good example. When casting streamers from a beach an intermediate sinking line often performs better than a floating line. The line sinks beneath the wave action, giving the angler a better feel for the fly and what it is doing.

Another example is sight fishing for tarpon in the Keys, or along the west coast. The fish often travel in water 10 or 12 feet deep. They might never see a fly cast on a floating line, but an intermediate sinking type pulls the fly down near their level.

Yet another example would be fishing in canals or at power plant outflows during the winter. The fish sometimes huddle together in incredibly tight masses right down on the bottom. A sink-tip or even a high density shooting head gets the fly down to the fish. A floating line keeps the fly near the surface and is completely useless in either of these situations.

The moral of this tale is that a fly fisher who intends to be prepared for all contingencies will have floating, slow sinking, and fast sinking lines available, and will not hesitate to change lines when the situation dictates.

Regardless of the line you choose, fill the reel as full as possible by adding backing underneath the fly line. Attach the backing, usually 20 pound test Dacron for an eight- or a nine-weight, at the rear of the fly line. Then a big fish can continue its run without coming up abruptly against the end of the line.

The strongest way to attach backing to fly line entails whipping a loop in the end of the line. Tie a Bimini twist in the backing, then simply loop the two together. A correctly looped connection resembles a square knot. This connection further has the advantage of making line changes on a single spool relatively easy. Just unloop one line off and loop on the next.

How much backing do you need? As much as you can fit on the reel. The line should come close to brushing the reel pillars when it's all wound onto the reel.

For smaller fish on lighter tackle, 20 pound Dacron is standard. For bonefish you need 150 to 200 yards of this. If you've got enough for bones, you'll be able to handle most anything that comes along that you would tackle with a 7-, 8-, or 9-weight rod.

For big tarpon, or sailfish or other offshore species, you need more and heavier backing. Two hundred fifty to 300 yards of 30 pound dacron is standard for tarpon, and offshore more is better. Special reels are available for big game offshore fly fishing which will hold 500 or even 600 yards of 30 pound Dacron.

One other word about backing- the braided, high tensile strength lines offered by several manufacturers is making Dacron obsolete, at least as backing for big game fish. Thirty pound braid has the diameter of eight pound mono, so any given spool can hold two to three times as many yards of the braid as Dacron- an obvious advantage when a 150 pound tuna heads for the African coast.

The braided line has almost no stretch, either. Doug Hannon told me he rolls tarpon over at 100 yards when using this braid. I've heard from other anglers that the small diameter and low stretch of this material can cause severe cuts if you touch it carelessly while it's under tension. Be forewarned.

10

Leader Systems

We all know that the most important link between any fisherman and the fish he seeks is the hook. Although it does happen, in most saltwater fly fishing a sharp hook seldom fails. Typically, the critical link between the fish and the fly fisherman is the leader. The leader is involved in most fly tackle system failures. Let's examine different types of leader systems for saltwater applications.

The first item of business is the line-to-leader connection. I present here my favorite way of making this connection, the whipped loop. It may not be elegant but it never fails. Other methods can be used.

To do this, make a loop in the end of the fly line by doubling it back on itself. Then use a piece of 15 or 20 pound monofilament to make a snell knot over the loop. If you learn to do this you can do it anywhere, and the only tool you need is a pair of pliers (which most of us carry) to pull the knot up. You can then easily connect the looped end of the leader butt to the loop at the end of the fly line.

For those who prefer, several brands of both knotless and knotted tapered leaders for saltwater are on the market. I prefer to make my own leaders, but if you don't you'll have no choice but to use these ready-made products.

Consider using fluorocarbon leader material for your tippets. Fluorocarbon has an index of refraction close to that of water, which supposedly makes it more difficult to see while in the water. I don't know about that but it definitely gets more strikes.

Fluorocarbon is also more dense than water, so it sinks readily. The manufacturers claim it has better knot strength and more abrasion resistance than nylon, and my own tests verify the latter claim. My tests also clearly show that leader-shy fish will hit flies tied to fluorocarbon tippets much more readily. Although fluorocarbon costs much more than nylon, you will get more strikes if you use fluorocarbon tippets. Considering the investment you have in your other tackle components, tippet material is a minor and worthwhile expense.

For those who prefer tying their own, the basic leader design is the tapered leader without a shock tippet. This works fine for nonabrasive species of fish, such as bonefish, permit, redfish, and seatrout. The basic formula for the tapered leader is 60-20-20, that is, 60 percent butt, 20 percent taper, and 20 percent class tippet. Please realize that this is only a starting point. Experiment with this until you get the result you want.

So, a typical ten foot bonefish leader for a seven through nine weight system consists of six feet of 30 pound test, a foot of 20, a foot of 15, and two feet of 10, with all the sections joined by blood or double surgeon's knots. Remember that leader length is a compromise and must be adjusted to suit conditions. Longer leaders spook fewer fish but cause more problems when casting, particularly with large or wind-resistant flies. Again, experimentation produces the best results.

If we wanted a leader for permit with a ten or eleven weight system we would increase the butt section to 40 pound test. The larger diameter of the fly line calls for a larger diameter monofilament in the butt of the leader. Then our taper section would consist of a foot of 20, a foot of 17, and lastly two feet of 14 pound fluorocarbon for the tippet (some permit angler make the entire leader out of fluorocarbon). Bigger fish, bigger flies, bigger system.

Having said all this, I never bother with tapered leaders anymore. I use big game style tippets for all saltwater applications. This leader has only two sections, a butt and a tippet, joined by a loop to loop connection. Fewer knots means fewer places for breakage.

The leader butt usually consists of five to seven feet of 30 pound mono for seven–

through nine-weights, or 40 or 50 pound mono for heavier rods. Both ends of the butt section have loops formed by a double surgeon's loop. One end is looped to the fly line, the other to a specially prepared 16 pound (or 12 pound, or 20 pound) class tippet.

To prepare the tippet, tie a small loop in one end using a Bimini twist. Tie a loop on the doubled end, using a double surgeon's loop. After trimming all the tags, loop it to the butt section. The tippet should be long enough to give you a leader of 10 feet or so in length.

Like my line to leader connection, this leader lacks elegance. It turns over well with most saltwater flies though, and most importantly the only place it ever breaks (other than at wind knots) is at the fly. The astute and well prepared angler will tie several of these up at home and carry them afield in a labeled ziplock bag.

If your target is a species of fish with an abrasive mouth you'll need to add a shock, or bite, tippet. Use 30 pound fluorocarbon for snook, ladyfish, and baby tarpon, 60 or 80 pound fluorocarbon for large tarpon, and single strand or Tyger wire for sharks, bluefish, or barracuda.

When adding a shock tippet, it should be as short as you think you can get by with. Short shock tippets are less noticeable to the fish. For those interested in IGFA regulations for record, the shock tippet must be less than 12 inches long including the knots. You can attach the class tippet to the shock by a variety of methods. Again, for those interested in records, the class tippet must be at least 16 inches long excluding the knots.

The standby for years used to attach shock to class tippets has been the Albright special. You can use other knots, including the double surgeon's or the Hufnagle, depending on the diameters of the two lines being joined. If the diameters are relatively close, the double surgeons works well. For a greater difference a Hufnagle is superior. All of these knots are supposed to permanently attach the shock leader to the class tippet.

When using a singlestrand wire trace for toothy critters, attach the wire (#2 or #3 single strand) to the fly with a haywire twist. Attach the other end of the wire, which should be three or four inches long, to a short piece of 30 pound mono with an Albright special. You then join the shock tippet to the class tippet by whatever means you like.

The new Tyger wire leader material makes it easier to use wire for bite tippets. You can tie knots in it as if it were nylon, which is a lot simpler than tying Haywire twists.

One thing to keep in mind is that adding any of this stuff to the far end of the leader usually makes casting more difficult. You may need to shorten your leader until casting becomes comfortable again.

All the above presupposes the use of a floating or an intermediate fly line. What about going deep by using a sink-tip line or a high density shooting head?

In deep water the splash of the line as it hits the water doesn't spook the fish. Since you want to get the fly down, use a short leader. A long leader allows the fly to ride up well above the level of the line. Short in this situation means only two or maybe three feet, nothing more.

You sacrifice delicacy of presentation here but with the fish deep this won't be important. Although some folks just use a section of 20 or 30 pound mono looped to the end of the fly line, I suggest you make sure that the tippet's breaking strength is less than that of your backing. Your system's weakest component will then be the leader. If something breaks, it will be the tippet. You won't lose the expensive fly line.

Remember to lubricate your knots before you pull them up (use saliva), then pull them up slowly. Always test your knots before using them. It's irritating when they break in your hand, but it's much less so than when they break on a fish.

Accessories

Fly fishing seems to attract folks who love gadgets. Manufacturers respond by offering scads of them. This section only discusses those items considered essential, leaving convenience items out of the picture.

You need a good pair of fishing pliers, preferably with a wire cutter. My own preference is the Gerber Multitool. This particular tool can easily be handled with one hand while you hold onto your fish with the other. It's also very corrosion resistant.

You absolutely must have and use a good hook file. The best hook sharpening devices for saltwater hooks are carbon steel files, about four inches long. Unfortunately, these rust like crazy so prepare to purchase several every year.

Delay the inevitable by making a holster for your file. Get a piece of corrugated cardboard and wrap it around your file. Cut it to size, then place it in a small polyethylene bag like those flies come in. Soak the cardboard with three-in-one oil, silicone spray, WD-40, or some combination of these. Wrap duct tape around the bag, and your holster is complete. Keep the file in its holster when not sharpening hooks and it will last quite a bit longer.

A stripping basket comes in very handy for surf fishing or wading in weedy places. When I wanted to know more about these I called John Bottko, owner of the Salty Feather Fly Shop in Jacksonville, since he fishes the surf a lot. John said that he finds carrying a small stripping basket just as inconvenient as carrying a big ones, so use the biggest you can find. He also said that for the do it yourselfer a Rubbermaid laundry basket works well if the bottom had a LOT of holes drilled in it. If you wade out too far, wave action in the basket may tangle the line. Commercially made baskets have projections which stick up from the bottom, designed to hold the line in place. Lefty Kreh told me it's easy to hot glue projections made from weed whacker string into the bottom of a laundry basket. If you are bothered by line tangling in your laundry/stripping basket, give this a try.

Two commercially available baskets recommended by John Bottko are the William Joseph Stripping Basket, which you can view at www.williamjoseph.net/basket.aspx, and the Charlie's Total Control Stripping Basket, which can be viewed at www.flyfishbasket.com.

Every year I have fishermen come aboard my boat who have the finest tackle made, but wear clip-on sunglasses over their regular prescription glasses. This shows misplaced priorities.

First of all, God gave you but one pair of eyes. When they're gone, they're gone. They deserve the finest protection you can give them.

Secondly, if you can't see the fish your catch will almost always be small. Good vision is way more important than fancy tackle. I wear prescription sunglasses, but have also worn clip-ons, and I can assure you that there's at least a 20 percent drop in how well you see with the clip-ons. You have four surfaces collecting dirt and causing glare instead of only two.

Finally, when you're not fishing your fancy tackle sits around collecting dust. A good pair of prescription sunglasses is the finest aid to driving comfort available (outside of a $50,000 automobile).

For flats fishing in sunlight dark amber is probably the best lens color. For overcast situations light amber is preferred. Offshore anglers prefer gray lenses. All the finer glasses do an excellent job, and in spite of manufacturer's claims probably none are probably intrinsically better than the others.

Find and purchase a quality pair of sunglasses. Treat them with care and they will give your eyes years of service and protection.

A good hat likewise will help you to see. While a ball cap will do the job, in Florida sun protection is also an issue. A broad brimmed hat will help to protect your face, ears, and neck from the sun and is a worthwhile investment. The Tilley Hat offers a lifetime guarantee!

Knots

Every fly fisher will have a love-hate relationship with knots. He'll love some and hate others, some of whose use unfortunately cannot be avoided.

Saltwater fly fishers should know how to tie the following knots: Bimini twist; double surgeon's knot and loop; Albright special; clinch knot; non-slip loop; and the haywire twist. Illustrated instructions for all of these knots follow, along with some short notes for their most appropriate uses.

Clinch Knot (courtesy of Stren Fishing Lines)

Use this easy-to-tie knot to use when tying a fly to a class tippet (no shock tippet).

1) Pass the line through the eye of the hook, swivel, or lure. Double back and make five turns around the standing line.
2) Holding the coils in place, thread the tag end of the first loop above the eye, then through the big loop.
3) Hold the tag end and standing line while pulling up the coils. Make sure the coils are in a spiral, not overlapping each other. Slide against the eye.
4) Clip the tag end.

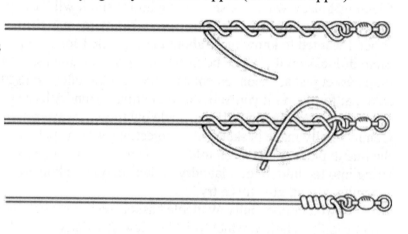

Non-slip Loop (courtesy of Stren Fishing Lines)

Use this knot to make a looped connection between the fly and the shock leader. The loop allows the fly to swing freely, giving it much more freedom of movement and better action, especially when a heavy shock leader is used.

This is an exceptionally strong loop when tied correctly. But be sure to use the right number of turns (as determined by the line's strength rating--see Step 2), and tighten your knot very carefully.

1) This is one of the few knots where you begin the knot before you insert the line in the hook's eye. Make a simple overhand knot. Bring the tag end through the eye and back through the overhand knot. You must return the tag end through the overhand knot the same way you entered it (see illustration).

2) Make the recommended number of turns with the tag end around the standing line.

Pound Test	Turns
6 to 8	7
8 to 12	5
15 to 40	4
50 to 60	3
60+	2

3) Return the tag end through the overhand knot the same way you exited the knot.

4) Draw on the tag end until the knot forms together. Then pull on the standing line to close the knot well. Finally, pull on both the tag end and standing line to assure the connection is as tight as possible.

<u>Sizing the Loop</u>

The size of the loop is determined by three factors:

1) The smaller the overhand knot, the smaller the loop. For small loops, try to make the overhand knot no more than 3/16 inch in diameter (about the size of a large split shot.

2) Once the tag end has been in-serted through the hook eye and back through the overhand knot, hold the overhand knot lightly, and pull on the tag end. This will carry the overhand knot down near the hook eye.

3) When finally closing the knot, pull out as much slack as possible between the tag end and standing line.

Bimini Twist

Use this to put a doubled line at the end of the backing so the fly line can be attached. Also use it in tying the big game leaders used for tarpon and billfish. When tied correctly, this knot maintains one-hundred percent of the line's breaking strength. Believe it or (k)not, the Bimini twist is actually an easy knot to tie. Practice it at home before you go on your trip, and it will be a snap to tie when you need it.

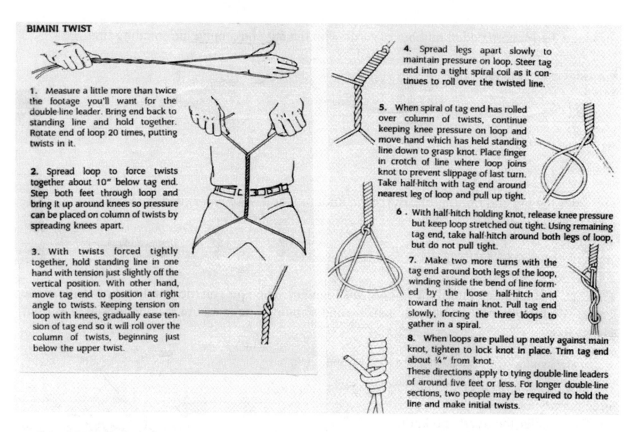

BIMINI TWIST

1. Measure a little more than twice the footage you'll want for the double-line leader. Bring end back to standing line and hold together. Rotate end of loop 20 times, putting twists in it.

2. Spread loop to force twists together about 10" below tag end. Step both feet through loop and bring it up around knees so pressure can be placed on column of twists by spreading knees apart.

3. With twists forced tightly together, hold standing line in one hand with tension just slightly off the vertical position. With other hand, move tag end to position at right angle to twists. Keeping tension on loop with knees, gradually ease tension of tag end so it will roll over the column of twists, beginning just below the upper twist.

4. Spread legs apart slowly to maintain pressure on loop. Steer tag end into a tight spiral coil as it continues to roll over the twisted line.

5. When spiral of tag end has rolled over column of twists, continue keeping knee pressure on loop and move hand which has held standing line down to grasp knot. Place finger in crotch of line where loop joins knot to prevent slippage of last turn. Take half-hitch with tag end around nearest leg of loop and pull up tight.

6. With half-hitch holding knot, release knee pressure but keep loop stretched out tight. Using remaining tag end, take half-hitch around both legs of loop, but do not pull tight.

7. Make two more turns with the tag end around both legs of the loop, winding inside the bend of line formed by the loose half-hitch and toward the main knot. Pull tag end slowly, forcing the three loops to gather in a spiral.

8. When loops are pulled up neatly against main knot, tighten to lock knot in place. Trim tag end about ¼" from knot.

These directions apply to tying double-line leaders of around five feet or less. For longer double-line sections, two people may be required to hold the line and make initial twists.

Albright Special

Use this knot to tie line to leader when the two are of dissimilar diameter, or when tying Spectra to other monofilament or fluorocarbon.

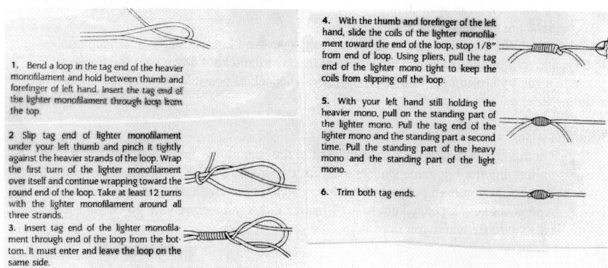

1. Bend a loop in the tag end of the heavier monofilament and hold between thumb and forefinger of left hand. Insert the tag end of the lighter monofilament through loop from the top.

2 Slip tag end of lighter monofilament under your left thumb and pinch it tightly against the heavier strands of the loop. Wrap the first turn of the lighter monofilament over itself and continue wrapping toward the round end of the loop. Take at least 12 turns with the lighter monofilament around all three strands.

3. Insert tag end of the lighter monofilament through end of the loop from the bottom. It must enter and leave the loop on the same side.

4. With the thumb and forefinger of the left hand, slide the coils of the lighter monofilament toward the end of the loop, stop 1/8" from end of loop. Using pliers, pull the tag end of the lighter mono tight to keep the coils from slipping off the loop.

5. With your left hand still holding the heavier mono, pull on the standing part of the lighter mono. Pull the tag end of the lighter mono and the standing part a second time. Pull the standing part of the heavy mono and the standing part of the light mono.

6. Trim both tag ends.

Haywire Twist

Use this to tie a hook or lure onto a piece of single strand, stainless steel wire leader.

1) Gently bend six inches of wire back onto itself. Do not put a kink in it! Twist the wires around each other.

16

2) When you have six twists in the wire, begin doing "barrel wraps" by twisting the tag end around the main piece of wire. You will need four to six barrel wraps depending on the diameter of the wire. It should look like the illustration.

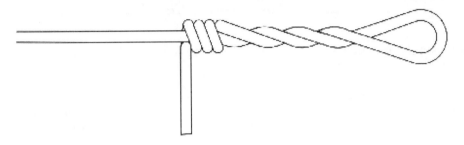

3) After finishing the barrel wraps complete the twist by placing the tag at 90 degrees to the loop. Bend the tag back and forth until it breaks off. If you do this it will not leave a sharp point, important for avoiding cuts when handling the leader.

Sometimes you'll need a bite tippet!

Double Surgeon's Knot/Loop (courtesy of Stren Fishing Lines)

   Use this to tie line to leader when their diameters are similar, or when tying a loop in the end of a piece of line.

1) Lay the line and leader alongside each other, overlapping six to eight inches.

2) Treating the two like a single line, tie an overhand knot, pulling the entire leader through the loop.

3) Leaving the loop of the overhand knot open, pull the tag ends of both the line and leader through again.

4) Hold both lines and both ends to pull the knot tight. Clip

ends close to avoid foul-ups in the rod guides.

Steve Bachman about to land a flounder from St. Joe Bay on a chilly November day.

Waders and Wading Gear

Winter in Florida often comes with windy weather. Fly casting from a boat in 20 knot winds challenges even the finest casters, and most of us just don't want to deal with it. Simply use the most elegant solution to this problem, one that trout fisherman up north have used practically forever- get in the water and wade.

Even during the summer months, many anglers find wading an effective way to fish. It's usually cooler than fishing from a boat, and allows the angler to approach the fish more closely. The aesthetics of being in the fish's own element while stalking them adds to the pleasure of fly fishing for many people.

During the summer months waders are hardly necessary (you'd sweat to death in no time), but specialized footwear makes wading more pleasant. Wading booties are the finest wading shoes made for wading Florida flats. A thick sole provides support and protection from oysters, crabs, sea urchins, and other hazards to the foot. The high, tight fitting boot top keeps sand, shells and other debris out of the boot and resists the incredible suction effect the soft marly bottoms have on shoes. They stay where they belong- on your feet.

During the winter in the northern half of the state chest waders are a must. Chest high nylon boot foot waders will work for the casual wader, but anyone who is serious will want to upgrade to neoprene or Gore-tex waders. While both these materials work well, Gore-tex waders are the ultimate in comfort.

Both neoprene and Gore-tex waders come as both boot foot and stocking foot styles. With stocking foot waders you'll need a shoe, and again, the neoprene flats booties are the best. Your standard summer booties will not fit over the waders, so you'll need a second pair about two sizes larger that your normal shoe size

If you're coming down from up north, please take my advice and leave your felt-soled wading boots at home. The muck in which most seagrasses grow sticks to that felt like you simply will not believe. In only a few minutes you'll be almost anchored to the bottom. Although you really need flats booties for serious wading here, a cheap pair of sneakers works in a pinch.

Boats

boat (bot), n. 1 a hole in the water into which one pours money

The boat. What a piece of equipment it is! Here in Florida many anglers take their boats VERY seriously. It's not unusual while on the water here to see state-of-the-art flats skiffs, only 18 feet long, which retail for well over $35,000 for a boat/motor/trailer package, especially during tarpon season. Something about tarpon brings out the true fanaticism in Florida anglers!

Undeniably these boats, the Hell's Bay, the Maverick, the Hewes, the Action Craft, and all of the other, newer boats that have appeared on the scene in the past few years, are incredibly fine fishing machines which are a joy to own and use. With some modifications and some trial and error learning how to best use it, even a johnboat can be turned into an efficient fishing boat, though. What features does a good saltwater fly fishing boat need? What makes it easy to fish from?

Generalizations are difficult due to the wide variety of fishing done here, but any boat used for fly fishing will need good rod storage to protect expensive rods and reels. A casting area free from protrusions of any type saves many headaches, heartaches, and sometimes broken toes and tackle. For fishing on flats a shallow draft, both for running and while actually fishing, is invaluable for getting into skinny areas where redfish, bonefish, trout, and snook can all be found a great deal of the time. If you spend much time on the pushpole you'll prefer a smaller, lighter vessel that tracks well and is easy to pole..

Boat noise is one of the most important considerations of all. When there is ripple on the water a noisy boat goes, "bloopbloopbloopbloopbloopbloop...". The fish can hear that noise, and believe me, here in Florida they have learned what it means. A quiet hull design means you are going to catch more fish in shallow water, and it's worth spending more money to get one.

For anglers who frequently fish along the beaches and out into the ocean a larger and more seaworthy vessel needs serious consideration. Fishermen who prefer to use live bait for chum will need a larger skiff with a good live well that will keep that bait frisky. Once a good fish is hooked, it's important to be able to move around inside the boat without tripping over lots of "stuff." A clean design with adequate storage space is very important. Unfortunately, no one boat handles all chores well, so unless you can afford to own several boats your decision on what to buy will always be a compromise.

For some reason jonboats get little respect. This is a shame since they really are useful

in shallow inshore and backcountry areas. You can rig them for fishing very easily and they work extremely well for exploring hazardous areas. My 14 foot MonArk has been dubbed the "Bang-O-Craft" because of its countless scrapes with rocks and oysters. Its tough metal hide absorbs punishment without complaint. It just bounces off and keeps right on motoring along. The noisy hull is a big drawback of jonboats, but they really do have many other redeeming qualities.

Two anglers fly fish from a jonboat in Pine Island Sound.

20

This isn't a boat show. Homosassa tarpon fishermen wait out a storm.

The number of car top boats seen here has exploded in recent years. Canoes and kayaks make excellent craft for getting back into areas that receive little if any fishing pressure. Kayaks paddle more easily, canoes can haul more "stuff" and allow friends to fish together. Both allow access to areas inaccessible to the wading angler, and deserve serious consideration.

Knowledgeable anglers fishing from canoes carry a pushpole in addition to their paddles. The pole allows both anglers to stand up while searching for fish. The bow man carries the rod while the stern man pushes the boat. After the bow man connects, they trade gear, turn the canoe around, and switch roles. The canoe now goes backwards, the stern man handles the rod, and the bow man poles the boat. It may sound crazy but it works very well for skilled anglers.

Boaters need accessories, too. We will use an anchor as our first example. It needs to hold the boat securely. More importantly, it sometimes needs to be abandoned quickly, especially when a big fish bites. When a big fish strips off line FAST it needs to be chased right now, and pulling the anchor up wastes valuable seconds. Most Florida fishermen use a float on their anchor rope so they can chase fish like this in a hurry. The anchor can be unclipped and left where it is. At the end of the battle the boater returns to retrieve the anchor, or reconnects it to the bow of the boat. The fishing can then continue in exactly the same spot.

Many shallow water anglers use a pushpole for propulsion across the flats. Pushpoles are relatively inexpensive and maintenance free. Some anglers use nothing else.

Electric motors become more popular every year. You'll see both bow mounts and stern mounts in use. Trim tab mounted electric motors from Lenco have also become very popular for many applications, such as beach fishing for tarpon and fishing around docks.

Bow mounts give excellent control of the boat and have the advantage that you only need one. They work in any depth water too, something that cannot be said of a pushpole. They and their operator always seem to get in the way of a fly fisher, though.

For effective use of stern mounts two are used. Steering requires a pushpole. In other words, the stern mounted electrics help the poler, rather than replacing him the way the bow mount does. The angler gets the entire front deck to himself, with no one or nothing to get in the way. Some guides use a combination of bow and stern mounts.

Lenco trim tab mounted electrics work by means of remote control and are extremely maneuverable. One can go forward while the other is in reverse, spinning the boat on a dime.

Use whatever combination of propulsion suits you best.

Patrick Phillips used a kayak to get to this redfish.

Guides

They should be your best friend, but might be your worst nightmare. Good ones are a bargain, bad ones a complete waste of money. Some anglers swear by them, others swear at them. The professional fishing guides of Florida are a diverse lot, and like any group of people anywhere hard to make generalizations about.

Anyone considering hiring a guide should ask him some questions before booking the day(s). "What do you charge?" is an obvious start. "What's included?" and "What type of fishing do you do?" are other easy questions. Most fly fishing guides supply tackle, flies, and license as part of the package. All good ones carry liability insurance.
Ask before you go.

A question I'm often asked by potential clients is, "What type of boat do you have?" A quality design will mean a more comfortable day for you. Some boats ride hard. Others are very wet. Still others are noisy. But unless you happen to be familiar with the various boat manufacturers, the answer to this question may not mean much to you.

During your conversation with the guide, tell him what you want to do. If you will be in the area for several days and need help finding places to fish after your day together, tell him. If you have concerns about your casting and would like some instruction, tell him. Honesty now will save misunderstanding and ill will later.

Speaking of ill will, I guide myself, and I can assure you that many people coming to fly fish in Florida have inflated views about both their angling skills, especially fly casting, and the numbers of fish willing to commit suicide on any given day by eating counterfeit food made from hair and feathers. Having realistic expectations will make for a better day for both you and your guide. If you can double haul and can quickly make an accurate 50 foot cast you can have good shots at most of the fish you see. If you can't don't expect to catch a load of fish.

If you can be flexible in your scheduling, ask what days are likely to be most productive. While the guide can't predict the weather or give guarantees, moon phase has a lot to do with fish behavior since it affects tides so much. The guide knows this and also has an experience base from past years on which he can prognosticate. Why book a date that he knows may be unproductive?

If you don't know his reputation ask the guide for references. Often guides develop long term relationships with some of their anglers and fish them the same week every year. Guides with a lot of return business generally entertain and instruct in addition to finding fish. Others could find fish in a bathtub but get little if any repeat business because they're obnoxious. Although you may catch fish, you could still hate the entire experience!

Any guide with an iota of business sense will ask for a deposit to reserve dates, a reasonable request. If an angler changes his mind at the last minute, the guide loses out on a day's wages. Guides get none of the fringe benefits that most salaried workers take for granted. When they're sick or if the weather's bad, they don't get paid. They do not earn retirement pay.

While it may look like peaches and cream to the angler, most guides work hard for their entire lives and seldom retire anywhere near what most folks would consider financial security. It's a tough way to earn a living, and most guides do so because they love it. The financial rewards are few for all but the very best. So don't complain about the deposit, and don't forget to give a good, hard working guide a well-deserved tip.

Hazards and Safety

Hazards? In Florida? Yes, accidents happen everywhere, and Florida isn't immune. Take a look at the hazards you may encounter on any trip in the Sunshine State.

Number one has to be insects, primarily mosquitoes, but biting flies and stinging insects can't be forgotten either. Insect repellant and protective clothing takes care of the biters. Controversy increases about the safety of DEET (the active ingredient in most insect repellants), but it definitely does repel insects. It also melts down fly lines, so be careful with it.

There isn't any controversy about the effects of the West Nile virus or encephalitis. DEET is the best way to protect yourself against mosquitoes carrying infectious disease.

Some folks like to use Avon's Skin So Soft or other non-DEET repellants. My own experience is that these do not work against anything but no-see-ums. I suspect the individual's attractiveness to and tolerance for bugs determines, in part at least, their effectiveness.

Nothing will repel a swarm of paper wasps should you be so unfortunate as to crash into their nest in the backcountry. Keep a careful eye out when traveling down overgrown creeks, and be prepared to clear out under power in a hurry should you hit one.

Next comes the sun. Sunburn is an ever present risk in Florida, and skin cancer rates continue rising everywhere. Protect yourself with sunscreen and protective clothing. Dr. William Barnard tells me that he uses the highest SPF sunscreen available whenever he goes fishing regardless of the season, and recommended that I do the same. I pass his advice on to you.

Lightning strikes more people in the state of Florida every year than all other states combined. The majority of those hit are either golfers or anglers. A graphite fly rod could well be the finest lightning rod ever designed. Is any fish worth a million volt jolt? Find and get under shelter when those threatening thunderheads come rolling your way.

Waders need to concern themselves with three forms of aquatic wildlife. Stingrays are the most prevalent hazard waders face. Seldom aggressive, the rays cover themselves with sand or mud and thus are hard to see. Step on one and it will drive the stinger deep into your leg. The stinger then breaks off while the ray goes about its business, leaving you with an excruciatingly painful souvenir of your encounter, one that takes a very long time to heal.

Drag your feet while wading. Do the well-known "stingray shuffle." The ray will swim away if you touch the wing. This may startle you, but leaves no lasting mementos.

Alligators swim all through coastal Florida waters. Many folks assume, mistakenly, that gators live only in freshwater. Although gators are seldom aggressive, if you see a big one paying attention to you, get out of the water. Whatever you do, don't drag fish on a stringer while gators are around!

Gators often rest on the bottom in shallow water- be careful when you wade. I seldom see gators in central Florida coastal waters during the winter months. We never worry about them then. During the warmer months we watch much more closely and in waters where there are lots of them we are much more hesitant about getting out of the boat.

Sharks present almost no danger, unless you are dragging a stringer of fish. However, they certainly deserve respect, especially when the surf gets full of big ones. The mullet run will bring large sharks in close to shore. Consider fishing from the beach then!

Other boaters possibly present the greatest hazard of all. Florida has the highest boating fatality rate in the nation. Alcohol is often a contributing factor in boating accidents. Stay sober and consider wearing a life vest when traveling from spot to spot.

All modern outboard equipped boats come with a kill switch lanyard. I seldom see operators wearing these. The chance of falling from a boat under power is greater than the casual observer may realize. If you as an operator do fall out of such a vessel, you can rest assured that the boat will not continue in a straight line. It will turn in a circle, and will eventually run you over. The marks that the prop of a fishing skiff will make on human flesh are horrible to contemplate, but anglers in Florida are injured or killed just this way every year.

It takes only a moment to attach this lanyard to your belt buckle. If you're operating the boat get in the habit of doing this. If you're not the operator, make sure he uses this important piece of safety equipment.

A well prepared angler knows the hazards and acts accordingly. In addition, common sense dictates always carrying a first aid kit. All anglers, all adults need to know basic first aid techniques. Although you hope you never need them, you never know when you will. Take a standard first aid course at your earliest opportunity.

Chapter 2 Angling Techniques

Poling my canoe across the shallows on my first visit to Everglades National Park's Mud Lake the thought entered my mind, "There will never be any fish in this shallow water." No sooner had the thought completed than a clearly visible and quite substantial fish appeared. A quick cast put the fly in front of it and the fish immediately charged and ate the fly. Five minutes later my hand grasped seven pounds of unhappy redfish, which was quickly unhooked and released. Several more redfish followed and Mud Lake fast became a favorite place to fish.

This chapter examines in depth various techniques used to catch Florida's saltwater gamefish. Many of the methods used here differ considerable from those used elsewhere, necessitating some explanation.

For starters, many of our fish often hunt for food in ridiculously shallow water. Redfish and bonefish in particular will look for crabs and minnows in water that does not even cover their back. Bob Stearns showed me six foot long tarpon outside of Flamingo, fish cruising through grass with their backs out of the water. It takes an enormous change in the mindset that "big fish only use deep water" to get the confidence to look in these shallow areas.

Much of Florida's saltwater fishing requires a substantial amount of hunting first, and the fly never enters the water until the fish are located. Let's take a look at how to find fish, then at sight-fishing, blind-casting, chumming, fighting and handling fish, and other important angling techniques.

Searching For and Finding Fish

Here's the scenario- two anglers have a boat, and have begun fishing in a large bay in which neither have fished before. Do they have any chance of success?

It depends on how hard they search. A situation like this often requires extensive hunting. Many tips follow which will hopefully make the hunt a more successful one.

Begin the search by moving fairly rapidly, looking for any signs of life, especially bait. An area showing obvious signs of life will much more likely hold fish than a location which otherwise looks good, but has no bait. Sharks and rays may also indicate fish.

Work different types of habitats until you find fish. Points with water movement (especially with fallen trees), creeks, creek mouths, the windy side of bays, the sheltered side of bays, deep bays, shallow bays, drop-offs, channels, and oyster bars, are all locations that could hold fish. Work them all in succession, using common sense to guide your search.

For example, don't try the south side of a bay with the wind from the north and the temperature in the fifties. A more likely location on a day like this would be a mud-bottomed, wind-sheltered shoreline with sunshine warming the shallows. The fish could maintain a comfortable body temperature here, and could be persuaded to eat a well-presented fly. The windy side of a bay might be good on a warm day. The wave action oxygenates the water, and blows baitfish against the windward shoreline.

As a general rule, work creek mouths when water flows out of, rather than into, them. The current carries bait and gamefish know that.

Try around oyster bars or mangrove shorelines on the rising tide. The fish like to hunt in areas not accessible to them when the tide was low. Both the oysters and the mangroves hold plenty of small baitfish as well as shrimp and crabs, all of which your saltwater gamefish hold in high esteem as edibles.

Search aggressively! If you don't find the fish holding on a particular habitat type, for example oysters, don't waste time fishing around other oyster bars unless you actually see fish working there.

Birds have long been used by savvy anglers to locate fish. Anytime terns start diving and screaming, it's easy to figure out that fish are underneath, piling into bait.

Wading birds such as great blue herons or great egrets also feed on baitfish. Anytime several of these birds work together in one area, they indicate the presence of bait. Most of the time predatory fish like snook or redfish will be there too, and sometimes the birds and the fish play the bait off of each other. Congregations of wading birds can certainly mean more to the fly fisher than simple aesthetics.

One technique which almost always works, but which requires a bit of observation and patience, involves looking for guide boats. Often several guides will be drifting with the current, casting through a productive zone. Once they finish passing through it, they'll motor back upcurrent BEING CAREFUL NOT TO MOTOR NEAR THE FISHY AREA, and make another drift. If you watch what they are doing and closely emulate it without getting in their way or spooking the fish, they will usually not mind your joining them.

Quite understandably, guides get touchy about sports who ruin the fishing. Keep in mind that in shallow water an outboard spooks fish from a long way off. Keep your approach quiet and treat others with respect and you will usually be welcomed.

Sight Fishing

Few angling experiences compare with actually seeing the fish in shallow water, casting to it, manipulating the fly, and watching the fish take. In order to succeed consistently you must have two items of equipment. The first is a billed or broad brimmed hat. The underside of the bill should be a dark color. The dark color reflects less light onto the face, reducing glare. You also need a pair of quality polarized sunglasses. The polarizing filters cut reflection from the water surface, making it easier to see into the water. The right glasses are very important.

The right attitude is even more important than the right equipment. It takes a certain degree of mental toughness and perseverance to get up in a boat or wade all day and really concentrate, trying to read signs that indicate fish. Concentration definitely is the key here, for without it success is impossible.

When you concentrate you see more fish. Seeing more fish means more shots at fish. The odds dictate that with more opportunities, you have more hookups. Now let's discuss what to look for.

Sometimes a fish betrays its presence in shallow water

A redfish cruising through shallow water.

by causing disturbances on the water's surface. Fins, whether dorsal or caudal, are easy to spot, particularly when in motion. Sunlight sometimes reflects off of the caudal fins of tailing reds or bonefish, and you can see the flash from a surprising distance.

A fish cruising in shallow water pushes a wave up above it, a wave known as a wake. To visualize what this looks like, think of a submarine moving through the water only five feet below the surface. Would it make a disturbance on the surface? You bet it would!

Obviously, fish are smaller than submarines, but the principle is identical. Wakes are easily seen when it's calm. They're harder to see if it's windy, but it can still be done. Although a choppy water surface has a chaotic pattern to it, moving waves have a pattern. They all move in the same direction. The heights are all in a certain range. ANYTHING that breaks this pattern, that looks even slightly different, could be a fish and should be investigated, either visually or by casting up ahead of it.

The importance of looking into the water was stated earlier. Most fish on the flats do not put up flags telling their enemies of their whereabouts. Fish enter shallow water looking for a meal, but they still try to hide as well as they can. If you want to see them you have to train yourself to look and to see.

Again, look into the water. This is most easily done when there is little or no wind, the sun is high in the sky and at your back, there are no clouds, and the bottom is light in color. That you need clean water should go without saying. Tilt your head back and forth to find the most effective angle for your sunglasses.

Avoid staring at one spot. Keep your eyes scanning along the bottom, looking for any break in the patterns you see there. Scan in a pattern, back and forth, from close in to the boat to the limit of visibility and then back in close again. Develop your peripheral vision as well. Your skill and ability will improve as you practice.

What do you look for? Not a fish, but anything that might be a fish. Don't expect to see a goldfish in a bowl. Most of the time you are looking for subtle clues that betray the presence of a fish. There are different kinds of clues. Muds are easily seen and are almost always caused by fish. Although the fish making them may be mullet or stingrays, gamefish frequently follow both. Investigate with a cast or two.

Look for any movement that breaks the patterns. The ubiquitous waves cast moving shadows on the bottom, a pattern that has already been mentioned. Look for any movement contrary to the patterns produced by the waves.

Sometimes you see the movement of the fish itself, or sometimes you see its shadow moving along the bottom as it swims. Either way you know there's something there. Large tarpon over light sand bottoms are about the easiest of all fish to see this way. They look like big logs cruising through the water. I find seeing bonefish and seatrout the most difficult.

Look for flashes. When fish turn or roll on their sides, particularly while they're feeding, their sides catch and reflect light. This lasts for only a brief moment, but is easy to see and is a dead giveaway to the presence of fish. Tarpon and redfish will both do this for no apparent reason when they're happy. A flashing fish is a good thing to see.

Look for differences in color. The light cream color of their pectoral fins are often the only visible clue to the presence of redfish when they cruise over a dark grass bottom. Bonefish have a peculiar emerald color, unique and sometimes hard to see. Tough to spot, permit have silvery sides that reflect the bottom with incredible effectiveness. They do, however, have a dark outline which can be discerned by careful observation. Check out everything which might be a fish!

Watch underneath any birds like cormorants, pelicans, or great blue herons when they fly close to the water surface. As they pass over fish, the fish spook and jump, as if someone yelled "BOO!" at them without warning. I've taken some fine fish after a wading bird in flight tipped me off to their presence.

Sometimes your ears can direct you to your quarry. On a cold, windy day one winter I had an angler from Buffalo, N.Y. out on what I thought would be a futile search for fish. I heard a splash and went to investigate, expecting to find mullet. We were happily surprised to see a big redfish tail waving at us in the chilly breeze. Tailing fish splash. Quiet anglers can hear them. The distinct feeding pops of trout or snook are very easy to hear. When a school of jacks jumps on a school of mullet it can sound like someone is dropping bowling balls into the water!

Another thing to look for are fishy-looking shapes. Sometimes the fish lay up. They're not cruising. They're not moving. They may be in an ambush mode, or sleeping, or just sunning themselves, but they certainly are motionless. Needless to say, they're hard to see and frequently very hard to catch when they do this.

If you see something that looks like it might be a fish, cast to it! Many times I have let my curiosity get the best of me and approached too closely. The fish let me know that it was actually a fish and not a piece of wood by streaking off towards deeper water, leaving me feeling fishless and foolish.

You usually can't see the entire fish. Seatrout are one of the hardest of all fish to spot. Their dark backs blend in perfectly with grass. They often lie motionless over grassy bottoms, particularly around the edges of sandy areas. While they do this they are almost impossible to see. Often the only clue you have to a trout's presence is its tail, a little lighter in color than the background, with a darker band along the back edge. Check it out with a cast!

Seatrout, especially the larger specimens, are one of the spookiest of all fish. They seldom let you get very close, and rarely eat after they flush. A good cast is the best form of investigation, unless you'd rather see fish than catch them.

One time I spotted what I thought was the motionless tail of a redfish in Mud Lake, a shallow, brackish Everglades pond. I cast beyond where the head should be, and was rewarded with a strike. It turned out to be one of my most unusual catches ever, a sawfish of about twenty-five pounds. Never ignore anything. You're a hunter and have to behave like one.

Try these techniques and practice. Practice a lot! As your seeing skills develop, you derive a lot of pleasure and pride in being able to see things that others can't. Not only will you catch more fish, you will get more enjoyment from all of your fishing. You'll be amazed at all the sights you were missing!

Blind-casting

Imagine for a moment in your mind's eye the perfect bonefishing scene. On a lovely, warm day you stand on the bow of a guided skiff. A gentle, cooling breeze ripples the surface of the shallow, crystal clear water. Bright sunshine illuminates the white sand bottom, clearly displaying the school of hundreds of bonefish greedily tailing for crabs and other crustaceans. The biggest bone of all time devours your perfectly presented fly, and you're off to the races.

Now let's talk reality. The highest tide in ten years picks the same weekend as your bonefishing trip, covering the flat with three feet of water. A heavy overcast with intermittent rain squalls combines with a hard wind blowing at 20 miles an hour with gusts. Can bonefish still be caught?

When Mother Nature gives you overcast skies, blind casting may still produce a few fish.

Both of these situations have happened to me, from heavenly to hellish and everything in between. With perseverance and some luck, bonefish can be caught in all of them.

Let's face it, most of us would rather sightfish. It's more interesting, and more exciting. But Mother Nature doesn't always cooperate. Wind, clouds, and high or dirty water can conspire to make sighting conditions less than ideal. If you want to hear the magic song of a reel in stress, you fish anyway. Simply deal with lousy conditions by blindcasting.

Let's discuss a few general rules for blindcasting. It really does involve more than just mindlessly casting a fly out into the water. If fishing a flat, pick one where you know fish feed. Obviously you won't catch any fish where there are none. All other things being equal, the fish feed on their favorite flats whenever the weather conditions allow. If you're there, you just might get a few.

Use the tips described in the sightfishing section to search the water you can see into for fish. If you see any, cast to them! There's no sense in turning down any good opportunities.

Keep casting your fly into the water where you cannot see. Although it depends on your direction of movement relative to the position of the sun, this will usually be the deeper water. Believe that fish are in there, and just keep casting.

Make long casts. You cover more water this way, giving more fish the chance to see your offering. You may periodically line fish, and you'll see the boils and muds they make as they flee. You may look at it as a fish you won't catch, but instead look at it as proof that you are working the right area. Spooked fish mean the fish are there! If you just keep casting you'll eventually get some.

As always, fly choice here can make the difference between success and failure. While sight fishing you usually want to use a fly that resembles a typical food item of the targeted species. When blind casting a brightly colored (or noisy) attractor pattern is often a better choice. Poppers, flies with rattles, flies that push a lot of water, or a fly rod lure like the Dupre Spoon-Fly would all be appropriate choices.

In many locations in the state you may not be fishing flats. Bass fishermen in freshwater tune in to the concept of structure. Many saltwater fish relate to structure, too. Stumps, docks, oyster bars, rocks, wrecks, points, fallen timber, drop-offs, creek mouths, seawalls, edges of grass beds and sandy bottoms; all of these types of irregularities and more attract and hold many species of fish. In snook country, points of land extending out into a current often hold fish, and if a fallen tree lies there so much the better. Experienced anglers recognize fishy looking areas. Use your judgment and trust your instincts.

Teasers

Most anglers associate teasers with offshore fishing, and certainly the concept has reached its most rapid evolution in the arena of fly fishing for billfish. Billfish teasers often resemble a large popping plug without hooks, but it could be a freshly dead or frozen baitfish such as a ballyhoo or mullet rigged without a hook.

During billfishing the teaser is trolled about 100 feet behind the boat until a fish rises to it. The teaser is then manipulated to excite the fish and lure it to within fly casting range, usually only about 30 to 40 feet behind the boat. At this point one of two things happens, depending on whether the teaser is a real fish or an artificial.

When teasing with an artificial, the reeler gives it a mighty jerk, pulling it into the boat. The fly fisher yells, "Neutral!" and the captain takes the boat out of gear. In the meantime the excited fish frantically wonders where the teaser went. The fly fisher delivers the fly, and hopefully the fish eats the fly and a hookup ensues.

When teasing with a baitfish, a similar thing happens except that the reeler allows the fish to mouth the bait before pulling it away. After the fish gets the flavor of the bait in its mouth and loses it, delivering a fly anywhere near the head of the fish usually results in an immediate and vicious strike. Most fly-caught billfish succumb to this technique.

Teasing can be used inshore too. Large jack crevalle are tremendous fly rod targets, but usually flies are simply too small and move too slowly to interest them. A pair of anglers can team up to catch these fish.

Get a large popping plug and remove the hooks. Tie this modified plug on the line of a spinning rod (if you don't own one of these you can usually borrow one from one of the neighborhood kids). The "teaser" casts the plug out where the jacks are and reels it in as fast and with as much commotion as possible.

In the meantime the fly fisher has his line in the air, with a large popping bug or streamer on the business end. When the jacks start chasing the plug, the fly fisher drops his bait on the plug while the teaser simultaneously pulls it from the water.

Smart snook anglers in the Palm Beach/greater Miami area tease, too. Many bridges over canals and rivers in that part of the state shelter some enormous snook. These fish feed mostly at night, and prefer large mouthfuls. Fly fishers using standard techniques have little chance of success. But two fishermen working together can sometimes hook up with these monsters, although landing them around these bridges when the fish have those pilings to work around is another thing altogether.

Equipment needs for bridge teasing are basic. All you need are a few live mullet in the six to eight inch size range, a large rigging needle, and a stout cane pole to which is tied a section of 50 pound (more or less) monofilament. At daybreak (this is an early morning operation) use the rigging needle to tie the mullet to the line on the cane pole. The teaser then works the mullet around the bridge pilings, tempting the snook to come up and blast it. If the snook cooperates, the teaser pulls the mullet away, then puts it right back down again. When the snook comes back, the teaser might let the snook mouth the bait, but then pulls it away again. The idea is to get the fish so angry that when the fly fisher finally tosses the feather duster over, the snook is ready to smash anything. It works.

Wading

Tails, fish tails, reddish bronze tipped with a bluish tinge, protruded from the water's surface all around us. Although the fish were obviously feeding, while in such in shallow water they were very spooky. Every time we maneuvered the boat close enough for a cast the tails would vanish, while further away beyond casting range tails continued to wave. It was another frustrating situation.

Fortunately, both Joe Mulson and I had with us the needed piece of equipment that would allow us to get close to our wary prey. No, it wasn't a spinning rod with a long cast spool. Joe and I were wearing chest high waders. We simply abandoned the boat and went after the reds on foot.

One of the most effective ways to approach game fish, as well as one of the most enjoyable of all the ways to fish involves getting into the fish's element and wading. The angler has a low profile and keeps the disturbance of the water to a minimum, allowing him to sneak up on feeding fish without spooking them.

It's often possible to hook shallow water reds with literally just the leader out of the fly rod's tiptop. The fish come so close, all one need do is to dangle the fly in their faces. This makes for tremendously exciting fishing!

For many species of fish which swim in our salty inshore areas, wading will actually be more effective in many situations than fishing from a boat. For example, in areas where

Joe Mulson wades to a school of redfish.

redfish are heavily pursued by anglers in boats, they soon learn that boats are trouble. Getting into casting range from a boat can be tough. A wading angler who knows how to keep quiet can literally wade right up to the fish.

On many days in the winter and spring, strong winds make even the most skilled boat handler want to scream in frustration. Fly fishing is difficult when the boat is moving too fast because of strong winds. It's tough to strip the line fast enough to keep contact with the fly. A wading angler can fish in almost any kind of breeze.

In Florida during the summer months, shorts and some type of protective footwear are all that you need for comfortable wading. I stepped on a flounder one time while wading barefoot, and although nothing happened as far as injury goes, I nearly soiled my pants! The incident convinced me that some sort of shoe was really a good idea. Crabs, shells, broken bottles, and other hazards to the feet make barefoot wading a stupid thing to do.

The best footwear for wading is neoprene wading boots. Several manufacturers make these. Since they're ankle high, they keep sand and shells out, and resist the suction effect that soft bottomed areas sometimes dish out. Take it from me- losing your shoe in bottom ooze in thigh deep water is not fun.

In central and north Florida, waders make winter wading possible. Those who wade only occasionally can get by with the boot foot type of nylon wader. Red Ball waders will give several years of service. Neoprenes work well, but you will get damp inside and on warm winter days they get positively steamy. For those for whom wading is a way of life, stocking foot

Gore-tex waders are the only way to go.

Stocking foot waders need wading boots. The area fished dictates the type of boot worn, and some anglers may need more than one type. Freshwater trout fishermen are familiar with felt-soled wading boots. These work best where slick, algae coated rocks cover the bottom. Some anglers wear chains or crampons when working around treacherous rocky areas. On soft muddy bottoms chains aren't needed and muck sticks to the sole of the felt boots and makes wading impossible.

Where the bottom is sandy or muddy (most places in Florida) the hard soled neoprene wading booties like those mentioned above work best. You will need to purchase a second pair for use with the neoprene waders, usually two sizes larger than your shoe size.

Waders also need to carry all their paraphernalia. In the winter wading vests provide a terrific way to carry tackle and accessories. Many fine vests are on the market. Make sure the one you buy has enough storage space for everything that you need.

An important consideration on wading vests, pouches, or whatever you choose to use to carry your gear is that zippers made out of anything other than plastic will quickly corrode and fail. Try to find nylon zippers and pulls, or use a vest with Velcro closures.

In the summer vests are too hot to be comfortable. The only thing to do is carry less stuff. Some fishermen carry extra flies on their hat, others carry accessories in an over the shoulder or around the waist type of bag. Nu-Mark Manufacturing, a tackle manufacturer in Houston, specializes in quality accessories for the wading angler. Look for their products at your favorite tackle store.

What accessories will you need? This depends on the type of fishing done. Anglers need extra flies, fly boxes, floatant for hair bugs, pliers, and a glove for handling fish as an absolute minimum. Leader material, water, food, and more get added to the essentials. You end up carrying a lot of stuff. It adds up fast if care is not used.

What techniques can waders use to find fish?

Oftentimes waders use a boat to find fish, then anchor up, slip out, and start wading. Two (or more) wading anglers work a long stretch of shoreline by "leapfrogging", that is, one angler hops out of the boat and starts wading. The other takes the boat downwind (or sun or tide) several hundred yards, anchors it, and starts wading. When the first angler reaches the boat, he takes it a few hundred yards down the shoreline and they repeat the process. If four anglers do this, they can work new water all day long and never have to fish alone. If one is right-handed and the other's a lefty, it works even better.

If you are wading down a flat the fish seem scarce, do what guides do and zigzag. Go in close to shore and then work farther out. The fish may be on the flat in slightly deeper or shallower water. By looking in different depths on the flat your chances of finding fish improve.

Of necessity much of the angling time spent wading consists of casting blindly. In general, flies that make noise, especially surface baits like poppers, often work the best for two reasons. First of all, watching and working a popper that you can see is more interesting than retrieving a subsurface lure or streamer that cannot be seen. Secondly, the noise a popper makes attracts fish that might never see an underwater bait. They hear the popper and come to investigate. And although this is somewhat of an intangible, surface strikes are so much more exciting than underwater ones. Keep in mind that poppers won't work for some species.

Cast to any areas that you think might hold fish. Cast along oyster beds, rocks, stumps, pilings, drop-offs, the edges of grassy and sandy areas, or any other area or structure that might hide a fish. In addition to increasing the odds for a strike, your targeting specific locations before every cast improves your casting skills and this pays big dividends on future trips.

Always look for signs of fish while wading. If you see one, try to get into the best possible position from which to cast. Sometimes you have to take any shot that's offered, but other times the fish move slowly and you can get a head on presentation, the kind most likely to produce a strike. The first cast is usually your best opportunity. Try to make it count.

Lastly, use care and common sense when wading, especially in new areas. Make sure the bottom is firm enough to hold you before hopping out of a boat. On the Gulf side of the Keys, and in most places in Everglades National Park, the bottom is very soft and the muck is very deep. If you just jump out you may find yourself up to your waist in marl with no easy way to get out. Also, if you step off a drop while wearing waders you will discover to your dismay that waders were not designed with swimming in mind.

Stingrays are definitely a cause for caution. Do the "stingray shuffle," never lifting your feet from the bottom. Kicking the ray's wing will cause it to swim away. Pinning it to the bottom will lead to a pierced leg and a trip to the emergency room.

In waters with sharks or alligators (and where aren't they?), dragging a stringer with fish invites huge trouble. Most fly fishers don't kill many fish anyway, and these predators provide another good reason not to. And finally, although wading can be done as a solo act, safety considerations dictate that you fish with a buddy. So find another fishing maniac and go chase those fish together!

Chumming

When all else fails, attract the fish to you. Use chum. Depending on the fish you want there are several different approaches to this technique. The best way to do this for bonefish is to use live shrimp and a chumming tube. Allow me to explain.

The least troublesome way to chum for bonefish, redfish, or other flats fish involves breaking live shrimp into pieces and just throwing the pieces out where you want the fish to show up. The trouble with this is that every fish in the area that eats shrimp gets a free meal. Most of these fish are little guys like pinfish. You won't want to catch most of these fish, and your chum won't last very long.

Live bait chumming offshore pulls lots of fish to the boat.

These anglers are tossing nets to catch live chum, outside of Jupiter Inlet.

A chumming tube is a piece of PVC pipe. A one and a half inch diameter piece about twenty inches long is plenty, but any PVC scraps you happen to have will do. Cap one end permanently by using PVC cement. Use a drill to fill the pipe full of approximately quarter inch holes. Hole size isn't critical. Put another cap on the other end, but don't cement it on. Drill holes through the pipe and cap so that a nylon cord can be tied through the holes to tether the tube to the boat and hold the cap in place.

Next, go to a known bonefish flat. Anchor the boat about 30 feet upcurrent of a white sand patch. Take 25 or so live shrimp, break them up into pieces, and put them into the chum tube. Add six or eight whole live ones, too. Put the cap on, tie the tube to the tether line, and heave it out onto the near side of the sand patch. The chum now does its work. Bones can smell the shrimp from a long way off and will follow the odor to its source. At this point the fly fisher waits and watches for fish to come into the chum line. When he sees them, a fly imitating a shrimp is delivered. Many, many fly fishers caught their first bonefish this way.

Anglers fishing for bluefish use a similar technique, using ground up fish (usually menhaden) instead of shrimp. The chum "soup" is ladled sparingly over the side of the boat in an area where bluefish are known to be. The blues come into the chum line, and the angler works the fly into it. The fly for this is the bloody chum fly, a hunk of brown marabou tied to the hook. Dead drift the fly with the chum. Any motion imparted to it only puts the fish off.

On Florida's west coast guides often chum fish into feeding frenzies by using "whitebait," or pilchards, which they catch in cast nets. They anchor the boat up current of a location where redfish, snook, and sometimes seatrout are known to be. They then throw handfuls of the live baitfish hard onto the water's surface, stunning them. As these injured and struggling minnows drift down current, predators who recognize an easy meal when they see one start feeding on them. Ten minutes or so of this, and the fish will hit almost anything thrown their way.

On the Atlantic coast from Jupiter south to Key West, offshore guides use pilchards or other small baitfish to lure little tunny, big crevalle, yellowfin and blackfin tuna, large sharks, wahoo, dolphin, billfish, and other pelagic species within casting range of a fly. They purchase by-catch (cold beer is the medium of exchange!) from shrimpers to use as chum. Again, many pelagic species (especially bonito and blackfin tuna) follow these boats, waiting for the smorgasbord of small dead fish that shrimpers throw away after every time they pull their nets.

Captain Jake Jordan does most of his fishing out of Marathon Key. Although Jake fishes for permit, bonefish, and tarpon in shallow water, he's best known for pioneering deep-water fly fishing techniques for permit over spring holes in the open Gulf. These fish school up on the

34

surface over spring holes. The water there will be from sixty to over one hundred feet deep, so dropping your crab fly to the bottom isn't too practical, and is unnecessary anyway.

When Jake locates a school of permit, he dips a live, silver dollar sized blue crab out of his bait well, and tosses it into the middle of the milling permit. He says the crab instinctively heads for the bottom, and will make it down ten feet or so before a fish gobbles it. He gets another crab and tosses it out. This one will only make it down about seven feet. The next one only makes it a few feet down, and pretty soon the fish are racing each other to hit the crabs before they hit the water.

The angler, meantime, picks the fish to which he wants to cast, and when the school is sufficiently worked up, he delivers his fly. Jake's clients have taken several permit of over thirty pounds by using this technique, so it's obviously effective. Jake claims that the pattern out here is relatively unimportant, too. The fish are so worked up from the free handouts that they forget to be fussy. If the fly looks remotely like a crab, they jump on it.

In all the discussions above, regardless of the fish being sought or the technique used to chum them, the common denominator is simple- in order for chum to work there must be fish present. Chum will not pull fish into an area they are not using. If the fish are there but being uncooperative, chumming can turn a mediocre day into a great one.

How to Fight Fish

"There's a fish at three o'clock!" Captain Tommy Locke directed my casting from his position on the poling tower. I couldn't see the fish in the glare of the early morning sun, but I cast where he told me to. The fish inhaled the fly and in a heartbeat I was hooked up to what at that time was the biggest fish of my life.

Forty minutes later this magnificent fish was alongside the boat, where Captain Jim Weber lipped it. Jim and Tommy both estimated its weight at 130 pounds. After some resuscitation the fish swam away strongly. I felt like I needed an oxygen tent, but I had whipped this fish in a relatively short period of time. We were all very pleased with the vigor the fish had shown as it disappeared into the emerald waters.

Regardless of their size, fish to be released benefit greatly from a short, hard fight. Most of us can recall (even if it was way back there when we had physical education classes in school) over-exercising. The next day our muscles were sore and stiff, making it difficult and painful to move.

For most of us this was not a life threatening situation. But a fish played too long develops the same lactic acid compounds in its muscle tissue that we do when we over-exercise, and a fish that can't move well often falls prey to one of its many enemies.

Oxygen dissolves better in cold water than warm. While here in Florida we never find truly cold water, the cooler temperatures of winter often put more fight into the fish we catch, particularly redfish. Fish caught at this time of year suffer less stress because of the relatively plentiful oxygen supply in the water. Without having done any research on the subject, common sense leads me to believe that post-release mortality is lower during the winter months.

In summer, fighting fish hard is more important simply because the water has less oxygen. The fish is in a situation somewhat analogous to the marathon runner who trains at sea level and then has to run a race at 10,000 feet- there is simply not enough oxygen. Concerned anglers will fight the fish hard during the summer in consideration for their quarry, and bring the fight to a conclusion as quickly as possible.

Jim Weber with the author's first big tarpon. If you want to enjoy a scene like this up close and personal, you must be able to fight fish skillfully.

Why else should anglers try to fight the fish hard? The least altruistic reason is that the longer the fight, the more likely it is that the fish will get away. The hook wears a larger and larger hole in the tissue and a brief moment of slack allows it to fall out. Abrasion on the leader leads to breakage. The angler tires, makes a mistake, and the fish breaks off. It just makes more sense for everyone involved to fight the fish hard and beat it quickly.

Let's take a look at seven general rules for fighting fish which hold for any type of tackle, and which lead to a higher success rate for any angler lucky enough, or skillful enough, to hang a big fish every now and then.

-Rule 1: Use the heaviest line that's practical. Why use six pound tippet if ten pound will work just as well? I take exception with anglers who tell me ultralight tackle is more "sporting". They may have more fun with it but it really beats up on the fish. I was speaking with a guide recently who told me that his client fought a 30 pound plus redfish for an hour and a half on fly tackle before the hook pulled out. My response was the guy should learn how to fight fish. The guide said he did a good job but was using six pound tippet. WHY?

Why would anyone chasing 30 pound reds use six pound tippet unless he was specifically trying for a world record? In my own saltwater fly fishing I seldom use less than twelve pound tippet, with the exception of bonefishing.

-Rule 2: Set the drag correctly. When using fly tackle set the drag at 25% of the breaking strength of the tippet. To determine the drag setting get a good scale and tie the leader to it. Then tie the other end of the scale to a tree or some other immovable object. Point the rod directly at the scale and pull until the drag starts to release. The reading on the scale is the actual,

36

measured drag setting on the reel.

-Rule 3: Learn to put maximum pressure on the fish. While we're still tied to the tree, start putting some bend in the rod while holding the reel to prevent drag slip. How much pressure can you put on the line before it breaks? Try this two different ways.

First, use the method already described, and second, try lifting a ten pound mushroom anchor off the floor while standing on a table. Use twelve-weight fly tackle with 16 pound class tippet. Using the scale, with all their strength, the maximum pressure the most skilled anglers can put on that 16 pound tippet will be only twelve pounds or so.

During a demonstration with a 10 pound anchor, several men in succession stood on a table and tried to use a 12-weight rod to lift the anchor. Most of us just barely moved it and it was the rod that broke, rather than the leader. The obvious conclusion is that with 16 pound tippet the average fisherman will never break the line no matter how hard he pulls on it, and with twelve pound tippet we can use 90% of our pulling strength and still be safe as long as we let go when the fish surges.

I've seen many different men try this with 12-weight tackle. Most of them only got the scale up to four or five pounds, and the highest I've ever seen anybody get it was 14 pounds. Don't believe me? Try it yourself!

While your neighbors might call for the men in the white coats if they see you fighting trees with your fishing tackle, if you want to learn to put maximum pressure on the fish you hook, few things are more valuable.

-Rule 4: When the fish swims away, don't try to stop it. While you can't pull hard enough to break a 16 pound class tippet, plenty of fish can. If the fish surges or makes a run and you try to stop it, something will break. While the fish runs it uses up its energy reserves. Let it go.

Snook fishing around mangroves or other structure provides one exception to this rule. If a fish runs toward the roots, you have a decision to make. If he gets in there, he's gone. Should you try to stop him? Every time!

I vividly remember trying to stop a snook in the Everglades that I had hooked on a surface plug. I locked up the reel, trying to keep that fish from the trees. The eight pound test line went slack and the plug floated to the surface. I reeled it in and checked it- the hooks had straightened before the eight pound line broke.

-Rule 5: Either you or the fish should be gaining line. When the fish stops its run, you should immediately attack it and start gaining line. Never let up or let the fish rest. While neither of you takes line, he is resting. He recovers faster than you, so a standoff only prolongs the fight. Show the fish you want to win. Like Billy Pate said, "You have to want the fish more than he wants to get away, and the fish thinks he's going to die."

-Rule 6: Learn to use side pressure. In shallow water, or if the fish is at the surface in deep water, pulling up on its head does little or nothing to tire it or break its spirit. The fish spreads its pectoral fins and resists with almost no effort. If you pull to the side, or better yet pull down (the famous "down-and-dirty" move), the fish has no defense and has to use muscle power to overcome the pull. Furthermore, once it has been rolled over once or twice, the fish will give up more quickly. Always pull opposite to the direction the fish is moving. In other words, if the fish is moving to the left, pull to the right and vice versa.

Rule 7: Change the angle of pull frequently. This one is particularly important for lifting fish from deep water. If you maintain a constant angle of pull, the fish can easily adjust to it, spread its pectoral fins, and resist with minimum effort. If you change the angle of pull constantly by "wagging" the rod, the fish will usually come right up. He may go right back down again, but

This angler is applying side pressure to a big Banana River Lagoon redfish.

he has to work to do this, and thus gets tired. It is very important while doing this to have the butt of the rod pointing down at the fish rather than up at the sky. High sticking does not move the fish and leads to broken tackle.

Learn and use these seven techniques for fighting fish. You will catch more of the fish you hook, the fish you release will have a better survival rate, and those around you will know that they are in the presence of a world class fisherman.

Mike Deegan with a fine Indian River Lagoon redfish. Not only does cradling the fish this way make for a great photograph, it is much better for the fish than hanging it by its jaw.

Handling Fish

Before you beat the fish, you decide whether to kill or release it. The only good reason to kill a fish involves eating it. I think killing a trophy fish to eat it is a tremendous waste. Eat the smaller fish and release the trophies so they can pass on those genes!

At the very least put table-bound fish on ice immediately for maximum quality. Most fish headed for the table benefit from being bled and gutted before being iced down. Some, like bluefish and mackerel, become almost inedible without this treatment.

Handle fish you intend to release as little as possible. Many times just letting small fish shake in the water at boatside or at your feet will free them with no handling whatsoever. You can safely handle most small fish that won't unhook themselves with a bare, wet hand. Roll the fish on its back and remove the hook. Most times it will come out easily.

A better approach than handling fish unnecessarily is to use a de-hooker. Several varieties are available commercially, or you can make your own. What they all have in common is a handle on one end and a large, blunt hook on the other. The bend of the hook on the de-hooker is slid down to the bend of the fish hook, and the fish is simply shaken off the hook. You never touch the fish and the entire process usually takes only two or three seconds. Everyone should carry one of these handy tools.

Larger fish require a different approach. I use a cloth glove covered with squiggly rubber lines to handle many of the fish I catch. With this glove to protect your hand you can "lip" many species of fish just like you would a largemouth bass. Redfish, snook, tarpon, and cobia can all be handled this way. The glove protects your hand while you "tail" some of the other species, like larger jack crevalle, Spanish mackerel, permit, dolphin, kingfish, and bonito. And of course the de-hooker also works on large fish, too.

A BogaGrip is an invaluable fish handling tool, probably better than the glove. The BogaGrip won't remove slime from the fish, and once the fish is on the BogaGrip it will not come off until you let it. It's easy to hold on to, and even has an accurate scale built into it. Although not inexpensive, I recommend these tools highly.

Really big fish usually require the use of a gaff. A lip gaff is recommended for tarpon too big to handle any other way, barracuda, large kingfish, and large tuna headed for release. After piercing the thin membrane behind the lower jaw, pin the gaff against the underside of the boat gunwale, preventing the fish from jumping off the hook.

Kill gaffs are used on large fish not intended for release. Most fly casters won't ever need one.

I try never to use a net unless I'm going to kill the fish. Nets remove the slime layer and often damage the eyes as well. Their use is not recommended for catch and release anglers.

If you want to photograph a catch, please keep in mind that fish suffocate when kept in the air. Have the camera equipment ready before the fish comes along side. Once you remove the fish from the water, work quickly! If you hold your breath while you work you have a better idea of when the fish needs to breathe again, too.

If you want a mount, get a few photos so you can get accurate color rendition and tape the fish to get its length and girth. Almost all taxidermists use fiberglass mounts these days. Glass mounts look better and last longer, and allow you to release your trophy unharmed. Let another angler experience the same thrill you just did!

Chapter 3 The Fishes

Anglers visiting Florida's saltwater for the first time could easily compare their experience to that of finding a treasure chest. Almost everyone has heard about the "Big Three"- tarpon, bonefish, and permit- but so many other fish here take flies and catching them is either fun, interesting, challenging, or all three combined, that to just discuss the most popular species would be a disservice to the reader. Instead, this chapter takes a look at most of the common fly caught species with information about specialized tackle, techniques, times of year, and various other interesting tidbits. I intend to paint as complete a picture as possible for each of these fish in the short space allowed in this book.

Barracuda *Sphryaena barracuda*

Blake Matherly with a barracuda caught in the Marquesas Keys.

The barracuda, or cuda for short, is one of fly fishing's most underrated gamefish. Lightning fast and possessing keen eyesight, big cudas (anything over about 15 pounds) don't get fooled easily. Although they lack stamina, the speed of their strike and runs and their spectacular leaps make barracuda very exciting fish to catch.

Cuda can be sight-fished on Keys flats in a manner similar to tarpon or bonefish. The best season for this is during the winter, when big barracuda come into the shallows to sun themselves. You'll see them cruising slowly, or laid up over white spots on the flat.

Cuda require a somewhat different approach than other flats dwellers. The fly should never land near (within about five feet) the fish, but rather is cast beyond the cuda 10 feet or so and then stripped as fast as possible in hope of enticing a strike. If the fish follows without striking, the fly is moving too slowly.

Sometimes pulling the fly from the water and casting it back out so that the fish intercepts it as it returns to its resting place works well. Sometimes the rod needs to be tucked under the arm and a two-handed retrieve used in order to give the fly sufficient velocity.

Another way to entice a flats cuda to strike is to cast the fly, then immediately backcast and pull the fly from the water. Repeat this from four to six times. Then, let the fly fall and retrieve it quickly. The cuda gets so excited by seeing all these flies blast by that he just crushes it on that last cast when you retrieve normally. Remember though, if the cuda sees you, and they see quite well, the chance for a strike greatly diminishes.

Cuda can be caught by blind casting on the flats. They tend to use sandy holes in grass flats as ambush points. If weather or sky conditions don't allow sight fishing, long casts past sandy areas and rapid retrieves will often raise a few fish. Expect to work hard!

You can fish cuda over wrecks or around channel markers, channel edges, or other structure, using the same techniques already described. In these offshore situations, chumming with live baitfish like pilchards or sardines will usually get them in the mood.

Cuda flies tend toward the long and thin, usually made from synthetic materials. A fly from six to eight inches long tied on a 1/0 hook is a good choice. The bulk of the fly seems to be relatively unimportant, so the fly should be no thicker than a pencil. Bright colors work best most of the time. Remember to use three to four inches of single strand wire or most fish you hook will be off with your fly before you ever knew they were there.

Cuda will also take poppers. The same rules apply. Long and thin, fast movement, long casts, and bright colors will bring the most action. Don't use poppers you value- they won't last long. Usually with cudas it's one fish per fly, regardless of fly type.

The all around rod described in Chapter 1 makes an excellent cuda stick. These fish lack stamina, so they give the best account of themselves on the lightest tackle practical. Seven weight outfits will toss the cuda flies an adequate distance if the wind isn't too strong.

The best locations for sight fishing cuda on the flats include all of the Keys waters and Biscayne Bay. On the east coast they will sometimes be found inshore, but this fishery lacks consistency. Rare in the Everglades and inshore on the west coast, cudas can be found in most offshore waters from about Cape Canaveral/Tampa Bay south, especially during the summer.

Although barracuda flesh has excellent taste and texture, the fish often carry ciguatoxin, a nerve poison that can be fatal. Handle all your barracuda carefully (those teeth are every bit as dangerous as they look) but gently, and after getting a photo or two release them to fight again.

Black Drum *Pogonias cromus*

A happy Greg Ritland with a black drum from the Banana River Manatee Refuge.

Black drum are not usually thought of as a fly rod fish, and in most places they completely ignore flies. But in the Banana River Manatee Refuge, especially during the winter months, big black drum tail on the flats and will eat certain flies with a surprising degree of consistency. These fish start at 20 pounds and go up from there! I don't know just how big they get, since the biggest ones always seem to break off. But my own personal best here was 45 inches long with a 35 inch girth. We estimated its weight at about 52 pounds.

Should you visit this area, throw Clouser minnows in brown or black, or crab imitations in brown. Drop the fly close to the fish and allow it to sink to the bottom, then move it very slowly. Keep working on the fish until it eats or moves off. Sometimes, if it's tailing, you can chase an individual fish for as long as ten or fifteen minutes before it finally sees your offering and decides to take!

Once hooked most of these fish fight like bulldozers. Unless you want to be messing with one fish for a long time use a heavy tippet (at least 15 pound) and put it to him immediately. I try to keep them from running at all, but on the other hand I break off quite a few fish and sometimes end up with bloody knuckles. Even with this approach, expect a hard fought 10 to 20 minute battle.

These big fish aren't edible unless you enjoy eating coarse flesh that's loaded with parasites. Revive your catch, which won't take long (these fish are RUGGED) and release it so it can make more baby drum.

42

Bluefish *Pomatomus saltatrix*

Capt. Merrily Dunn with a Sarasota Bay bluefish.

Unfortunately, normally Florida bluefish just don't create the same type of excitement that they do up north. Since the average Florida bluefish only weighs between one and two pounds, that isn't really surprising. Every spring though, a horde of big, hungry choppers migrates north along the east coast following baitfish schools. If easterly, especially southeasterly, winds push the bait near shore the blues will be right along the beaches, terrorizing mullet, bathers, and anything else that's in the water.

Inlets seem to attract these fish as much as anything else. Coming up the coast, St. Lucie, Fort Pierce, Sebastian, Ponce, and Matanzas Inlets, Port Canaveral, the St. Johns river mouth and Nassau Sound are all possible sites for the blues to come ashore. Some years they never do come in, and are north of the Florida state line and probably up to Cape Hatteras before ever making landfall.

The smaller blues hang around inlets and river mouths along the east coast all winter. They move into river systems and we've caught them in the Indian River system as far from the ocean as the power plants in Titusville, at least 40 miles from Ponce Inlet. Like their bigger relatives they strike pretty much anything when they feed. Heavy mono leaders and durable, flashy flies imitating minnows are suggested. Poppers sometimes bring very exciting fishing.

Bluefish also run along the west coast. These again tend to be smaller fish. Up in the Panhandle bluefish are caught all summer, but along the rest of the west coast it is primarily a winter and spring fishery, again concentrated around cuts and passes.

Bonefish *Albula vulpes*

Somewhat surprisingly, bonefish can be very easy to catch with flies. As could be expected, they can be practically impossible, too. Among the biggest found anywhere, Florida bonefish average about six pounds and frequently reach weights in double digits.

Bones can consistently be found from Biscayne Bay south all the way into the Marquesas Keys. They feed on small fish, various crustaceans, marine worms, and other invertebrates, and classic angling for them takes place on shallow flats where they feed, locations where anglers typically watch all of the action.

Fortunately for the boatless, lots of good wade fishing can be found in the Keys and even around Miami. Ocean side flats tend to be firm and support the weight of even husky fly fishers. Waders have the advantage of stealth on their side, an especially big help in those heavily fished Keys waters.

Good bonefishing can be found all year long, weather conditions permitting. During the winter periods bones tend to feed between fronts, especially after the afternoon sun has warmed up the water a bit. Spring is good and fall is probably the best time to fish for bones. You'll find the best summer fishing in the morning, as intense heat and sunlight during the day make the flats uncomfortable for fish and angler alike. Evening fishing during the summer also produces.

During the spring and fall the fish feed on the flats any time of day. It gets windy this

Capt. Rick DePaiva with a Marquesas Keys bonefish.

44

time of year. If the water gets muddy the game is over at that spot. You'll have to try to find clean water. But good weather often brings tremendous fishing. Relatively few people fish the Keys during the autumn, and you may have the entire flat to yourself.

During the winter, water temperature again becomes critical. During cool weather, do your fishing during the afternoon hours. The water will be warmest then.

Given the choice, fish an incoming tide (winter excepted). Also, whether fishing in a boat or wading, try to move with the current, since the fish always move into it. By "going with the flow," casts to fish will generally be head-on shots, too- the best kind.

Expert bonefisherman Chico Fernandez describes bonefish feeding behavior this way: "When the tide is low and the fish first move onto the flats, they are hungry. After they've been feeding for a few hours they become much more selective." It makes sense. Bones are usually easier early in the tide.

This having been said, sometimes time of day becomes more critical than tide phase. Again, normally this occurs during summer, when morning fishing is best, and during winter, when evening fishing is best.

If you must fish during the day in the summer, fish an incoming tide. Cooler ocean water coming onto the flat allows the fish a degree of comfort they would not have otherwise. The situation reverses during the winter. The sun warms up water that's been on the flat a while enough to allow the fish to use it. This happens during the later stages of the incoming tide and the early stages of the outgoing.

Slowly wade or pole with the current looking for anything which might be a bonefish. If there are no fish tailing or pushing wakes look for muds in somewhat deeper water. Muds are made by feeding fish. Make your casts fall short a few feet, letting the fly sink to the bottom if necessary. The fly will be between you and the fish, but if you are moving with the current they're moving toward you. As soon as you think they can see it, move it slowly. Make sure that you keep watching the fish!

If they see it there will be no doubts about it. They do one of three things- flee in abject terror, come check it out and refuse it, or come check it out and eat it.

If they flee, the fly was fouled with grass, or moved at them, or was too close to them before it moved. If they refuse it, check the fly. If it is not fouled with grass or algae, change to a different size or color. If they eat it, set the hook GENTLY. When the fish takes off, it will take care of hook setting.

If you see fish pushing up a wake, cast several feet ahead of it and move the fly SLOWLY. Sometimes when the fish are pushing a wake, they swim fast, with an obvious agenda, and aren't interested in eating. If they don't strike don't let this bother you- they probably wouldn't have taken a live shrimp!

Tailing fish are eating, though. A small crab fly made from wool, or my Son of Clouser pattern, are good choices for this situation. These flies hit the water with a soft, seductive "splat," sink rapidly into the feeding zone, and imitate a favorite bonefish food. Crab flies don't even need to be moved. If the fish sees it and wasn't spooked by the presentation they usually eat it immediately.

If this is your first bonefish, at this point your life may change forever! First, clear the line. If it fouls on anything the leader instantly breaks, you have a super adrenaline rush, and you own one less fly. Once the fish is on the reel extend the rod high into the air. The fish run right along the bottom, so you want to hold the line up to prevent the leader from fraying on coral, rocks, or sea fans.

Let the fish run. If you try to stop it he'll break off. Make sure the drag is set only tightly enough to prevent the reel from forming a backlash.

Once that first incredible run ends he will take a couple shorter ones. Once you've beaten him, handle the fish gently. Leave him in the water if possible. If not, hold the fish parallel to the water's surface and belly up. They have no teeth or spines and are quite safe to handle. Remove the fly, revive him until he can swim away, and release him to grow and thrill another fisherman. And congratulations to you!

All of the above supposes that you have good visibility. But if you fish early or late in the day, or if it is overcast, or if you are not used to looking for fish, seeing bonefish in the water can be very difficult. They can still be caught. Try blindcasting for bones.

All other things being equal, the fish feed on their favorite flats when weather conditions allow. If you're there you might just get a couple.

When you use this blind casting technique for bonefish, fly choice is important. You want a fly with which you can cover a lot of water reasonably quickly. The Clouser minnow works well for this. Search the water you can see into for fish. If you see any, cast to them! There's no sense in turning down any good opportunities.

Keep your fly in the water into which you cannot see. Generally this will be the deeper water, but fish feed there as well as in the skinny stuff. Keep casting! Fish every cast as if you expect to hook a fish. Sooner or later you will.

Make long casts. You cover more water this way, giving more fish a chance to see your offering. Also, the fish oftentimes follows your fly for quite a distance before finally making up its mind. Long retrieves give them the opportunity to do this.

Once you hook up, play the fish as explained above.

Cobia *Rachycentron canadum*

Cobia rank as one of Florida's most exciting nearshore gamefish. Found along both coasts in water as shallow as three feet and out into depths of over 100 feet, they often eat flies with little hesitation, although on some days they completely ignore feathered offerings.

Cobia love structure and often cruise around channel markers, buoys, floating debris, ocean going ships at anchor, and other inanimate objects. They also swim with other "denizens of the deep." Along the Atlantic coast they often swim with manta rays off the beaches. They sometimes associate with sea turtles. I've seen big cobia swimming with manatees in Charlotte Harbor, and in the Homosassa area they follow stingrays in shallow water in the early spring, making for a great sight fishery before tarpon season starts.

These fish, like many other fish found off the beaches, can be chummed up with live baitfish. The baitfish get them feeding and then they're much more likely to hit a fly.

Cobia make seasonal runs up and down both Florida coasts, heading north in the spring and to a lesser degree south again in the fall. During these migrations angler excitement rises to a fever pitch.

At least a nine-weight outfit is usually used when chasing these fish, depending on where you are. In the Panhandle during the spring cobia run an 11- or 12-weight outfit may be more appropriate. Cobia there get big, over 100 pounds, and they're strong. Plenty of backing is needed. Their mouth is rough, so use a 40-50 pound shock tippet.

Cobia eat a wide variety of marine organisms. They hold small fish, eels, shrimp, crabs, and squid in high regard. Consequently, flies imitating any of these foods (or even nothing in

The author's sons, Alex and Maxx, with a handsome cobia caught off a buoy out of Port Canaveral.

particular) all work well. For example in Homosassa dark colored flies, especially rabbit strip patterns, are popular. Up in the Panhandle they like big white ties, sometimes with some pink thrown in. These flies supposedly imitate squid, another favorite cobia food.

There's not much of a catch and release fishery for cobia. Excellent on the table, they are seldom released once they grow larger than the minimum size limit of 33 inches.

Dolphin *Coryphaena hippurus*

The dolphin rates high as an offshore fly rod target. They strike explosively and their fight is spectacular with frequent acrobatic leaps. In addition, their stunning coloration and high quality on the table make them extremely popular with Florida anglers.

They are usually found by trolling, but any type of offshore flotsam often holds dolphin, especially in the summer months. A minnow imitation or popping bug thrown near the floating material will often garner a savage strike. Once a fish is hooked, other fish in the school often follow it, making multiple hookups possible and prolonged action a distinct possibility.

Tackle size depends on the size of the fish encountered. Small chickens can be caught on freshwater trout tackle. Nine-weight tackle is considered light for the real dolphin, since the average east coast fish ranges from five to 15 pounds. They get much larger, up to 50 or even 60 pounds. If you're lucky enough to hook a trophy like this you'll need plenty of backing on the reel, as big ones are incredibly strong, will make long, fast runs when hooked, and frequently need to be lifted out of deep water.

Maxx Kumiski with a "chicken" dolphin caught in waters off of Big Pine Key. Although small, the fish gave a great account of itself on the three-weight rod he was using.

Like many other fish, dolphin respond well to chumming, using small baitfish like pilchards, or even cut up chunks of mullet, balao, bonito, or whatever. Once they are in a frenzy behind the stern, the fly fisher usually has an easy time getting them to strike.

Dolphin grow fast and are short-lived. They mature sexually at the age of nine months and rarely live longer than four years.

Crevalle Jack *Caranx hippos*

Crevalle of over six pounds or so are one of my favorite fish. Big, fast, tough, and aggressive, they willingly eat flies (especially poppers), and they are common enough that catching one doesn't require an exodus to some far-off location.

The late, great A.J. McClane had this to say about the crevalle:
"One of the several things in the crevalle's favor is the fact that it's a first-class light-tackle fish which can be caught on fly gear. Small crevalle of 6 to 7 pounds are gregarious and travel in schools. As they become older, big jacks occur in pods, or sometimes you'll see a single or a pair 'running' at top speed.

"The individual crevalle takes its feeding seriously. Here and there one mullet will rise above the surface, doing front and back flips, then leaping madly in all directions with a telltale swirl countering each shift. If the hapless baitfish is lucky, it may elude the jack for two or three jumps, but sooner or later the mullet will land in the crevalle's jaws. You can actually drift through acres of frantic mullet and observe this single-minded pursuit."

McClane added this about the jack's fighting ability: "In common with the permit, large jacks always seem to have an extra ounce of energy in reserve. Their tactics are dogged and unrelenting. It's not uncommon to play a 20 pounder for an hour or more on light tackle."

You can find jacks throughout the state, both in inshore and nearshore waters. They frequently patrol around structures like seawalls and jetties, and are attracted to inlets and river mouths. When they corner or surround a school of baitfish little doubt remains about what's going on- the bait leaps frantically into the air as the crevalle churn the surface to a froth. This makes for heart-attack action as long as the fish stay on top!

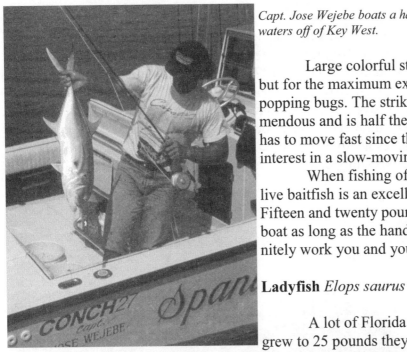

Capt. Jose Wejebe boats a handsome crevalle jack caught in waters off of Key West.

Large colorful streamer flies work well for jacks but for the maximum excitement from these fish use popping bugs. The strike from a good sized jack is tremendous and is half the fun of catching them. The bug has to move fast since they usually don't show much interest in a slow-moving bait.

When fishing off the beaches, chumming with live baitfish is an excellent way to catch large jacks. Fifteen and twenty pounders will stay right under the boat as long as the handouts continue. They will definitely work you and your fishing buddies to exhaustion.

Ladyfish *Elops saurus*

A lot of Florida fly fishers have said if ladyfish grew to 25 pounds they would fish for nothing else. Small ladyfish can be a nuisance, but when this animal hits three pounds it fights far out of proportion to its size. After hookup it takes off on a lightning run, which usually ends with a spectacular leap. They're fast, they jump, they're tough, and they take flies eagerly. Too bad they only grow to about five pounds!

These bigger ladyfish school in certain areas and seldom use others. Two hotspots during the winter are both of the electric generating station outflows, south of Titusville on U.S.1. It is not unusual here to hook and lose two or three of these beasts on a single cast. Unfortunately, these power stations are now closed to all entry between November 15 and March 31 in the name of manatee protection. The Indian River Lagoon in the vicinity of the St. Lucie Inlet holds some good concentrations of big ladies, as does the Loxahatchee River.

Ladies have very abrasive mouths and are rough on flies. Fortunately, they hit almost anything. When I target ladyfish I clean my fly box of all the uglies, the failed experiments, the

Handle ladyfish with a towel, or better yet, don't handle them at all. A dehooker will remove hooks without your having to touch the fish.

49

flies that are just too beat up to use for anything else. That having been said, Clouser minnows in chartreuse and white are always a good choice. Coating the fly's head with epoxy will extend its life significantly. In many areas they also hit surface bugs, always an exciting way to fish.

Light tackle maximizes the sport with ladyfish. A six-weight does a good job. Be sure to use a good long length of 30 pound fluorocarbon as a shock tippet. The mouths of the ladies wear out the shock quickly and you have to cut off and re-tie your fly frequently.

Ladyfish are rumored to be edible. However, I don't know anyone who knows anyone who eats them! So handle your ladies gently and release them as quickly as you can. And be sure to bring a towel- the ladyfish is a slimy creature, and you'll need the towel for cleaning that slime from your hands.

Little Tunny *Euthynnus alletteratus*

Fly fishers take little tunny, usually called bonito in Florida, all along both coasts during the summer months. These are the same fish usually referred to as false albacore from the Carolinas north. They are an incredible fly rod target- fast, strong, and willing, frequently eager, to take flies. Although you can sometimes find and cast to breaking fish, most anglers targeting bonito use pilchards or other live baitfish to chum them up. We've also used frozen glass minnows and shrimper's by-catch with good success.

Once the bonito are chummed up they are not fussy about the fly pattern, and almost any white fly

Tom Mitzlaff with a Little Tunny he caught near the Gulf Stream off of Jupiter.

imitating a minnow works, especially if it matches the chum in size. Poppers will often work just as well, and the strikes are just awesome. With any type of fly their strike is spectacular. They may see and charge the fly from 30 to 40 feet away and have a good head of steam up when they hit it, often coming clear out of the water.

The first run is something to experience, long and very fast. They sound and then go out away from the boat at close to warp speed. Like all members of the tuna family they are swift, powerful swimmers. This run will test, and frequently break, your tackle. Tunny will find and exploit any flaw in your tackle system. The fight tends to be long and tough, with some serious lifting needed when fishing in water over 50 feet deep.

Using live pilchards as chum you can keep the bonito around your boat all day. However, at the end of such a day you'll need an application of a muscle cream like Flex-All!

The Mackerels *Scombridae* family

Florida waters hold three different species of mackerel- Spanish, cero, and king. You find Spanish and kings along both coasts the length of the state; ceros are found mostly from Miami south into the Keys. Ceros and Spanish are

The Spanish mackerel is a toothy, aggressive critter, great fun on a light fly rod.

quite similar- schooling fish that average two to six pounds, are found in ocean waters from right off the beaches to several miles offshore, and feed primarily on glass minnows, pilchards, sardines, anchovies and other small baitfish. From here on when I mention Spanish I'm talking about both fishes.

King mackerel (or kingfish) range in size from "snakes" in single digit weights, to "smokers" of 50 or 60 pounds. They are usually found farther offshore in water more or less 100 feet deep, around wrecks, buoys, or other structure, offshore from inlets, or other areas where their primary food (menhaden and other large baitfish) is abundant.

Spanish make excellent fly rod targets when they work on bait schools. Terns are especially helpful in pinpointing schools of Spanish. Small flies imitating glass minnows or other small bait work well, flies like the Glass Minnow pattern, small Clouser minnows, or the Surf Candy pattern. Although Spanish (and all the other mackerels) have sharp teeth, if you use a wire trace you'll get many fewer strikes. Thirty pound mono gives a reasonable compromise between strikes and cutoffs. Bring a lot of extra flies!

For anglers without boats, Spanish can often be caught from the beach, especially around sunrise and sunset. Rod Smith, Gary Berkson, and I were casting for snook off Satellite Beach one summer morning. The snook were uncooperative and we could see the Spanish going nuts on glass minnows just out of casting range. We took the canoe off my car and launched it through the surf, and proceeded to catch several nice Spanish mackerel on small chartreuse Clouser minnows. I must say that three of us in the canoe was a bit of a crowd!

Spanish are good eating, especially if they are bled and put on ice immediately. They don't freeze well, so don't fill the boat up with the idea of saving them for a rainy day.

Kingfish are another animal entirely. For one thing, few kings are caught from shore- a boat is pretty much a necessity. Secondly, you are not likely to find kings at the surface feeding ravenously the way Spanish do. Without a special approach, fly fishing for them successfully is difficult to accomplish at best, and could probably be considered impossible.

What the serious kingfish angler needs in order to catch them on flies (and this should come as no surprise) is a livewell filled with pilchards or other small baitfish. The successful fly fishing king mackerel angler chums the kings within casting range of the boat. Once they're there and actively feeding, catching them follows naturally.

Captain Tommy Locke specializes in catching kings on flies. Based in the Boca Grand area, Tommy fishes along the buoy line leading out into the Gulf from Boca Grand Pass when the kings are running. The buoys serve as fish attractors.

Tommy tosses pilchards over a few at a time until he gets the kings' attention. They literally boil on the pilchards right behind the boat. While in this frenzy the kings take a white fly resembling a pilchard without hesitation. You'd better have a wire trace between the fly and the leader. Kings have <u>extremely</u> sharp teeth.

You'd also better have a lot of backing on the reel, and be prepared to reel a lot of line. Kings swim long and fast once hooked up, and the bigger they are the farther they go. They don't call them "smokers" for nothing! Some of Tommy's anglers have taken kings over 40 pounds this way.

Tackle for these big kings starts with nine-weight rods, which are definitely on the light side. Ten- and eleven-weight tackle gives the angler better lifting power when the fish sound.

While Capt. Locke uses this technique in the Boca Grande area, other charter captains use the same technique elsewhere along the coast. In order to work effectively, there must be something present to concentrate the fish- a reef, a wreck, a buoy line, a spring hole, or some other type of structure.

King mackerel make excellent table fare.

Permit *Trachinotus falcatus*

The author with one of the few permit he's caught.

Permit are one of the great trophies of the Florida Keys. A Keys Grand Slam consists of catching a bonefish, a tarpon, and a permit on flies all in the same day. Most anglers who try and fail to achieve this distinction stumble over the permit way more often than the other two.

Up until about twenty years ago permit were an extraordinarily rare fly rod catch. Due to the pioneering efforts of guides like Nat Ragland, Steve Huff, Jeffrey Cardenas, and Dexter Simmons and anglers like George Anderson and Del Brown, catching permit on flies, while still not easy, happens with reasonable frequency.

These "permit pioneers" recognized that permit love eating crabs and also recognized that sink rate was an important factor in fly construction. They then designed crab imitations that permit actually ate. Ragland developed the Puff, Anderson developed the McCrab, and Brown developed the Merkin. These flies revolutionized fly fishing for permit.

Anglers who want to catch a permit on a fly are strongly advised to hire a guide. I typically prefer the do it yourself approach and the desire to help others who feel the same way was one of the driving forces behind my writing this book. However, I have tried on my own unsuccessfully for years to take a permit on a fly. I hardly ever see them, much less get them to eat.

Having said all that, you may want to try anyway. Like kingfish tackle, a nine-weight is considered light for permit. Unlike kings, no wire is needed, and a shock tippet is actually a handicap. A 14 or 16 pound test fluorocarbon tippet supplies all the protection you need.

Look for permit near the edges of flats, or near rock piles. Sometimes the fish "fin out," lying just beneath the surface with the tips of their dorsal and caudal fins in the air. They often tail, rooting in the bottom for crabs just like bonefish do. You'll see them cruising along the flat in water three or four feet deep.

Guides differ in their recommendations on how far to lead the permit, but all of them agree on the following point- once the fish sees the fly (a crab imitation, of course) that fly should be allowed to drop to the bottom and should not move again until the fish has either taken it, or refused it and started swimming off. If the former occurs, strip strike with the line hand to make sure the fish actually has the fly. Once you determine that the fish is actually on, use the rod to strike several more times. The mouth of a permit has about the same consistency as the tires on your car. You really need to stick them.

53

If the fish refuses your fly, all is not lost. When it starts to swim off, move the fly just a little and see if it comes back. If it does, do not move the fly until it takes or refuses. You might have to play this game a few times. If the fish really does move off, try to get the fly airborne and deliver it out front again. Don't give up until the fish is out of sight!

If you are lucky enough to hook up, prepare for a long tough fight. A good sized permit can easily be over thirty pounds. Like other members of the jack family, permit are incredibly strong. They run like a bonefish when hooked, but swim much farther than bonefish do. If hooked near the edge of a flat the permit usually heads toward deeper water.

In one way, they are kind of like snook or largemouth bass. If they can tangle your line up on a snag, they will. They will find plenty of snags between the flat and deep water, things like sea fans, coral heads, crab trap lines, and others. They also rub their snout in the bottom, trying to dislodge the hook. They successfully use their broad sides to resist to the utmost. If you are lucky enough to boat the fish, it may be miles from where you hooked up.

Permit are reputed to be delicious on the table. Most serious fly fishers would rather lose their casting arm than kill such a magnificent fish.

Redfish *Sciaenops ocellatus*

Mark Marsh with a trophy redfish from the Indian River Lagoon.

Redfish may keep more guides working than any other fish in Florida. Schools of hundreds of redfish averaging between five and ten pounds are fairly common sights on flats all over the state. You'll also find them as singles, doubles, or small pods of fish.

In the Indian River Lagoon you may see schools of fish in the twenty to thirty pound range, hundreds of fish sometimes. It is a truly incredible sight. The Indian River Lagoon offers the planet's finest sight fishing for these big reds.

You may see redfish laid up on the bottom, pushing up wakes, tailing, or "backing," that is, feeding in water so shallow that they are not even covered and their backs are out of the water. Best of all, redfish eagerly (well, most of the time) gobble flies of all kinds, including all the various minnow imitations, poppers and sliders, and flies imitating crabs, a favorite food.

Reds are made to order for the do-it-yourself angler. Various techniques work well for reds, and they're found in most parts of the state. You can catch them from the beach, by wading on shallow flats, or of course by casting from a boat. Typically fished for with flies in water from six inches to three feet deep, they make a superb fly rod target.

Tackle for reds typically includes rods in the seven- to nine-weight range. Line choice depends on where you fish, but for flats floating weight forward lines work best. A leader about the length of the rod tapered to a 12 or 15 pound tippet, and the fly of your choice finish the rig.

Popular flies for reds include bendbacks, deceivers, seaducers, popper/slider types, divers, Clouser minnows, and crab patterns. As mentioned earlier, reds usually aren't too fussy. If you have a fish refuse, change to a smaller and/or darker colored fly.

Effective fly sizes range from #4 at the small end to 2/0 at the big end. Larger flies are better when it's warm. Choose smaller darker flies in the winter.

Florida currently protects red drum with a slot size limit and a one fish per day bag limit.. Fish smaller than 18 inches or larger than 27 inches must be released. Legal-sized fish make for excellent eating.

Seatrout *Cynoscion nebulosus*

Seatrout are probably the most popular sportfish in Florida. Unfortunately, finding large seatrout (over six or seven pounds) is fairly rare. Finding a concentration of large seatrout is VERY rare. Still, it does happen, and a decent sized trout is a worthwhile catch on a fly, particularly on a popping bug.

Seatrout feed primarily on other fish and shrimp. Therefore, the fly fisher should try to imitate these foods. All of the popular minnow imitations will work well, and trout have a weakness for brightly colored flies. Hair bugs or other types of poppers also produce, and are my own personal favorites for these fish. And of course seatrout are suckers for flies that mimic shrimp. The fly fisher can successfully use a wide variety of flies.

Seatrout are unspectacular at the end of the line. A Pfleuger Medalist 1498 is all the reel needed. In other words, state of the art tackle is unnecessary. Really nice trout will make runs, but they won't be very long. The only reason you would need more than fifty yards or so of backing is if some other type of fish ate your fly instead of a trout. This is a very real possibility, so don't get complacent!

Rod size is determined by wind and fly size more than anything else. A seven weight will be ample, and nine-weights overpower almost all trout hooked.

Waders (and everyone else who looks) find trout on grass flats all over the state. Trout like areas of mixed sand and grass bottom, and use the edges between the two as ambush points. Sand holes in grass flats make good targets for your fly when fish can't be seen, especially when the weather is cool. As concerns depth they could be anywhere from mere inches of water

Capt. Dan Malzone with a handsome trout from Tampa Bay.

to five or six feet. Generally speaking, they will be more shallow early and late in the day.

Blind casting over healthy grass flats with any type of surface fly can be extremely effective, especially early or late in the day. On flats big trout will often be found cruising under schools of finger mullet, waiting for one to make an error. Cast around and into these schools. When mullet make muds, seatrout will definitely be in the vicinity, looking for an easy meal.

When iced down after capture, seatrout are excellent eating. Seatrout now have a slot limit and closed seasons which depend on where in the state you happen to be fishing. If you catch any over about 20 inches, please allow them to pass their genes on to future generations.

Sharks Phylum *Chondreicthyes*

SHARK! To the average person, the word is synonymous with fear bordering on terror. To the angler, sharks supply a source of wonder and another target for our flies. We marvel at the grace they show as they move through the water, even as we try to keep our distance. We are no strangers to fear either, we fishermen. It makes no sense to go looking for trouble.

Many different species of sharks swim in Florida waters. Several make exciting fly rod sport. Some, like the nurse shark, are dull, sluggish creatures. Others, like the hammerhead, often grow to lengths which make them longer than the boats from which the anglers are fishing. Tangling with a fish like this from a small boat could prove exceedingly dangerous!

Several species of sharks patrol shallow flats and can be stalked and cast to like other flats fish. Blacktips, lemon sharks, bonnetheads, and bull sharks all like to hunt in the shallows

56

and use water so skinny their backs are exposed to the air. They are extremely spooky in these shallows and you need to use the greatest skill in stalking and care in presentation in order to elicit a strike.

They take brightly colored streamer flies, if you place the fly off to the side of their head where they can see it and turn on it. Joe Mulson and I had shot after shot at some blacktip sharks one time while in Everglades National Park. We watched in frustration as the shark would come up behind the fly ready to eat and would lose sight of the fly after getting it under its snout. The poor shark kept trying to eat this morsel and opened up and missed time after time! I still don't know who was more frustrated, the shark or us.

You can sightfish sharks with poppers on slightly deeper flats. In very shallow water the popping of the fly can spook the shark, but with a foot or more of water under them they become much more aggressive. You'll find watching a shark tracking and then attacking your popper tremendously exciting!

Finally, whether on the flats or offshore, sharks respond very well to chum. Get a small fish of some kind (barracuda, blue runner, ladyfish, and crevalle all work well) and partially fillet both sides. Hang it in the water. The current will spread the scent and sharks will follow it to your boat.

Tackle for shallow water sharking depends on the anticipated size of the shark. For smaller sharks to fifty pounds or so seven- to nine-weight outfits work well. Blacktips, bulls, and lemons all reach triple figures in the poundage department, though. Going after these brutes without sufficient firepower is sheer folly.

When one of these sharks realizes it's in trouble in the shallows it streaks off for deeper water as or more powerfully as any other fish is capable of doing. Under the best of circumstances you'll be in for a long, hard fight. Go undergunned and you've probably lost before you start. I hooked some 200 to 400 pound bull sharks off the beach at Jupiter one time with a 12-weight outfit. I could have been using sewing thread for as much difference as it made to them.

Bigger sharks can be had offshore. They are usually chummed in by using live baitfish or a combination of live bait and ground menhaden, balao, or other oily fish. This can be very serious business, with sharks the size of the boat entering the chumline a distinct possibility.

The legendary hammerhead called Old Hitler may be encountered. Old Hitler has been seen in various locations in Florida, usually during the tarpon run. These locations include Boca Grande Pass and some of the Keys bridges. This monster's length is estimated at between 17 and 21 feet. Hooking a shark like this on a mega fifteen weight would still be folly- he might never realize he was hooked!

Captain Tommy Busciglio told me one of the best true shark stories I've ever heard. Tommy was fishing with clients in the Marquesas Islands off of Key West when they came upon a large school of hundred pound plus tarpon. These huge "baitfish" had been packed into a tight ball on a deep flat by three hammerheads between 12 and 15 feet long. While two sharks kept the tarpon corralled, the third would charge into the pack and eat. The tarpon were showering like gigantic terrified mullet as these sharks took turns feeding. Tommy said it was the single most awesome thing he's ever seen in a lifetime of fishing.

Hooking a shark like that from a small skiff in shallow water would be indescribably exciting. But imitating a six foot long tarpon with a fly (and casting it if you could) would be difficult at best!

Needless to say, regardless of the type of shark you chase or where you choose to chase them, you need some wire on the business end of the leader. Some anglers prefer single strand, but for big sharks it can easily kink and break during the battle. About twelve inches of plastic-coated Sevenstrand works better for the big boys. A small swivel between the wire and the class tippet will help prevent line twist while fighting the shark. Blacktips especially like to spin during their often spectacular leaps!

When tying flies for sharking, use bronze hooks. The fly isn't worth your fingers. Cut the wire leader and the bronze hook will quickly rust out (we all hope), leaving no permanent damage to the fish.

Bonnetheads aren't one of the great trophies of the flats, but they are fun and can save a day.

58

Snapper *Lutjanidae* Family

    Snapper aren't usually thought of as fly rod targets, but in Florida both mutton snapper and mangrove snapper sometimes fall to fly rodders. Muttons in particular like to follow stingrays along Keys flats, and when they do this they are at their most "catchable" by fly fishers. Ordinarily it's difficult to fool a mutton with a fly, but when one is following a ray that's kicking up some groceries it's much easier to convince it to take. Muttons are a great fly rod trophy,

very hard to fool. Flies similar to those used for bonefish or permit do the trick.

    Small mangrove snapper are commonly caught while fishing for other species, especially in the Everglades and Keys. Bigger ones (more than a couple of pounds) are suspicious of everything. They respond well to frozen chum blocks though, and can be taken with flies dead drifted behind the boat with the chum.

    Both mutton and mangrove snappers are delicious.

This is a small mutton snapper, but it was taken on a fly. Only a small percentage of fly fishers ever accomplish this feat.

Snook *Centropomus undecimalis*

    If snook ranged all over the United States the way black bass do, they would undeniably be the most popular fish in North America. They certainly hold a special place in the hearts of Florida fishermen. They make a superb fly rod target. They take flies readily (when they're in the mood, and they can be very moody), they're strong, they're tough, they jump, they use structure to break you off, and they get fairly large (over 30 pounds). Quite simply, they are one of Florida's most popular and challenging game fish.

    Snook inhabit shallow coastal waters, estuaries, and brackish lagoons. They may range into fresh water, especially during the winter months. They can be caught by both sight-fishing and blind-casting along beaches, by chumming with live bait off of beaches, in passes, along mangrove shorelines, by blind-casting, sight-fishing, or chumming on flats, in creeks, around oyster bars, and more. They have many of the same habits as the aforementioned black bass, take many of the same flies, and can be caught with the same tackle.

    Like bass, snook seldom make long runs. They lunge with incredible power for bridge abutments, pilings, roots, or whatever else is available to them. If they reach the cover the game

59

Barry Kent with a beautiful snook caught near Blowing Rocks.

usually ends. Once in a while a stupid snook gets hooked and heads out to open water, but such dumb specimens usually don't live long, since snook make a fine table fish.

Snook are found roughly from Tampa Bay on the west side and Port Canaveral on the east side, south. Snook are caught north of this line on both coasts, but it becomes a very specialized fishery requiring local knowledge.

Tackle needs as usual are dictated by the size of the fish targeted and the type of terrain to be fished. Fishing for big fish around mangroves requires a rod and leader system with guts. Nine weight rods do nicely. If you hook a big fish near mangroves he'll likely try to run into them. You must try to stop him. A wimpy leader will just give way. A strong one of 20 or 30 pound test will give you some hand-sizzling action, and although those line burns smart, this leader is much more likely to hold the fish.

Snook possess raspy, abrasive lips and a sharp leader (and hand) cutting device on their gill plates. You must use a shock leader. Different opinions exist on what the optimum thickness is for this shock, but 30 pound fluorocarbon is probably the most popular choice.

Even if the fish run large a skilled angler snook fishing on grass flats could easily get by with a seven-weight. With nothing to tangle the line on, the fish will make short runs and jump until she tires. Then she's yours! That's all there is to it!

Strict laws on bag limits, minimum and maximum sizes, and closed seasons protect snook. The Florida Fish and Wildlife Conservation Commission website at www.marinefisheries.org has the latest information. Catch and release angling is allowed any time.

Tarpon *Megalops atlanticus*

In my humble opinion, tarpon of any size are <u>the</u> supreme shallow water fish for fly casters. First of all, although smaller tarpon are as game as any fish, tarpon get to be as large or larger than the average angler. Second of all, tarpon are often sight-fished in water so shallow and clear that the angler can watch the entire drama of the fish tracking and eating the fly which as another point they take quite willingly (on occasion). Thirdly, after being hooked tarpon make these incredible, indescribable leaps, somersaults, tailwalks, and other out-of-water displays, sometimes so violently that they severely injure themselves. Their response to being hooked is so extreme that they sometimes leap into the angler's boat, trashing gear, injuring occupants, and occasionally causing smaller craft to capsize! You have to <u>love</u> a fish like that!

Tarpon aren't all 100 pounders, and frequently these smaller fish are a lot more fun. This one came out of the Indian River Lagoon.

Tackle needs depend on the size of the tarpon being targeted. As one might expect, fishing for tarpon in the 80 pound and up category requires specialized tackle like eleven- and twelve-weight rods, matching high quality reels, and specialized lines and leader systems. Very skilled anglers could take on and beat tarpon in the 50 to 70 pound range on nine- or ten-weight rods, but most anglers shouldn't go after these fish under-gunned. It puts too much stress on the fish to fight for a long time, making them susceptible to attack by their mortal enemy- big sharks. Stu Apte routinely whips even very big tarpon on twelve pound tippets in 20 minutes or less. Doing this is in the best interests of the fish.

Tarpon eat almost any type of fly designed for use in saltwater. The standard flies tied for tarpon are based on the Keys style tarpon streamer, developed by Stu Apte and others in the Florida Keys. Typically, they're tied on hooks from size 3/0 to 5/0 (although smaller flies are getting more popular) for big fish of over 100 pounds. The popularity of this style stems from its tendency not to foul as much as the fish's willingness to take it.

This style is far from the only kind of fly that the silver kings will eat. Minnow imitations like the PolarFiber Minnow, the flies by Enrico Puglisi, or my own SexyFlies, are all excellent tarpon patterns. They have the advantage that every tarpon in Florida hasn't seen them hundreds of times yet. Tarpon live a long time (as much as 30 years), and although the Cockroach is still surprisingly effective sometimes, every big fish out there has seen several every year for its entire life.

Flies for big tarpon are usually pre-rigged to the leaders and stored in a "tarpon box" to keep them from tangling.

Leader systems for the bigger fish are quite specialized too. Most anglers prefer the "big game" style of leader with a (usually) 80 pound fluorocarbon shock tippet, a section of class tippet of 12, 16, or 20 pounds, and a long (five to eight feet, or sometimes even more) butt section connected to the end of the fly line.

Although the Keys and Homosassa have justly deserved reputations as tarpon fishing meccas, tarpon can be found anywhere in the state during the summer, sometimes in surprising places. The big fish attract a directed fishery all along the west coast during the traditional "tarpon season" during May and June. Smaller fish can literally be found almost anywhere, sometimes all year long. In the fall tarpon of all sizes follow the mullet run down along the east coast beaches. Hanging a hundred pound tarpon from the beach with a fly rod would make for an exciting but short fight! Goodbye, fly line!

Many anglers fish for years for big tarpon without success. To catch big ones consistently, you really need to hire a good guide. Even then, bad weather can ruin the fishing in a flash. Many, many anglers have spent a week fishing for tarpon with the best guides in the business and never hooked a single fish. I spent seven years trying myself before I got that first 100 pound fish. So when things look bad and the fish won't bite and you're tempted to blame the guide, the weather, the moon phase, or (heaven forbid!) even yourself, don't. Just remember that the answer to the anguished question "WHY???" is, "Because they are tarpon."

Many tarpon kill tournaments used to be held in Florida. Almost all of these have been replaced by release tournaments, in which all fish are measured and released. Anyone wanting to kill a tarpon must first purchase a tarpon tag, similar to a hunter's deer tag. This tag costs 50 dollars. All taxidermists now make fiberglass mounts, so there is absolutely no reason to kill them for mounting. In the U.S. tarpon are not used as a food fish, so there's really no reason to kill a tarpon at all.

Tarpon are very delicate fish, surprisingly so for one which reacts so violently to the sting of the hook. If you are lucky enough to catch a silver king, try not to remove it from the water. Take as much time as necessary to revive it. And the thrill you get as you watch that warrior swim away will be as intense as the thrill you got when he rocketed out of the water on that first breathtaking leap.

Tripletail *Lobotes surinamensis*

Most fly fishers have never heard of the tripletail, never mind caught one. This really is a shame. A common if unusual looking fish, tripletail readily take a well presented fly.

Tripletail are found along both Florida coasts, usually off the beaches but within sight of land. They like to hang out around any floating objects in the water, such as buoys, boards, mats of seaweed, or other objects. I've even seen them under dead jack crevalle which had been discarded by mackerel netters. They often lie on their sides directly underneath the object in question, looking like anything but a desirable gamefish.

During the stone crab season in southwest Florida, tripletail specialists make a point of running the line of crab trap buoys first thing in the morning. They check each buoy with several casts to see if there are any tripletail present. This is really exciting fishing, for when a big tripletail gets hooked he tries to foul the leader in the buoy line. Stopping them is difficult, and lots of big 'tails break off.

What is big for a tripletail? They routinely reach double digit weights, but any fish over 10 pounds is a nice one. The all tackle world record exceeds 45 pounds. These fish are very strong and will sometimes even jump.

Tripletail seem to eat most types of flies with equal vigor. Seaducers, Clouser minnows, shrimp patterns, even popping bugs, all work at times. The standard eight- or nine-weight outfit performs well. Tripletail have firm white flesh and make fine eating.

Tuna *Thunnus* species

Tuna! What exciting fly rod fish! Here in Florida three species of tuna are of interest to fly fishers- the blackfin (Thunnus atlanticus), the yellowfin (Thunnus albacares), and the little tunny, or false albacore (Euthynnus alletteratus). While the little tunny can be caught quite close to shore and have already been discussed, the blackfin and the yellowfin are usually taken well offshore, either by following the bycatch trail of shrimpers or by chumming the fish into range with pilchards or other small species of baitfish.

Anyone chasing tuna of any type had better have top quality tackle, especially a quality reel. These fish swim as fast as almost anything else in the sea, and go for quite a distance. Additionally, yellowfins, due to the size they attain, can easily and rapidly strip any fly reel currently in production. The largest tippet class fly rod world record for the yellowfin is around 60 pounds, but the all tackle world record is close to four hundred. You can see that there might be a problem if you hook a fish like this on fly! You'll have about eight seconds of reel-smoking ecstasy. Of course you'll have to replace leader, line, and all the backing, but it sure was fun!

While experienced offshore fly fishers could probably track down some blackfins or yellowfins and have the proper gear for them, anglers not experienced in this type of fishing who want to try it should hire a guide who specializes in offshore fly fishing. Although tuna are caught all along the east coast, most of this activity centers in the Keys, especially Key West. In the next section of this book details will be given about who fishes tuna (and on fly that's not very many) and when the best times are.

Blackfin tuna are excellent eating and yellowfin are simply sublime.

Miscellaneous Fishes

Other fish swim in Florida's salt, fish not often taken by fly fishers and so ignored in this work until now. While chumming offshore, especially over wrecks, some surprises should be expected to show up in the chum line. Fish like wahoo, amberjack, African pompano, even sailfish are all distinct possibilities.

The late Bob Huttemeyer told me about a morning when he was fishing for little tunny and hooked one of about 15 pounds (on conventional tackle). While he was playing his fish a magnificent blue marlin suddenly appeared, then attacked and ate his fish. Now he was hooked up to a several hundred pound marlin, fishing from a small boat, using fifteen pound test line. This "Old Man and the Sea" drama lasted well into the afternoon, when the marlin finally got serious and broke the line. Especially when fishing offshore, always expect the unexpected!

A few surprises may await inshore too. Unfortunately these are usually much less spectacular than blue marlin. You certainly may take flounder while fishing for reds or seatrout, especially in north Florida, always a pleasant surprise.

Other species may take your fly. Fishing with a hair bug for baby tarpon in Sebastian River one time, I had a strike. The fish was hooked and it was immediately obvious that it was not a tarpon. Much to my dismay, a minute later a hardhead catfish came alongside the boat, my hair bug stuck in its jaw. Blowfish, sailcats and lizardfish are other types of unexpected (undesired?) inshore fish that are all known to take flies sometimes.

64

This puffer fish nailed a rattle fly in the Mosquito Lagoon. You probably won't need a Tibor to boat one of these.

The Quick Reference Guide

On the next page you'll find a quick reference guide which tells you at a glance which tackle and flies to use for the most popular species of fish. A few words of explanation will allow you to interpret the chart:

-Rod weights- the most commonly used rods to take the species in question. Experienced anglers can use lighter rods than those listed.

-Line type- the most commonly used line. Due to space limitations a simple code is used. F= floating, FS= sinktip, and S= sinking, from intermediate to Wet Cel #4. Understand all lines are weight forward types.

-Leader- again a code was needed. T= tapered, using the standard leader formula described in chapter 1. Use the strength class tippet you prefer, usually between 12 and 16 pound test.

-Fly type and size- self explanatory.

-Water temperature- the first number tells the lower avoidance temperature, the second tells the upper avoidance temperature. Fish will be hard to find and usually won't eat near these extremes. The best temperature tells that temperature at which the fish stay most active.

When the water temperature is below the optimum range but warming fish will often feed. When the water temperature is above the optimum temperature but cooling fish will often feed. When the temperature changes toward either the high or low extremes, fish will be hard to find and even harder to fool with a feathered fake.

SPECIES	ROD WEIGHT	LINE TYPE	LEADER	FLY TYPE AND SIZE	WATER TEMP.
Barracuda	6-7-8	Floating	9'-12' T w/ wire	cuda fly, 4-8" long, 1-1/0 hook	60-82; 75 best
Bluefish	6-7-8-9	F; FS; S	depends on line type. Need wire!	poppers, surf candies, other durable baitfish imitations	50-84; 68 best
Bonefish	6-7-8-9	floating	9'-12' tapered to 10 or 12 lb.	#4-#1 depending on depth, MOE, crab, or reverse tie	60-93; 75 best
Cobia	9-10-11	floating	9' big game w/ 30-50 lb. shock	big deceivers, rabbit strip flies, other large flies 2/0-5/0	
Dolphin	8-9-10	floating or monocore	9' big game w/ 50-80 lb. shock	minnow imitations, 3/0- 5/0	70-82; 75 best
Crevalle Jack	from 6 to 10, depending on size of fish	F; FS; S	depends on line type- need 30 lb shock	minnow imitations and poppers #4- 5/0 depending on size of fish	70-90; 80 best
King Mackerel	9-10-11	floating	9' big game w/wire	minnow imitation or chum fly- match size of chum	70-88; 78 best
Permit	9-10-11	floating	10'-15' tapered to 12- 16 lb.	crab flies or Clouser minnows #2- 2/0	65-92; 72 best
Redfish	6-7-8-9	floating	9'-12' tapered w/ 20 lb. shock	wide variety, #4-3/0 crab flies, minnows, poppers	52-90; 71 best
Seatrout	6-7-8	floating	9'-12' tapered	minnow or shrimp imitations, poppers #2- 1/0	50-81; 72 best
Snook	7-8-9-10	floating	9'-12' T or BG w/ 30- 50 lb. shock	poppers or minnows, #2- 3/0	60-90, 70-75
Tarpon, baby (5-30 lbs)	5-6-7	floating	9' tapered w/ 20-30 lb. shock	minnows or poppers, #4- 1	74-100, 76 best
Tarpon (30-70 lbs)	8-9-10	floating or monocore	9'-12' tapered or big game, 50- 80 lb. shock	primarily minnow patterns (standard tarpon streamers) 1/0- 3/0	same
Big Tarpon (over 80 lbs.)	11-12-13	floating or monocore	10'-14' big game w/ 80-120 lb. shock	standard tarpon streamers 2/0- 5/0	same
Tuna, blackfin	9-10	intermediate or full sink	8'-10' BG w/ 30 lb. 4' w/ 30 lb.	minnow imitations or chum flies to match chum 1/0- 2/0	70-82; 74 best

Part 2 Where to Go

Introduction to the Second Section

Florida is a big state. "Vast" may be a better description. Starting from Orlando in the middle of the state, Key West requires about an eight hour drive on excellent modern highways. Similarly, Panama City lies about six hours in the opposite direction, and there's plenty of space between Panama City and Pensacola.

Since Florida is a peninsula, it has a tremendously long coastline. No one individual can possibly know it all. So when putting this section together I called saltwater fishing guides from around the state, guides who specialize in fly fishing, and interviewed them in order to learn about readily available opportunities for fly fishers in their areas. They freely gave information, and that information is shared with you here.

In this new edition I have filled some gaps that were in the original edition. New coverage areas include Amelia Island, Fort Pierce, Jupiter, Marco Island, Steinhatchee, and Appalachicola Bay. The areas covered in the original book have been maintained, and that coverage has been completely updated.

Also in the original edition, in every coverage section there were short sections for waders, inshore boaters, offshore boaters, and beach fishing. In this edition "offshore" has been changed to a more accurate "nearshore," and hand powered boats like canoes and kayaks, almost completely ignored in the original book, have been added. Where they are available, boat rental information has been obtained.

Let's take a moment to discuss hand powered boats. While these can be used to take extended trips, I am assuming for the purpose of this section of this book that anyone using one will remain within a few miles of the launch site. I am also assuming that large open water crossings will not be done. While I launch my canoe and kayaks through the surf sometimes to fish in the ocean when the weather allows it, I am not recommending that the reader do this. Unless the weather is perfect, hand powered boats are best used in sheltered waters or close to the launch site. My recommendations here will reflect that premise.

How is this information arranged in a geographical sense? If you were to start at the northeast side of the state at Florida state line, drive south along the east coast to the Keys, and then proceed north up the Gulf coast to Pensacola, you would be following the same sequence as the fishing areas that are presented here.

Aerial photographs from the US Geologic Survey have been included to make visualization of the areas easier. If you need more detailed aerial photos they are available over the Internet at www.terraserver.com, a superb resource for any serious angler.

If you will be doing any driving in the Sunshine State I cannot recommend highly enough DeLorme Publishing Company's Florida Atlas and Gazetteer. The Gazetteer contains detailed maps of every area of the state. I used it extensively in preparing this section. See the Resource Catalog in the back of this book for information on how to order the Gazetteer.

Amelia Island

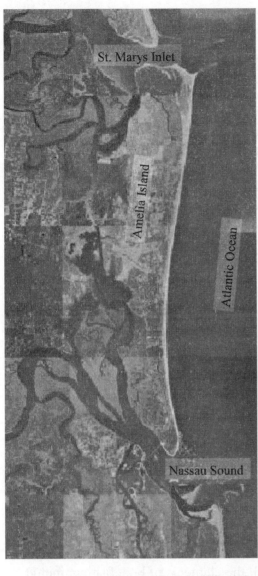

St. Marys Inlet

Amelia Island

Atlantic Ocean

Nassau Sound

Overview

Amelia Island is a lovely barrier island located in the extreme northeast corner of Florida. To the north the St. Marys Inlet separates Amelia Island from Cumberland Island, Georgia. On the east side the Atlantic laps miles of white sand beaches. To the south the waters of Nassau Sound slice between Little Talbot Island and Amelia Island. And on the west thousands of acres of *Spartina* grass and oyster marsh and the Amelia River form a protective moat, insulating the island from the Florida mainland. The route A1A/200 causeway allows landlubbers to access the piscatorial riches Amelia Island holds.

Capt. Russell Tharin described some of the diverse fishery available to fly fishers visiting Amelia Island. Russell showed me a stack of photos of monster jack crevalle that his clients catch- fish well in excess of 30 pounds, with some exceeding 40. "We broke three 12-weights in one week on these jacks this past spring," Russell told me. Other species commonly available in the surf or out in the ocean include Spanish and king mackerel, barracuda, redfish, sharks, and sometimes tarpon, cobia, and tripletail.

"We have the highest tidal range in Florida," says Russell. "It usually ranges between six and eight feet depending on the moon phase. These big tides, the marsh, the rivers, and the ocean give us a very diverse fishery in a relatively small area."

In the salt marsh behind the island, backing redfish swim through inches deep water at low tide, searching for minnows and shrimp, their dorsal fins glistening in the early morning light. When the tide floods, the reds get back in the grass and tail. Although it reminds one of fishing in a wheat field, it is a very interesting and entertaining fishery.

Seatrout range through many of the same waters as do redfish. On low tide phases flounder feed very aggressively, often leaping clear of the water as they chase minnows. And although neither can be sight fished as the redfish can, both flounder and seatrout will readily take flies.

Opportunities for the Do-It-Yourself Fly Fisher

-Wading: Wading access is on short supply here, and what there is might be better described as surf fishing. At the south end of the island there is access for the boatless. Look for reds of other fish cruising along the beach.

-Hand Powered Boat: All of the salt marsh in the back is readily accessed by kayak or canoe. You can fish from the boats on normal tide ranges, working around oyster bars and the edge of the *Spartina* grass. The mud on the bottom is every bit as soft and clingy as it looks. On flood

69

tides you can abandon the boat and walk through the marsh grass searching for tailing reds and the occasional huge sheepshead, themselves up in the grass searching for fiddler crabs. Although difficult to fool, these fish will also take flies in this situation and they could easily be seven or eight pounds, truly a trophy fish.

-Inshore Boat: The main sight fishing targets here are redfish, but seatrout, flounder, crevalle jacks, ladyfish, and other species may present themselves, depending on the time of year and other factors. These other species usually require blind casting. Fishing in the marsh requires a great deal of local knowledge due to the tidal range, frequently heavy currents, braided channels, and the omnipresent oyster bars. If you go out on your own here be very careful navigating. The best sightfishing ordinarily is at lower tide phases.

-From the Beach: Surfcasting here can produce the usual Florida surf species– pompano, whiting, bluefish, and Spanish mackerel. Crevalle jacks and flounder are always a possibility, and redfish certainly are too. Use an intermediate line, and size your flies to the size of your intended quarry. A small fly designed to look and act like a sand flea is always a good choice.

-Nearshore Boat: A wide variety of desirable fishes swim through the ocean here. Bluefish, big redfish, Spanish and king mackerel, cobia, tarpon, sharks, and more can be found. In the summer big bait pods (principally menhaden, locally called pogies) attract all kinds of predators. Look for diving birds. In the fall mullet run down the beach in vast quantities, another excellent time to fish here. Jetties at St. Marys Inlet provide anglers with a very obvious fish attractor.

Flies and Techniques

Russell loves black Clouser Minnows in size 2 for casting to backing fish over mud bottoms and around oyster bars. If you intend to tie your own be sure to bring a lot- you frequently lose them in the oysters.

For fishing in the grass a fly that resists hanging up is essential. Bendbacks with weedguards, or the Dupre Spoonfly, work extremely well for this.

In the surf a fairly large (#1 or 1/0) and heavily weighted white minnow imitation proves effective. John Bottko's Surfin' Wooly is one good choice, as is the Sar-Mul-Mac. Other similar patterns work too.

Russell says, "I specialize in shallow water sight fishing for redfish year round on the pristine flats of Amelia Island. This type of fishing has all the elements of bonefishing, including hunting, stalking, seeing the fish, and making a stealthy presentation with heart-pounding anticipation. The hookups are just a huge bonus.

"Redfish are large and numerous here and they can be caught under several different and exciting scenarios. Nowhere in the state of Florida do you have the tides that range from five to seven feet in a six and a half hour period. This means that we must be in the right place at the right time.

"There is no best season. Redfish do not migrate and fishing can be good all year long, as long as the weather is good. There are three main ways that we sight fish for reds. First, I like to start fishing about two hours before dead low tide and fish the incoming water on the flats all year round. Second, in spring, summer, and fall, we sight fish for redfish in the surf on the incoming to flood tides as long as we have clear water and sunny days. Wading works best here. Third, we fish the flood tides in the marsh. Spring, summer, and fall work best for redfish tailing in the marsh grass and it happens only on our highest tides.

"Spring, summer, and fall, are the best times to sight fish along the beaches for migratory fish like bonito, barracuda, bluefish, cobia, jack crevalle, ladyfish, Spanish mackerel, king mackerel, sharks and tarpon. These fish can be found around (or under) bait pods, frequently striking into them repeatedly. We can find these bait pods and striking fish on the surface by watching for diving birds."

Access
For Waders– there isn't much in the back country. Beach access is available at the southern end of the island in the Amelia Island State Recreation Area, off of SR A1A, at Fort Clinch State Park at the north end of the island of SR 105A, and at various points along the beach.
For Boaters- Fort Clinch State Park, at the north end of the island of SR 105A, has a good boat ramp.
-Amelia Island State Recreation Area, off of SR A1A has a boat ramp.
-Amelia Island Yacht Basin $, 904.277.4615.
-Tiger Point Marina $, 904.277.2720.
-Fernandina Harbor Marina $, 904.261.0353

Fly Shops
Tidewater Outfitters, 904.261.2202, they have a small selection of fly equipment.

Guides
Capt. Russell Tharin, 904.491.4799, captrt@bellsouth.net; www.flyfishingameliaisland.com. Russell is a native Floridian, born and raised on the banks of the St. Johns River. Russell first began fly fishing in 1966 when he was 10 years old and purchased his first fly rod with two green stamp books. He has been an avid fly fisherman and sportsman ever since. He is Orvis endorsed, and a Master Fly Casting Instructor certified by the Federation of Fly Fishers.

Boat Rentals
To the best of my knowledge, at the time of this writing there are none available.

State Parks and Other Attractions
-Fort Clinch State Park, 904.277.7274. Located at the north end of Amelia Island. 62 campsites.
-Amelia Island State Recreation Area, 904.261.4878. Located on the southern tip of Amelia Island. No camping available.
-Little Talbot Island State Park, 904.251.2320. Located on the south side of Nassau Sound, across from Amelia Island. 40 campsites.
Information about all these parks can be found online at www.floridastateparks.org.

Accommodations
-Amelia Island Destinations, Inc., 800.685.1065, www.ameliaisland.com
-Amelia Island Chamber of Commerce, 800.2AMELIA (226.3542); www.ameliaisland.org. The Chamber can give you information on places to stay, local events, restaurants, and other travel needs.

Jacksonville

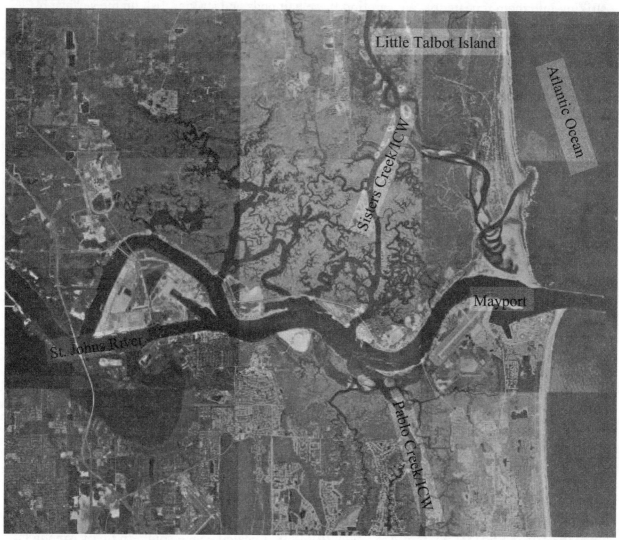

Overview

Not usually thought of as an angling destination, the Jacksonville area offers many fine saltwater fly fishing opportunities. The St. Johns River and a large network of tidal creeks offer a variety of inshore fishing. The Atlantic lies to the east, with miles of beaches and three different openings to the sea, at Nassau Sound, Fort George Inlet, and Mayport. You'll find seatrout, redfish, and flounder inshore, and bluefish, jack crevalle, tarpon, cobia, and Spanish and king mackerel along and off the beaches. Of course other fishes are available. Anglers without boats will find some excellent fishing while those with boats will be hard pressed to decide what to do. Capt. John Bottko, owner of the Salty Feather Fly Shop, supplied the following information.

Opportunities for Do-It-Yourself Fly Fishers

-Inshore Wading: Fly fishers can fish for redfish, seatrout, and flounder in Simpson Creek (north of Jacksonville in the Talbot Island State Parks), and in some areas in Sister's Creek (the Intracoastal Waterway north of Jacksonville) and Clapboard Creek. The best fishing for reds happens at low tide when fish come into very shallow water to feed. They can be seen splashing in the shallows then, and flies can be presented to individual fish. Also, when extreme high tides occur (5.5 feet or more) reds get up into marsh grass and feed on fiddler crabs. These fish tail and can be cast to. Access these creeks from SR 105 north of Jacksonville.

Whether wading or fishing from a boat, tides are very important to an angler's success in Jacksonville's backcountry creeks. John Bottko at the Salty Feather Fly Shop can supply you with the necessary tide information.

-Hand Powered Boat: In Guana River State Park south of Jacksonville some excellent angling for redfish is available for fishermen with canoes or other small boats. Below the dam if you hit it right (low outgoing tide, preferable early in the morning) you'll find backing redfish in inches of water. Flounder will be found in all these creeks. Tarpon get into these creeks during the summer. Above the dam it's more like a saltwater impoundment, with tides no longer an influence. Fish the shorelines, blind casting the snags, for trout, reds, and largemouth bass.

Hand powered boats can be used in all the backcountry areas here. The many tidal creeks, clearly visible in the aerial photograph, provide an excellent venue for them.

-Inshore Boat: Sister's and Clapboard Creeks provide excellent fishing for redfish and are really better fished from a small, even a hand powered, boat. The Intracoastal Waterway (ICW) north and south of town provides many fly fishing opportunities. In the ICW and in all the tidal creeks, the best fishing happens on a low outgoing tide. The reds get in very shallow water feeding on shrimp, crabs and minnows. Their backs are often in the air as their bellies rub the bottom! As the water comes up they get harder to catch, and when the oysters are covered and the water gets up to the grass it's time, with one exception, to do something else.

That exception happens during the highest spring tides, when the *Spartina* marsh completely floods. Then the redfish and some huge sheepshead venture on top of the usually dry marsh to search for fiddler crabs. Fish in this situation usually feed aggressively and are suckers for a well presented fly.

When the weather is good, fish along the jetties at the mouth of the St. John's River for jacks, Spanish mackerel, and bluefish. Look for congregations of anglers, or for fish busting bait on the surface, or just blind cast to the jetties.

Another good idea is to cruise along the beaches looking for cobia. They'll be found around floating debris, weed lines, rays, or other objects in the water.

-From the Beach: Little Talbot Island State Park, north of Jacksonville, offers a unique beach sight-fishing opportunity for redfish. The fish usually hold up by Nassau Sound, about a two mile walk up the beach from the parking lot. You walk along the beach looking for fish in knee-deep water, either holding their positions or cruising along looking for groceries. You may see singles or schools of 50 to 100 individual fish. You'll find the same fishing at the southern end of Amelia Island.

You'll see many sharks here and you can also try to catch them. I have hooked a couple but have yet to catch one with a fly myself. John Bottko told me about a big redfish he hooked off the beach which was attacked and eaten by a shark as he was fighting it. John got only the head, which weighed between eight and nine pounds.

-Nearshore: Fish in shrimp boat bycatch lines or establish your own chum lines and you may catch jacks, barracuda, tarpon, kingfish, cobia, sharks, and other species that come into the chum. A buoy line out from the mouth of the St. John's River serves as a built-in fish attractor.

The jetties at the St. Johns River mouth also attract fish, quite a wide variety. While it's sometimes dead, at other times diving birds and breaking fish advertise the presence of what is often a wide variety of fish.

Flies and Techniques

John Bottko recommends dark Clouser minnows for fishing in the creeks. This creek fishing is best started on a low outgoing tide. The fish move into very shallow water, so much that their backs are exposed to the air. Catching these fish requires pinpoint casting accuracy- too far away and they'll never see the fly, but too close and they'll spook and bolt for deeper water. Look for splashing and thrashing right along the water's edge.

Along the beaches, Popovics' Surf Candy, Blanton's Sar-Mul-Mac, or the Surfin' Wooly, a fly by John Bottko, work well. Clouser minnows or crab patterns are also favorites. Walk the beach, alternately blind casting and looking for individuals, pods, or schools of fish.

Large Deceivers or synthetic minnow imitations work well offshore, especially if the fish have been chummed in close. Next to large bait pods is another good place to try your counterfeits. Poppers also garner strikes from feeding fish.

Access

For Waders- as detailed above.
For Boaters- There are boat ramps, some of which charge a fee for use, at the following places:
-on the east side of Sister's Creek off SR 105
-on the east side of the Ft. George River on SR 105 ($)
-on the east side of Clapboard Creek on SR 105 ($)
-on the north side of Nassau Sound off SR A1A/105.

A canoe or small boat can be launched at the dam on the Guana River in Guana River State Park off SR A1A. There is also a boat ramp at the Pine Island Fish Camp ($) off of US 1 south of Jacksonville which allow access to the Intracoastal Waterway.

Fly Shops

The Salty Feather Fly Shop, 2683 St. Johns Bluff Road, Jacksonville, FL 32246, 904.645.8998; www.saltyfeather.com. A full service shop.

Guides

Guides including John Bottko, are available through the Salty Feather Fly Shop.
-Capt. Larry Miniard, 904.285.7003.

Boat Rentals

A1A Watersports, 904.249.6666.

State Parks and Other Attractions

-Little Talbot Island State Park (camping) off SR 105, 904.251.3231.
-Guana River State Park off SR A1A, 904.825-5071
Information about all state parks can be found online at www.floridastateparks.org.

Accommodations

There are plenty of motels in the greater Jacksonville area. The phone number of the Jacksonville Convention and Visitors Bureau is 800.733.2668; www.visitjacksonville.com.

St. Augustine

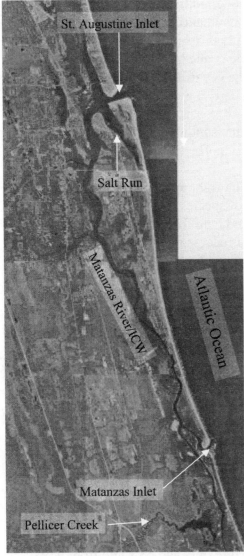

St. Augustine Inlet

Salt Run

Matanzas River/ICW

Atlantic Ocean

Matanzas Inlet

Pellicer Creek

Overview

St. Augustine, the nation's oldest city, seems to have more attractions, museums, and bed & breakfast inns per square foot than any city in the United States. Major attractions such as the Castillo De San Marcos (the old fort), the Lighthouse, and the Fountain of Youth to mention a few, are both interesting and educational for the entire family. The Oldest City stays busy year round with school field trips, bus tours and family vacationers. Also, over the years, this area has been steadily growing and maturing into a fishing destination.

Located between two fair-size inlets, St. Augustine has a unique fishery. The inlets create a "flushing action" as the tide falls and rises. While keeping the salinity very stable, it also keeps the habitat clean and clear most of the year.

From the Palm Valley Bridge (north of St. Augustine) to the canals of Palm Coast (to the south), the Intracoastal Waterway (ICW) offers excellent angling in a wide variety of habitats for redfish, seatrout, flounder, bluefish, jack crevalle, and tarpon. The two inlets, St. Augustine Inlet to the north and Matanzas Inlet to the south, give access to the ocean. The splendid, fast-sloping coquina beaches here offer excellent surf fishing. The rock pile along this stretch of beach is the only one on the northeast Florida coast.

The St. Augustine area serves as a temporary host for great migratory schools of forage species. This traveling smorgasbord is followed by the migratory predators – king mackerel, Spanish mackerel, cobia, crevalle jacks, little tunny, and the great "Silver King," the tarpon.

Capt. Steve Moore, a second generation guide and native of Northeast Florida, provided most of the information in this section.

Opportunities for the Do-It-Yourself Fly Fisher

-Inshore Wading: The Summer Haven River, south of St. Augustine off of SR A1A, offers seatrout, redfish, and flounder all year long, and bluefish in the winter. At Matanzas Inlet the same species are available, as well as tarpon to 100 pounds during the fall mullet run (but good luck landing a fish like that while wading!). Anywhere in the Matanzas River between Matanzas Inlet and Marineland off of SR A1A can provide good angling.

Waders can also wade around the Vilano Bridge area. Walk down close to the bridge on the southwest side. Wade through the shallow creek. Fish from the small jetty at Camachee Cove to the small boat ramp jetties. Various types of minnow patterns will work here.

In Salt Run you can wade the entire west side of the creek (it gets about waist deep during high tide). Enter from boat ramp on the south side or on the north side from the Anastasia

75

State Park ramp. Due to the proximity to the inlet there can be a wide variety of fish in here, including trout, redfish, flounder, bluefish, jacks, etc. Large trout show up during the spring.

If you find yourself near Matanzas Inlet you can find good fishing south from Crescent Beach to a half mile before the bridge. Take a left at the convenience store, follow it to the beach. You can wade after going under the bridge. This is great fishing. At low tide you can get to the large sandbar in front of the bridge. Fish the deep side of the bar.

On the south side of the Matanzas Inlet bridge on the ocean side it's very shallow to about 300 feet out. There are almost always trout and reds here in the summer. Fish it with a sinking tip line, using minnow or mullet patterns.

On the southwest side of SR 312 bridge you can wade south behind the oyster beds. There is a dirt road that leads to a point about 200 yards south. This is limited wading, but sometimes there's great fishing.

On the southeast side of SR 206 a dirt road takes you right to a point that you can wade around, but stay to the south. This area produces a variety of species.

-Hand Powered Boat: There are several opportunities around here for those using canoes or kayaks. Any of the wading spots listed above can be used as access points for those in hand powered boats. The boat ramps listed in the boat ramps section can be used by hand powered boats as well.

Starting from the north of St. Augustine and working south, Guana River State Park offers the impoundment above the dam and the tidal stretch of the Guana River below.

The Coastal Outdoor Center in Crescent Beach has extensive flats right behind the shop. They rent kayaks or will let you launch yours there. They also carry some fly tackle.

In the San Sebastian River you can wade starting from bridge at SR 16. This is a protected area, good on windy days. The few boats you'll see there will be small. Reds, trout, flounder, and small tarpon can be found here.

South of St. Augustine, Faver-Dykes State Park has a small boat ramp on Pellicer Creek, giving access to the Pellicer Flats. This can be a great area for redfish and seatrout.

-Inshore Boat: North of St. Augustine the ICW runs up through the Tolomato River. Fishing the ICW and the creeks along here you can sometimes find backing redfish on low tide, just like up in Jacksonville. Starting at the Palm Valley Bridge (CR210, from I-95 out to Ponte Vedra) heading south there are plenty of fish. Steve Moore says to look for the green channel markers "3" and "5" and fish the creek (identified by scattered marsh islands and sandbars) that you'll find on the east side. The creek goes about a mile up to the tree line, and reds and trout work right up by the shoreline in the thin grass.

Around Pine Island on the east shore all the way around back to the Intracoastal Waterway you should look for reds working around the oyster bars. Several openings will get you to the tree line at high tide.

A half mile or so south of Pine Island the sandbars at the mouth Capo Creek will be visible on the east side. Fish these at high tide for trout and flounder. If you like adventure, on a high rising tide follow the creek all the way back. At the apparent end take a left through the grass. It opens into a long, shallow area with thin grass against the shore. Redfish search for crabs in here. You can only stay here for an hour once the tide starts to fall.

The next creek south is on the west side, Stokes Creek. About a quarter mile up the creek there is a sunken barge. Fish the barge and the creek on left to the cove. Reds lay against the grass here. This is popper heaven.

Still north of St. Augustine and still working our way south, the Guana River is

76

the next creek, on the east side. Fish the oyster bars on the right. To the left at the first curve is a small cove, which sometimes has tailing reds. You may have to pick through the grass to get in. Go all the way up the creek to the dam. Fish below the dam and in the cove, as well as at the mouths of the feeder creeks.

The next creek is Robinson Creek. This one has great fishing in summer at high tide, particularly around the oyster beds at the mouth on outgoing tide. Follow the openings to the left through the grass islands as far as you can. Follow the tide.

Hospital Creek is the last one before St. Augustine Inlet. Fish all the way around to under the bridge. During the summer fish the high banks and the perimeter of the cove for snapper and redfish.

At the St. Augustine Inlet the bars give up many species of fish at the turn of the tides. Fish along the rocks with a sinking line and a Whistler or a large Deceiver during the summer for 20 to 40 pound tarpon. You can sometimes see these fish laying up in the rocks in the early morning on an outgoing tide. They will hit a large popper when they're close to the rocks like this. These jetties are good producers of tarpon during the fall mullet run. If you fish a big Clouser deep for reds you may get a few, but this action is spotty at best.

On the south side of the inlet you'll find Salt Run. It can have good fishing all the way down the west side. You'll find docks, oyster beds, clean sandbars and grass here. Always fish here on the higher tide phases. At low tide it's a complete waste of time. Reds, trout, flounder, and tarpon can all be found here in season, and some large trout are caught here every year.

As you head south down the ICW from St. Augustine you come to the mouth of the San Sebastian River on the west side of the channel. If you fish the left (south) side against the grass to the first dock you may encounter redfish or big jacks. Look for rolling tarpon.

Next you'll come to East Creek. You can find good fishing in the mouths of the feeders. Just inside the creek on right are scattered red mangrove and grass islands which are usually quite productive on an incoming tide. You should fish as far up as you can, and make sure to work the small coves.

As you continue south down the ICW look for channel marker "38", and fish south to Moses Creek. Work the edge of the grass for tailing reds as soon as water is eight to 10 inches deep. Silence and patience will reward you. On outgoing tide you can drift with the tide all the way north from Moses Creek, fishing shallow water with poppers or Deceivers. Any dark crab pattern will work great on a calm day.

At marker "75" on the west side of ICW you'll find scattered mangroves, grass islands, and oyster beds. This can be a productive area for a variety of fish.

Matanzas Inlet is the non-navigable inlet next encountered, although small outboard powered skiffs can and do run through. Fish the inside all the way from the inlet itself north to the Fort Matanzas National Monument boat dock. Fish the drop-off by the big sandbar in front of the bridge at low tide. Fish the breakers on the outside at high tide with a Mullet Fly or a large Deceiver on a sinking line.

South of Matanzas Inlet by marker "86" on the west side there's a creek with very productive fishing on both sides. Fish the feeder creeks at high tide and you can get all the way to the tree line. The depth will be about 18 inches at high tide. Reds and small tarpon use the little cove at the tree line. Stop your boat before the oyster bar at mouth of the cove and wade in. When you enter this creek, take the first creek on the right and fish the grass line all the way around the cove to which it leads.

Still going south, fish the passes on the west side that lead into Pellicer Flats. Access to the flats is at markers "92" and "97". On the flats, fish over the oyster beds at high tide and the edges on low tide. Redfish, trout and flounder will all be found here. During the summer you may see some small tarpon.

The canals of Palm Coast offer some excellent angling during the winter months.

-From the Beach: Fly fishers can catch whiting and pompano from the beach all year long, weather permitting. Bluefish appear during the winter months. Big bull redfish could show up at any time, with the possibility of fish approaching forty pounds in size. Spanish mackerel are another possibility, as are jack crevalle. An excellent place for the surf caster to try is at Washington Oaks, where a natural rock pile on the beach attracts many species of fish.

If you find yourself near Matanzas Inlet you can find good fishing south from Crescent Beach to a half mile before the bridge. Turn off of SR A1A at the convenience store north of the inlet and follow the road to the beach. This is great fishing. At low tide you can get to the large sandbar in front of the bridge. Fish the deep side of the bar.

On the south side of the Matanzas Inlet bridge on the ocean side it's very shallow to about 300 feet out. There are almost always trout and reds here in the summer. Fish it with a sinking tip line, using minnow or mullet patterns.

-Nearshore: Spanish mackerel, bluefish, little tunny, and more are all possibilities. Fish poppers close in, between the beach and about 200 yards out. Cobia are frequently seen, especially around manta rays in the spring and fall. Throw your fly on top of the ray and let it fall off.

Tarpon and kingfish can be caught off the beach by setting up a chum line. Actually, chumming between the St. Augustine and Matanzas Inlets about a half mile offshore can produce surprising catches at any time. Make sure to take a 12-weight with you!

Flies and Techniques

Steve Moore has very definite ideas about fly selection. For redfish he sometimes likes using poppers, with the Popovics Banger in silver or chartreuse being a favorite. He'll fish these along grass lines at dawn with slow pops (15 to 20 seconds delay between pulls). He also likes using smaller poppers to fish over oyster beds on calm days.

The Merkin Crab is another favorite redfish fly. Fish it with a slow 10 inch strip, or let drift deep with the current in passes or feeder creeks. It's also good around oyster beds.

Minnow patterns like the Lefty's Deceivers, the Seaducer, or the Clouser minnow are also effective on redfish. Use more subdued colors when the water is clear, and brighter colors when it's muddy.

The same flies, with the possible exception of the Merkins, are also effective on seatrout. Trout tend to be more aggressive than redfish, so try using a faster retrieve for them.

Flies for larger tarpon are larger (2/0, 3/0) tarpon standards– the Cockroach, the Homosassa Special. Whistlers are good in deep water around the jetties or off the beach.

Boat Rentals

-Devil's Elbow Fishing Resort, 904.471.0398. They rent kayaks, Carolina Skiffs, and pontoon boats.

-Anastasia State Recreation Area, 904.461.2033. They rent kayaks and canoes.

-Coastal Outdoor Center, 291 Cubbage Rd., St. Augustine, FL 32080, 904.471.4144. Kayak sales and rentals, extensive flats right behind the shop. They also carry some fly tackle.

Boat Ramps
-Bings Landing, (five miles south of Marineland on A1A), great ramp, good parking.
-Devil's Elbow Fishing Resort, Crescent Beach, good ramp for smaller boats, good parking.
-St. Augustine Lighthouse, on Salt Run, good ramp, no boats over 20 ft at low tide. Plenty of parking.
-Vilano Beach Ramp, SR A1A between Hospital Creek Bridge and Usina (Vilano Beach Bridge), good ramp, plenty of parking. Good on any tide. Can get crowded on weekends.

Fly Shops
Avid Angler, 904.824.8322, 2101 N. Ponce De Leon Blvd, St. Augustine, FL 32084

Guides
-Capt. Steve Moore, 904.824.2621, 904.540.6340; www.florida-fly-fishing.com, profishunt@se.rr.com. A second generation guide and native of Northeast Florida, Steve Moore has fished the fly on both Florida coasts for 35 years. Steve provided most of the information in this section.
-Capt. Chip Owen, 904,797.4007, 904.377.1115; www.captchipowen.com, chip007@bellsouth.net

State Parks and Other Attractions
        The St. Augustine area boasts many attractions, some of which have a rich history. A day exploring the town is well worth the time.
-Anastasia State Recreation Area, St. Augustine Beach, 904.461.2033. Two miles of beach and dunes. 139 tent sites, camping reservations a must.
-Faver Dykes State Park, Marineland, 904.794.0997. 30 wooded tent sites on Pellicer Creek.
-Guana River State Park, Ponte Vedra Beach, 904.852.5071.
Information about all state parks can be found online at www.floridastateparks.org.

Accommodations
-Devil's Elbow Fishing Resort, in Crescent Beach on SR A1A. 904.471.0398
24 guest cottages, boat slips and rentals. www.devilselbowfishingresort.com

There are many accommodations of all types in this area. The phone number of the Chamber of Commerce is 904.829.6477. The website is www.oldcity.com.

Daytona/New Smyrna Beaches

Overview

Tomoka Basin

Halifax River

Atlantic Ocean

Daytona Beach

Ponce de Leon Inlet

Daytona calls itself, "the World's Most Famous Beach." Speed Week, Bike Week, Spring Break, and other promotional events bring tens of thousands of visitors to the condo-lined beach every year. This famous beach stuff has nothing to do with fishing. Daytona Beach slopes very gently and consequently it, and neighboring New Smyrna Beach, usually have poor fishing except in the vicinity of Ponce de Leon inlet.

Locales in this vicinity which do attract and hold fish include the Intracoastal Waterway (ICW) behind the beach areas, Ponce de Leon Inlet (Ponce Inlet, locally), which separates Daytona from New Smyrna, the creeks feeding into the ICW, the northern end of the Mosquito Lagoon, and the Apollo Beach area of the Canaveral National Seashore. All offer good fly fishing opportunities. Captain Ron Rebeck, no longer guiding, shared much of the following information with me. Capt. Kent Gibbens and Capt. Mike Hakala filled out the information.

Opportunities for Do-It-Yourself Fly Fishers

-Inshore Wading: Good opportunities exist for redfish and seatrout at the north end of the Mosquito Lagoon in the Canaveral National Seashore, especially around Turtle Mound and parking lot 5. Find this at the south end of SR A1A south of New Smyrna.

Between Daytona and New Smyrna along US 1, Spruce Creek is wadable all the way up to the railroad bridge. Snook, redfish, seatrout, small tarpon, and jack crevalle can all be caught around islands and oyster bars.

Both sides of Ponce Inlet can be waded. There are parks along both sides. You'll find the fishing best during the fall mullet run, when bluefish and jack crevalle are the primary species. Other types of fish will also be found here, including redfish, seatrout, tarpon, Spanish mackerel, ladyfish, and sharks.

Behind the bowling alley in South Daytona is a wadable flat where tarpon to 50 pounds

80

hold during the summer months. You'll find these fish are tough to take on flies, although it can and does happen. Try fishing here early or late in the day.

In Ormond Beach, Tomoka Basin is wadable and produces seatrout, redfish, snook, jacks, and small tarpon for the fly rodder. High outgoing tide is best.

-Hand Powered Boat: As you can probably tell from the photo, there are many small creeks in this area which offer some excellent fishing. Spruce Creek, best accessed from US 1 between Daytona and New Smyrna, is one such creek. Calalisa Creek, accessed at Calalisa Park off SR 44 in New Smyrna Beach, is another. East of Edgewater there are several other creeks. North of Daytona is Ormond Beach, where the Tomoka River enters the Halifax River. Tomoka River is an excellent place to use a hand powered boat. All these creeks have snook, redfish, and trout, and get other species as well.

-Inshore Boat: Excellent night fishing opportunities exist for fly rodders under lighted docks all the way from J.B.'s Fish Camp in New Smyrna to Tomoka State Park in Ormond Beach. Moonfish (near the inlet), snook, seatrout, bluefish, and ladyfish are all likely catches.

During the summer tarpon can be taken between the two bridges in New Smyrna on a rising tide, after the clean seawater comes in. Try using standard tarpon streamers (when in doubt use a smaller fly), or baitfish imitations like SexyFlies or PolarFiber Minnows.

Fishing the jetties can be productive for jacks and bluefish, especially during the fall mullet run. Other fish frequently found around the jetties include tarpon (summer and fall), Spanish mackerel, (fall and winter), redfish (all year, but especially during the fall) and sharks.

In the Tomoka Basin fish the mosquito ditches on the high outgoing tide. Small tarpon, redfish, snook, jacks, and seatrout all wait at the run-outs for baitfish and shrimp to wash out.

All of the creeks on the west side of the ICW from Port Orange down south into New Smyrna will produce fish on outgoing tides. Again, predators wait in the run-out for baitfish to wash down to them. These creeks include Spruce Creek, Ten Mile Creek, Rose Bay, and others.

The docks along the Intracoastal from Edgewater north to Ormond Beach will hold such fish as snook, seatrout, bluefish, ladyfish, and redfish.

Lastly, the north end of the Mosquito Lagoon, including all of the islands in the Canaveral National Seashore, can produce fish during any time of the year.

-From the Beach: The only beach in the area with consistently good fishing is Apollo Beach in the Canaveral National Seashore south of New Smyrna. Pompano can be caught during the summer, and whiting are caught all year long. Jacks and bluefish can be taken during the fall. mullet run. Although winter and spring offer surf conditions which are usually too rough for fly casters, redfish are another possibility any time of the year. Again, the jetties at Ponce Inlet can sometimes provide good angling, but fall usually provides the most consistent fishing.

-Nearshore: Anglers running out from Ponce Inlet can find a number of targets all summer long, well into the autumn. The mullet run attracts all manner of fish to the jetties at Ponce Inlet. King and Spanish mackerel, crevalle jacks, bluefish, and tarpon can be found in nearshore waters here, ranging from the breakers along the beach to several miles out. While breaking fish under diving terns usually signal Spanish mackerel to the fly caster, kings will have to be chummed up. Tarpon, big ones, are usually found adjacent to bait pods, especially menhaden. Look for diving pelicans. Tripletail and cobia put in seasonal appearances too.

Flies and Techniques

Carry the following flies: Clouser minnows, especially for deeper water around docks. Big poppers and sliders work well when cast against seawalls or around docks, and produce explosive surface strikes. White flies, with luminescent materials tied in, work well under lights at night. Poppers and white surf candies work well in surf for bluefish.

It's often important to use sink-tip lines here due to the depth of the water. Using flies that make noise and/or push water is recommended. Try Whistlers, Siliclones, rattle flies, and similar patterns for sub-surface use, and big, noisy popping bugs when a topwater fly is needed. Bigger patterns work better in the discolored water frequently found in this area

Access

For Waders: Waders can access the grass flats at the north end of the Mosquito Lagoon and the best fish producing beaches in this entire area at the south end of SR A1A in the Canaveral National Seashore south of New Smyrna. Go all the way to Parking Lot 5 for the Mosquito Lagoon. Waders can also find easy access to the channels and sloughs of the Mosquito Lagoon North, also in the National Seashore, at Turtle Mound and the Eldora House.

There are parks on either side of Ponce Inlet where a wading fly fisher can park and get easy access to the inlet.

Waders wanting to fish Spruce Creek can park along U.S.1 between Daytona and New Smyrna where it crosses the creek.

Tomoka State Park, north of SR 40 in Ormond Beach, gives the wader access to the Tomoka Basin and Halifax River.

In South Daytona waders can park in the lot of the bowling alley and access the flat directly behind this building.

-For Boaters: There are a lot of boat ramps in the area. In the National Seashore there is one at the Visitor's Center and another at Turtle Mound. On the way down there is another at J.B.'s Fish Camp (J.B.'s is a popular weekend attraction with live music and the whole deal. Don't use this ramp on weekends if you're allergic to crowds of party-goers!).

There is a ramp in Edgewater, about two and a half miles south of SR 44. Take a left on Riverside Drive and the ramp is at Kennedy Park. There is a ramp about a mile west of the

North Causeway in New Smyrna Beach.

If you have a SMALL boat, you can launch it in Spruce Creek on the southeast side of the US 1 bridge. This is a poor excuse for a ramp, however. All of Spruce Creek is a slow speed manatee zone.

In Port Orange on Dunlawton Street there is a nice ramp.

Daytona has a ramp at Lighthouse Park.

There is a ramp at the Brigadoon Fish Camp on Rose Bay off of US 1.

Finally, in Ormond Beach there are ramps at Tomoka State Park and at the Granada Bridge.

Fly Shops

There are no fly shops in this area.

Guides

Capt. Kent Gibbens lives in Ormond Beach. Kent has lived in the Daytona area all his life and has fished Volusia and northern Brevard county waters extensively during that time. Kent is Orvis endorsed and can be reached at 386.672.8929, or through his website: www.backcountrycaptain.com

Capt. Mike Hakala has lived in New Smyrna Beach for 30 years, and has guided the Volusia and northern Brevard area for the more than ten years. He designs and sells Capt. Mike's Guide Proven Lures, available through his website at www.floridaysfishing.com. Mike can be reached at 386.428.8530 locally, or at 800.368.8340.

Boat Rentals

-East Coast Outdoors in New Smyrna Beach offers kayak rentals. Their phone number is 386.672.5003.

-Rental canoes are available at Tomoka State Park. See below.

-The Fishin' Store in New Smyrna Beach, 386.427.4514; www.fishinstore.com/rentals. Power-boat rentals.

State Parks and Other Attractions

-Canaveral National Seashore, 386.428.3384. Camping is allowed on the beach south of parking lot 5 during the winter months. There is also camping on many of the islands at the north end of the Mosquito Lagoon.

-Tomoka State Park is located three miles north of Ormond Beach on North Beach Street. 2009 North Beach Street, Ormond Beach 32174. 386.676.4050. Camping is possible here (100 sites) and there's a nice boat ramp. They also rent canoes. Information about all state parks can be found online at www.floridastateparks.org.

Accommodations

Not hard to find in this area! Daytona Beach Chamber of Commerce PO Box 2475, Daytona Beach 32115. 386.761.7163, www.daytonabeach.com.

New Smyrna Beach Chamber of Commerce, 115 Canal Street, New Smyrna, 32168. 386.996.5522, www.nsbfla.com.

Titusville

Overview

This area around Titusville, between Oak Hill and Cocoa, contains much of the Mosquito Lagoon, the northern end of the Indian River Lagoon, the northern end of the Banana River Lagoon, and Playalinda Beach, basically all the waters surrounding the Kennedy Space Center. Obviously, you find a wide variety of angling opportunities available here, and the season lasts all year long. These lagoons are completely landlocked in this section and therefore have very little to none whatsoever tidal influence. The redfish here are also landlocked, spawn in the lagoons, and offer the finest sight fishing for really big redfish that you can find any-where on the planet. Finally, because of the Kennedy Space Center, the Merritt Island National Wildlife Refuge, and Canaveral National Seashore, much of the lands surrounding these waters are undeveloped, offering a wonderful aesthetic to fishing here.

Opportunities for the Do-It-Yourself Fly Fisher

-Inshore Wading: Wading fly fishers can enjoy some fantastic sight fishing for redfish on the shallow grass flats of both the Mosquito Lagoon and the Indian River Lagoon. Dike roads run along the southwest side of the Mosquito Lagoon (accessible from SR 3) and along much of the east side of the Indian River Lagoon (accessible from SR 3, SR 406, and US 1) allowing access to these many of these flats. You can sometimes spot waking or tailing fish from your vehicle. There are no tides at all in these places, so fishing can be good at any time. Especially along the Mosquito Lagoon road, parking your vehicle and walking along the shoreline on a warm, sunny winter afternoon can lead to multiple hookups on tailing redfish.

The flats here tend to be soft, so expect to do some work when wading.

-Hand Powered Boat: From River Breeze Park south to LeFil's Fish Camp (both off of US 1 in Oak Hill), the islands east of the ICW in the north Mosquito Lagoon offer a maze of fishing op-portunities. Trout and redfish are the principle species, although flounder, jacks, ladyfish, and assorted odds and ends will also turn up. The same is true if you come down SR A1A from New Smyrna Beach. You're just coming in from the other side of the lagoon.

From the dike roads mentioned above, cartop boats can be launched almost anywhere.

For anglers who really enjoy paddling, the Banana River Manatee Sanctuary (locally referred to as the no motor zone), north of SR 528, provides some of the finest angling in the entire state. Boats with motors of any kind are prohibited from entering this area. Redfish, trout, black drum, snook, tarpon, and more can be caught in here. Since no motors are allowed, the area gets less fishing pressure than other areas.

-Inshore Boat: With a boat, more of the flats in the Mosquito Lagoon and Indian River Lagoon are available. The entire south end of the Lagoon is ringed by grass flats, and there is also a middle flat extending north from Pelican Island, at the south end of the Lagoon. North of the Haulover Canal, flats extend along the east shoreline of the lagoon all the way to Oak Hill. There are a lot of flats in the Mosquito Lagoon, and all of them hold fish at one time or another.

In the Indian River Lagoon, flats ring the entire lagoon north of the railroad trestle in Titusville. Flats extend southward along the east side of the Indian River to the NASA Cause-way and beyond. The spoil islands along the ICW can be reached, too, both in the Indian River Lagoon and north of the Haulover Canal on the west side of the Mosquito Lagoon.

Additionally, flats on both sides of the Banana River Lagoon between SR 520 and SR 528 can be fished. Redfish, seatrout, baby tarpon, snook, jack crevalle, and black drum are all found on the flats here.

Finally, the power stations off of US 1 south of Titusville can provide non-stop action for jacks, tarpon, and big ladyfish. These areas are now closed to all entry between November 15 and March 31 in the name of manatee protection.

-From the Beach: Playalinda Beach has good fishing when the weather allows. During the sum-mer months, anglers using light tackle with sinking lines and small weighted flies can catch pompano, whiting, and the occasional redfish. During the fall mullet run, jacks, Spanish mack-erel, bluefish, and sometimes other species can be added to the catch.

-<u>Nearshore</u>: Ocean access is through Port Canaveral. Some days there are so many fish in the Port itself it's hard to make it outside. In the Port you may find snook, bluefish, jacks, seatrout, and many other species. Night fishing under the lights is also possible, and can be extremely rewarding. Have you ever caught a ribbonfish on a fly?

The buoy line out of the Port attracts many types of fish. Cobia and tripletail love to lounge under the buoys and other flotsam. The buoy line also attracts king mackerel which can be chummed up. Expect little tunny and jacks to appear in the chum line! Spanish mackerel appear during the fall and can be found fairly consistently all winter when the weather allows.

Flies and Techniques

For fishing the flats in the lagoon systems floating lines are a must. A selection of flies should be carried that includes Clouser minnows in variety of colors, crab patterns for tailing fish, seaducers in yellow and grizzly and red and white, and surface flies such as poppers and sliders. Some of your flies need to have weedguards.

The surface flies are used mostly when blind casting, especially by waders. The sound of the fly attracts fish which cannot be seen. Use other patterns for sighted fish, depending on water depth, the amount of floating and bottom grasses, and what the fish are doing. For example, tailing redfish are usually suckers for a well presented crab pattern.

Since there are no tides in the lagoons, fish tend to move a lot. The most successful anglers have good hunting skills which they use to locate fish. For fly fishers it's definitely better to hunt first, then fish after you've found some. Blind casting without results gets old very quickly. Fish in the lagoon system could be scattered about in singles or pairs, or may be in schools containing hundreds of fish.

Beach flies depend on the target species. For whiting and pompano a small mole crab fly works best when delivered with a sinking line. For snook along Satellite Beach, large Deceivers or Blanton's Sar-Mul-Mac pattern tethered to a monocore line works best. Jacks and bluefish will slam poppers cast along the beach.

Off the beaches, Clouser deep minnows work well for Spanish mackerel and tripletail. The 'tails also like seaducers. Cobia and kings want a bigger mouthful, and large Deceivers in white and/or chartreuse work well. Any time you fish in a chum line the fly should reasonably imitate the chum.

Access

<u>For Waders</u>: several points allow access to the Mosquito Lagoon. On the southeast side of the lagoon try the boat ramp between parking lots 7 and 8 at Playalinda Beach. The flats in Eddy Creek and the flat to the north of Eddy Creek (getting here demands a major commitment by someone on foot) are often productive.

On the west side there is a dike road which runs along the bank, and can be accessed from BioLab Road off of SR 3. Look for a small sign which says "NASA Atmospheric Sciences". This road is about six miles north of the intersection with SR 402.

There are other access points to the north of the Haulover Canal along SR 3. These are dirt roads which are marked with small brown boat ramp signs. These roads will put you on the inside of the spoil islands on the west side of the lagoon along the ICW.

Indian River Lagoon Access- 100 yards south of the "NASA Atmospheric Sciences" sign (which marks the entrance to the Mosquito Lagoon dike road) is the L Pond Road on the opposite side of SR 3. This road accesses Dummit Cove, an excellent wade fishing spot off the

Indian River Lagoon. The road twists and turns its way around for a few miles before coming to what looks like a parking area, further identified by the culverts under the road. You'll find the bottom here is kind of soft.

Another excellent access to the east Indian River Lagoon flats lies one or two miles north of the Haulover Canal off of US 3. A dirt road on the west side of the road leads into a citrus grove and immediately turns and heads north along the east shore of the Indian River Lagoon. The flats all along this road are both wadable and productive.

On the west side of the Indian River Lagoon are access points off of US 1 in both Scottsmoor and Mims. The Florida Gazetteer shows both of these access points as boat ramps.

Lastly, to the south of SR 406 on Merritt Island is a dike road which gives waders access to Catfish Creek and Peacock Pocket. One word of warning- never try to cross the ditches which often separate the dike roads from the main river. The bottom of these ditches is soft and treacherous and could easily trap an unwary wader.

For boaters: Boat ramps can be found at the following places:

-Eddy Creek, between parking lots 7 and 8 at Playalinda Beach, giving access to the Mosquito Lagoon;

-at the Haulover Canal off of SR 3, giving access to both the Mosquito Lagoon and the Indian River Lagoon;

-on SR 402 just east of Titusville there's a ramp at Parrish Park, giving access to the Indian River Lagoon;

-off of US 1 just south of SR 50 there's a ramp at Kennedy Point Park, accessing the Indian River Lagoon;

-off of US 1 in Port St. John south of Titusville, giving access to the Indian River Lagoon and the excellent cold weather fishing at the power station discharges;

-at Kelly Park on Banana River Drive just south of SR 528, giving access to the Banana River Lagoon;

-at Port Canaveral, which accesses the Port and the Atlantic Ocean.

Canoeists can get into the Banana River Manatee Refuge on the east side just south of the Canaveral Air Force Station entrance on SR 401, and on the west side at the north end of Banana River Drive, just north of SR 528. Paddling north about two miles will bring you to the refuge. Don't get tunnel vision about reaching the refuge, you may see fish all along the flats here. *Since September 11, 2001 the entire east side of the no motor zone is closed to all entry.*
Beach access: Playalinda Beach has superb access. Take SR 406 east from Titusville, then bear right onto SR 402. Obey the posted speed limits– the rangers love to set up radar on this road!

Keep in mind this is a public beach and it can get mighty crowded on summer weekends. Try to get your fishing done early in the day.

Fly Shops
The Fly Fisherman, 1400 S. Washington Avenue, Titusville, FL 32780. 321.267.0348; www.flyfishermaninc.com. A full service fly shop.

Boat Rental
-Space Coast Watercraft Rental, Titusville, 321.267.7776; www.spacecoastwatercraft.com. Powerboat rentals.
-A Day Away, Titusville, 321.268.2655; www.nbbd.com/kayaktours. Kayak rentals.

Guides

-Captain John Kumiski, 407.977.5207; www.spottedtail.com. I can custom design various trips in this area: sightfishing for reds and other species in the Mosquito Lagoon, Indian River Lagoon, or Banana River lagoon; canoeing or kayaking in the Mosquito Lagoon or Manatee Refuge for reds, snook, seatrout, and baby tarpon; night fishing under the lights in Port Canaveral; fishing off the beach for cobia, tripletail, and Spanish mackerel; and more. I am a full service fishing guide, and an FFF certified fly casting instructor.
-Capt. Rob Blake, 321.633.0923; www.redfishonfly.com.
-Capt. John Turcot, 321.267.9818; www.backcountryonfly.com.

State Parks and Other Attractions

-Merritt Island National Wildlife Refuge, 321.861.0667, http://merrittisland.fws.gov
-Canaveral National Seashore, 321.267.1110, http://www.nps.gov/cana/
These two natural areas lie next to each other and provide tens of thousands of acres of wildlife habitat. MINWR is administered by the US Fish and Wildlife Service, CNS by the National Park Service. Birding here is especially rewarding. There are several nature trails and wildlife drives, and you may see dolphins, manatees, alligators, wild hogs, bobcats, otters, raccoons-any number of wild creatures. There are several places to camp in the Canaveral National Seashore (you'll need a permit, available at the Turtle Mound Ranger Station 386.428.3384x10), many of which are accessible only by boat.

Accommodations

There are lots of motels in Titusville. The Holiday Inn on US 1 in Titusville caters to fishermen and is right next to the Kennedy Point Park boat ramp. Their number is 321.269.2121. Ask for the Angler's Rate.
The phone number of the Titusville Chamber of Commerce is 321.267.3036.
The Space Coast Office of Tourism can be very helpful. Their number is 800.872.1969. The website is www.space-coast.com.

Mr. Kreh got this big red while fishing from the author's boat in the Indian River Lagoon.

Cocoa/Melbourne

Overview

The coastline between Cocoa Beach (Patrick Air Force Base, actually) and Melbourne boasts a terrific fishing beach with good access and big, strong fish, especially snook. The Indian River Lagoon system, behind the barrier islands, provides excellent shallow water sight fishing for many different species; as a matter of fact this lagoon is the most biologically diverse estuary in North America, with over 700 different species of fish having been catalogued from its waters.

The lagoon has the largest population of shallow water brood stock redfish anywhere in the country, with many fish reaching weights between 20 and 40 pounds. Since these fish are essentially landlocked, the fishery for them is not seasonal, but rather exists all year long.

This area definitely deserves a visit by the visitor anxious to see a relatively untapped fishery in an area not usually frequented by tourists.

Captain Rodney Smith lives in Satellite Beach, and from his home fishes along and offshore from the beaches, as well as in the Banana River Lagoon. He supplied the information that follows.

Opportunities for Do-It-Yourself Fly Fishers

-<u>Inshore Wading</u>: Lots of good access to shallow water flats awaits those wanting to wade for seatrout and redfish. Some of these areas include the following causeways: The Pineda Causeway (SR 404), the Eau Gallie Causeway (SR 518), and the SR 520 Causeway. Additional access is supplied by Tropical Trail on Merritt Island, and US 1 which runs along the west side of the lagoon system. Rodney says that access to the water from these roads is easy to find. He also says that waders need to use common sense when wading, since stingrays are ubiquitous here. Do the stingray shuffle!

Waders are requested to please respect homeowners' rights when parking vehicles and accessing the water.

-Hand Powered Boats: The No Motor Zone discussed in the last section lies north of SR 528 in the Banana River Lagoon. As of this writing only the west side is open. When the east side will re-open is not known.

The 1000 Islands area in the Banana River Lagoon behind Cocoa Beach is another protected area in which canoeists and kayakers can find some solitude and a good chance to find some snook, tarpon, redfish, and seatrout.

-Inshore Boat: In the lagoon system the top four gamefish targeted by most anglers include redfish, snook, seatrout, and small tarpon. You'll find other species of fish. Extensive grassflats along both shorelines of the Banana River Lagoon and the Thousand Islands area behind Cocoa Beach are good places to try. Additionally, an extensive system of canals behind Cocoa Beach holds tarpon during the summer and seatrout during the winter.

-From the Beach: Excellent surfcasting opportunities exist from the beach here, possibly the best in the state. Snook patrol the beaches from spring through fall, averaging from 8 to 15 pounds and sometimes topping thirty. Ladyfish, jack crevalle, barracuda, tarpon, Spanish mackerel, and other species also find their way to the rock reefs found along this stretch of beach. While casting in the surf a shooting head will help improve the presentation. Fast sinking lines are not recommended, but slow sinking lines are fine.

-Nearshore: In Port Canaveral itself there is sometimes excellent fishing for a variety of fish, including snook, jack crevalle, and bluefish. Fishing the lights at night in the Port is becoming increasingly popular, and with good reason. Out of Port Canaveral it's possible to catch multiple species in one day along the buoy line, under debris and weed lines, along the beaches, or well offshore, including cobia, tripletail, tarpon, large jack crevalle, blacktip sharks, Spanish and king mackerel, bonito, blackfin tuna, and dolphin.

If you want to fish inside the Port or north of the Port along the beach there are many security issues of which you need to be aware. Call the USCG station at Port Canaveral at 321.853.7601.

Flies and Techniques

Rodney says his favorite fly is whatever worked the day before. I guess we've all felt that way! He develops new patterns constantly, including the Schroach, the Last Chance Fly, and the Whitebait Fly. He also likes Ron Winn's Finger Mullet, the Glass Minnow pattern, Blanton's Sar-Mul-Mac, and the Popovic's Siliclone.

The technique used depends on the fishing being done, of course. Along the beach Rodney likes to look for activity from birds, or baitfish, or best of all from the targeted gamefish themselves. He likes the Sar-Mul-Mac in white and green for snook fishing here. He says that using a fast sinking line from these beaches is a bad idea, since you will snag on the rocks all the time. A floating or intermediate sinking line performs better.

Start at daybreak. You can cast from shore, or wade out to the first, second, or third reef (depending on the height of the tide) and fan cast around your position. Ordinarily you blind cast. Don't forget to cast toward the beach sometimes, since the fish will cruise along right in the wash. As in most beach fishing, a stripping basket comes in very handy, especially when there's some surf. This is a public beach, so when the sun bunnies start showing up, consider putting the fly rod away.

90

Fishing out of Port Canaveral, it's vital to start with a full tank of gasoline. Oftentimes a lot of water will need to be covered while you look for debris or weed lines. Work the buoys along the buoy line first, looking for tripletail and cobia. You need to start early in the morning in order to beat competitors to the buoys. If the buoys don't produce, you need to cruise along the beaches from one to ten miles out, searching for pieces of wood, plastic bags, or any other type of debris in the water. We've seen tripletail lying under all sorts of flotsam, even dead jack crevalle that had been discarded by mackerel netters.

Weed lines often have cobia working through them, searching for crabs and small fish. The weeds shelter barracuda and tripletail, too. Usually you will cruise slowly along the weeds, looking for fish. When you see them you cast to them. Very straightforward.

The other technique out of the Port is so obvious it barely deserves a mention. In the fall, especially in October, look for excited terns working. They are usually over Spanish mackerel, but little tunny are also a possibility. The fish get so thick sometimes you literally get tired of catching them since it's too easy. Glass minnows or Clouser minnows work well for this. Use a 30 pound fluorocarbon shock leader for the mackerel. You'll lose a lot of fish and flies but will get so many more strikes than if you used a section of wire trace.

In the lagoon system looking for redfish is done in much the same way as it's done elsewhere in the state. Waders blindcast while looking for signs of fish, preferably over a bottom with mixed sand and grass. Boaters pole (or electric motor) along the flats, looking for fish in groups as small as singles or in schools as large as hundreds of individuals. Bigger fish will generally be on the deeper flats, between three and four feet deep. These large redfish have become conditioned to boat and motors, which often makes it difficult to approach them with trolling motors. A silent approach is vital for success!

Smaller, slot-sized fish will go in closer to shore, sometimes right against the bank if they're looking for crabs. Check the flat from edge to edge.

If you fish anywhere in Florida during the summer months, it's important to fight your fish hard, get them in quickly, and make sure they're revived before releasing them.

Access
For Waders- see wading opportunities, above.
For Boaters- Boat ramps can be found at the following locations-
-Kelly Park, on Banana River Drive just south of SR 528. Access to Banana River Lagoon.
-Lee Wenner Park in Cocoa, on the southwest side of SR 520. Access to the Indian River Lagoon.
-at Port Canaveral there is an excellent ramp, accessing the Port and the Atlantic Ocean.
-at both ends of the Pineda Causeways over both the Indian and Banana River Lagoons.
-at the Eau Gallie Causeway, on the east side. Accesses both the Banana and Indian River Lagoons.
-off Ramp Road in Cocoa Beach, access to the Banana River Lagoon.
-on the southwest side of the Melbourne Causeway there's an excellent ramp, accessing the Indian River Lagoon. Harry Goode's Outdoor Shop is right across the street.
-at Sebastian Inlet- access to both the Indian River Lagoon and the Atlantic Ocean through Sebastian Inlet.

Fly Shops
Harry Goode's Outdoor Shop in Melbourne, 321.723.4751. This is an excellent shop staffed

with knowledgeable, helpful people

Boat Rental
-Mariner Club & Boat Rental, Indian Harbor Beach, 321.777.4386; www.marinerboatrental.com. Powerboat rentals.

Guides
Captain Rodney Smith, 265 South Robert Way, Satellite Beach, FL 32937. 321.777.2773, 888. 800.9794; www.camirl.com, www.Floridaguidelines.com

State Parks and Other Attractions
The Banana River Manatee Refuge is part of the Merritt Island National Wildlife Refuge. Cocoa Beach has plenty to see and do for any non-anglers in the party, including "World Famous" Ron Jon's Surf Shop.
The Kennedy Space Center is worth at least a day's visit if you're in this part of the world. Pick a windy day– fishing would be tough anyway!

Accommodations
There are lots and lots of hotels and motels along the beach on SR A1A. The Space Coast Office of Tourism will be able to recommend some. 800.872.1969, or www.space-coast.com.

Big redfish and big black drum like this one displayed by Barry Kent are why people will gladly put in 10 and 12 mile days in the Banana River no motor zone.

92

Sebastian Inlet and Vicinity

Overview

The reputation Sebastian Inlet holds as a premier snook hole in Florida is well deserved. Most of the successful snook fishermen at the inlet use (dare I even use the word in a fly fishing book?) BAIT. Fly fishing for snook at the inlet is usually difficult at best. The currents are usually too strong to easily get a fly down into the strike zone and there are almost always too many people around!

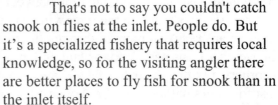

That's not to say you couldn't catch snook on flies at the inlet. People do. But it's a specialized fishery that requires local knowledge, so for the visiting angler there are better places to fly fish for snook than in the inlet itself.

The region around the inlet, with the Indian River Lagoon system to the west and the Atlantic Ocean to the east, probably has as large a variety of fish species available as any other area in Florida. Seatrout, redfish, snook, tarpon, jacks, snapper, Spanish and king mackerel, barracuda, cobia, sharks, and more all call this area home. Several fly rod world records have been set in the vicinity of the inlet on various species. No matter the time of year, nor the weather, there are angling opportunities in a wide variety of fishing situations. Canals, estuaries, back bays, flats, inlets, beaches, and creeks are all available.

Terry Parsons, who has lived here for over 30 years, guides the entire area between Melbourne and Ft. Pierce, specializing in the Sebastian area. Eric Davis grew up in Brevard County, owns The Back Country (a fine shop) in Vero Beach, and has been guiding here for 10 years.

Opportunities for the Do-It-Yourself Fly Fisher

-Inshore Wading: good access to the Indian River Lagoon for waders will be found along SR A1A south of Sebastian Inlet. Healthy grass-flats here support a good population of seatrout. Other species will sometimes be encountered.

North of the inlet along A1A about a mile is Long Point Park. Waders can park here and wade in the Indian River Lagoon. The primary target will be seatrout but again, other species will sometimes be encountered, including jacks, ladyfish, redfish, and snook. You can continue driving north along A1A and find river access all along the way. The species of fish you will most likely tangle with will be seatrout and redfish.

On the west side of the lagoon south of Sebastian River, Indian River Drive gives waders access. The oyster bars here provide good hunting for redfish looking to pick up a meal.
-Hand Powered Boat: Since the entire Sebastian River is a slow speed manatee zone, it's ideal for hand powered boats. Snook, tarpon, and jacks are the main species, but redfish, trout, sharks, ladyfish, and others will also be encountered. Launch at Micco Marina in Micco, or at Donald McDonald Park off of CR 505, west of US 1 on the south side of the Sebastian River.

The Sebastian River has many opportunities that change during the year. Tarpon inhabit the river all year long, with the time between May and October probably the most productive. The many docks that line the river will produce snook, snapper and some redfish. Jacks and ladyfish are very common all through the river. It's very sheltered and a good place to be when the weather turns nasty and the lagoon looks like a washing machine. The tarpon here are about as ornery a critter as you'll find anywhere. You can literally be surrounded by rolling fish and cast for hours without a strike. My best luck has been very early or late in the day, or on overcast, rainy days that are most definitely not chamber of commerce weather. Fish range from about 10 to 40 pounds, with bigger fish seen rarely. All of Sebastian River is a slow speed manatee zone. There are quite a few manatees in it most of the time.
-Inshore Boat: there are 14 boat ramps within 10 miles of Sebastian. Every kind of fish found inshore in Florida can be found here, with the exception of bonefish. Also, a good part of this area is posted as slow speed manatee zones. Marine Patrol officers work this area on a regular basis and the fine for speeding is almost $300.00. Learn the manatee areas and obey the law.

In the inlet itself you can find schools of crevalle tearing up mullet, especially during the mullet migrations. The flats adjacent to the inlet can provide a wide variety of different species, including snook, reds, and trout. The flats to the north of the inlet are especially productive.

South of the inlet by Sebastian the docks and canals on the western shoreline can provide good action for seatrout. As is the case all through this area, other species could show up at any time. On the opposite side of the lagoon the points and islands produce trout and reds on a regular basis, and deserve exploration.

North of the inlet the area around Long Point Park often produces trout, reds, and snook. If you go a little further north, the canal system known as the Honest John Canals support a well-known winter trout fishery which has produced several world record seatrout. Snook and reds in addition to trout can be found in this area all year long.

Drop-offs on the west side of the lagoon around the spoil islands often produce trout. All of the spoil islands both north and south of the Inlet have sand bars that protrude to either the east or west side, or sometimes both sides, of these islands. They usually have good current flow, forming a feeding lane for trout, jacks, ladyfish, and other common species of the lagoon.

The clam leases that are both to the north and the south of the Sebastian Inlet are good places to stop and take a few casts. Taking a couple of drifts while blind casting with a popper or other attractor pattern will usually determine whether you should invest much time here.

South of the inlet, the area that lies between the Wabasso Bridge (SR 510) and the Barber Bridge (SR 60) is commonly called The Narrows. This is a good area, especially when the weather gets bad.

The community called Grand Harbor has a marina which almost always holds huge snook. Going south past the 17th St. Causeway in Vero Beach is an open part of the lagoon that has many flats both east and west of the ICW. The entire west shore is a good place for redfish and trout.

94

On the east shoreline in Vero Beach is an area called The Moorings. This residential community has deep canals, some that are 18 to 24 feet. They will hold tarpon and big snook all year long. The flats that are around and a little south of The Moorings are some of the best around. They get some fishing pressure, but still provide good fishing.

Farther south and on the western shore is a strip of land that juts out to the lagoon almost to the ICW, commonly called Harbor Branch. There are productive flats both to the north and south of this. A deep channel cuts down the middle of this peninsula, making it a good place to get out of the hard northeast winds. You can catch anything in this area.

From Harbor Branch south a half a mile or so is a slow speed zone for the entire lagoon. Just to the south of the slow speed zone on the east shoreline is an area that has extensive mangrove shorelines where you can find great redfish and snook action. You can explore to your heart's content back here. Kayakers and canoeists will find plenty of protected waters. This mangrove area ends at the north bridge in Ft. Pierce.

-Along the Beach: the fishing along the beach here is arguably the best in the state. North of the inlet the beach is sandy, but has a fast slope. South of the inlet rock reefs run parallel to the beach. With clean water both beaches will attract fish.

Snook and to a lesser degree tarpon can be caught off the beach all summer long. Other species, especially jacks, will crash the party from time to time. If you like pompano, you can sight fish them from the beach when conditions are right.

During the fall Spanish mackerel will show up and can be caught all winter long. Bluefish are a common winter catch. Whiting can be caught year round.

Undoubtedly the highlight of any surf fisherman's year is the annual mullet run in the fall. As mullet move along the beach every other fish that eats them follows. Fishing for snook, jack crevalle, bluefish, and other species can be spectacular. It is quite possible to hook tarpon in excess of a hundred pounds from the beach. Good luck landing them!

-Nearshore: All of the same species mentioned in the section on Port Canaveral can be caught here, by exactly the same techniques, although if anything fishing is better here. Please refer to that section (p.92) for nearshore fishing information.

Flies and Techniques

Parsons has very definite ideas about fly selection. His number one selection for potluck fishing is a Clouser minnow on a #1 hook. However, he prefers using surface flies such as poppers and will always use them if conditions allow it. His favorite fishing is snook on fly, and he strongly believes that most folks use flies which are much too small. Using 9- or 10-weight rods he'll throw 3-D or slab flies tied on 4/0 and 5/0 hooks, flies which are seven or eight inches long. Most of this is casting to docks or other structure rather than sight fishing, since the water is usually too murky to see the fish.

Those tough Sebastian River tarpon are fished with small (#4) brown flies on a slow sinking line like a monocore. Terry says they are most easily caught when in four to six feet of water, and he likes bright, flashy patterns like Clousers and Polar Fiber Minnows. He only likes dark patterns on overcast days.

Terry likes to sightfish for reds whenever possible. He'll hunt for tailing fish, or fish pushing wakes, or even try to see them if the water is clear. He likes chartreuse Clousers when sight fishing for reds.

Eric Davis likes fishing for summer tarpon on the Atlantic. For this work he likes a Polar Fiber Minnow tied on hooks from 3/0 to 5/0. When fishing in the lagoon he still likes this fly in smaller sizes, although he says that the Clouser minnow is a versatile, all around fly.

Access

For waders- see the section on wading opportunities, too.

-The SR 510 bridge in Wabasso has a ramp and plenty of area to wade.

-The very east end of 69th Street (N. Winter Beach Road) in Vero Beach has good wading with oyster bars both north and south of the access.

-The very east end of 45th Street in Vero Beach has good wading conditions, and a dock.

-The east end of Oslo Road south of Vero Beach is a small ramp, and wading. North tends to bring more action. If you don't mind some deep wading, one can walk east to the spoil islands that are out in front of Oslo Road. Warning! Do not leave anything in your car here!

-SR A1A just south of the Inlet has good wading and plenty of area. Good deep water very close to shore.

-From Sebastian Inlet to Ft. Pierce there are well over a dozen access points along SR A1A that can get you on the beach.

For Boaters- You can find ramps at the following locations along the east side of the Indian River Lagoon:

-at Sebastian Inlet State Park.

-Honest John's Fish Camp, off of A1A north of the inlet ($).

-south of the SR 510 Causeway in Wabasso.

On the west side of the lagoon you can find more ramps at:

-Grant, off of US 1.

-Micco Marina, just west of US 1 and north of the Sebastian River Bridge on Sand Point Road.

-At both Dale Wimbrow Park and Donald McDonald Park on the south fork of the Sebastian River, off of CR 505.

-at the town landing in Sebastian, off of US 1.

-Round Island Park just south of Vero Beach on the east side of the Indian River Lagoon is a good ramp and has some limited wading access.

Boat Rentals

Treasure Coast Marina, 5185 S. Hwy. US 1, Grant, FL; 321.733.3390. Pontoon and fishing boats, kayak and canoe rentals. Located just off the Intracoastal Waterway between ICW markers #35 and #36, in the middle of the aquatic preserve and among the islands of the Pelican National Wildlife Refuge. www.treasure-coast-marina.com; email: treasurecoast-marina@yahoo.com

Fly Shops

-The Back Country, 634 21st Street, Vero Beach, Fl. 32960, 772-567-6665. www.verobackcountry.com. A complete outdoor outfitter and fly shop, open 7 days a week. They have a huge fly and fly tying selection.

-Wabasso Tackle Shop. Call Terry Parsons- it's his shop! 772.589.8518

Guides

-Captain Eric Davis, owner of The Back Country in Vero Beach, guides here a lot. 772-567.6665; www.verobackcountry.com

-Captain Charlie Fornabio also guides this area. 772.388.9773.

-Capt. Tod Hagan, 321.951.0223; www.fishingcaptain.com.
-Capt. Terry Parsons says in his modest way that he's the guy to fish with because he knows all the spots! Terry is Orvis endorsed, and can be reached at 772.589.7782 or 772.589.8518.
-Capt. Mike Peppe, 772-581-0062; www.tarpondancer.com

State Parks and Other Attractions
Sebastian Inlet State Recreation Area- the focal point for snook fishing on Florida's east coast. 9700 South A1A, Melbourne Beach, 32951. 772. 984.4852. Camping sites are available here. Information about all state parks can be found online at www.floridastateparks.org.

Accommodations
The phone number for the Melbourne-Palm Bay Chamber of Commerce is 321.724.5200. For the Sebastian River Area Chamber of Commerce the number is 772.589.5969.
And again, for Brevard County locations the Space Coast Office of Tourism will be helpful. 800.872.1969, or the website URL is www.space-coast.com.

-Ferndale Lodge, Sebastian, 772.589.5247 – efficiencies available.
-Key West Inn, Sebastian, 772.388.8588.
-Penwood Motor Inn, Wabasso, 772.589.3855.

The area around Sebastian Inlet is a great place to score with snook like this one.

Fort Pierce/Jensen Beach/Stuart

Atlantic Ocean

Fort Pierce Inlet

Fort Pierce

Hutchison Island

Indian River Lagoon

Overview

Twenty-two fish-filled miles separate the Fort Pierce Inlet from the St. Lucie Inlet. Due to the proximity of the two inlets, the Indian River Lagoon here has good water flow, making fishing over the miles of grass flats, bars, and docks here somewhat tidal dependent. Like every inlet from Sebastian south, the Fort Pierce Inlet and the St. Lucie Inlet concentrate snook all summer long. Snook are also found along the beaches and in the lagoon, as are tarpon, seatrout, crevalle, ladyfish, to a lesser degree redfish, and several other species.

In addition to the Indian River Lagoon, the Saint Lucie River (north and south forks), and of course the Atlantic Ocean add even more variety to the mix.

This area boasts a summer snook fishery that is second to none, and tarpon fishing can equal any elsewhere in the state. The tarpon fishing in the North Fork of the Saint Lucie from June to September can be fast and furious with what Capt. Marcia Foosaner calls "starter tarpon," fish in the 10 to 40 pound range. Lush grass flats in the Indian River Lagoon hold plenty of seatrout of the "gator" variety and redfish seem to be making a comeback in the area.

The winter months bring hoards of Spanish mackerel to an area south of the Saint Lucie Inlet called Peck Lake. Both bluefish and pompano invade the Lagoon and beaches. Large schools of jack crevalle in the 20 to 40 pound class roam the beaches from mid-winter to mid-summer. Nearshore offers the usual fare of cobia, kingfish, crevalle, little tunny, and dolphin.

From either inlet, the Gulf Stream is only five to ten miles offshore. Its warm flow attracts marlin, sailfish, yellowfin tuna, kingfish, wahoo, dolphin, and little tunny. Closer in, king mackerel, Spanish mackerel, and cobia are popular targets.

While a power boat certainly comes in handy here, the paddler and wader can find happiness too. For the angler this area offers an enormous variety of options.

Capt. Marcia Foosaner supplied most of the information in this section.

Opportunities for the Do-It-Yourself-Fly Fisher

-<u>Inshore wading</u>: Along the Stuart Causeway and Jensen Beach Causeway there is plenty of wading access. The west shoreline north and south of the Stuart Causeway offers docks to cast to as well as thick grass beds. Mosquito bridges at either end of the draw bridge offer good water flow and structure.

Hutchison Island offers loads of riverside access to the west and ocean access to the east. Look for the cars of locals to help you find these places. Local bait and tackle shops or fly shops can provide reliable information, with many supplying a map of wading areas.

The areas around Herman's Bay, Little Mud Creek, or Bear Point would be good places to start. The west bank of the Indian River Lagoon from Jensen Beach to Fort Pierce also provides a few areas of wading access, with the Walton Road area a good one.

During the summer a mosquito jacket and insect repellant is advised for anyone entering areas in close proximity to mangrove shorelines. For summer wading you need only wear a pair of the nylon shorts, zip-off- leg trousers (the latter for protection from small jellyfish), and a pair of wading booties. A fishing vest is helpful. Don't forget to shuffle your feet while wading! Early or later in the day is best, but not imperative, for a good day in the water.

Anglers wading during the winter should use chest waders, as water temperatures can and do drop into the mid- to high 50's.

-Hand Powered boats: There is not a grass flat or spoil island in the Indian River Lagoon from the Saint Lucie Inlet to Fort Pierce Inlet that is not accessible by kayak or canoe. Indeed, these hand powered boats are becoming commonplace. They are perfect alternatives to flats boats. While some anglers fish from them, most prefer to use them as transportation to the fishing destination, hopping out to wade upon arrival at a flat or spoil island.

-Inshore Boat: From the Fort Pierce Inlet to Saint Lucie Inlet a boater has all of the Indian River Lagoon and the Saint Lucie River to explore. Snook, tarpon, reds, and trout lead the list of predators, with ladyfish and jack crevalle close behind. Snook and tarpon of all sizes are available all summer long. Loads of flats as well as some bars are found in the Indian River Lagoon. Covered with thick grass, these flats hold big snook and trout. Look for concentrations of bait and the chances are good that the predators you seek will be there, especially if the water is moving well. Try Little Mud Creek for tarpon.

The inlets produce exceptional snook action- as a matter of fact, the 20 pound tippet IGFA world record snook was caught at the St. Lucie Inlet. Grassflats along the river produce snook, reds, and seatrout.

The North and South Forks of the Saint Lucie River are scenic fish habitat. The North

Fork harbors many big snook and tarpon. It is a very fishy looking and productive area. It's safe

An aerial view from the east of the Fort Pierce Inlet.

as far as running your boat goes, too, with very few rocks around. Both forks are lined with mangroves and have plenty of canals, bridges, and coves. Development along some stretches of shoreline has provided plenty of docks to which you can throw your favorite fly.

A very active night time fishery has developed in both the Indian and Saint Lucie Rivers, since the lights and structure attract bait for the predators.

-Nearshore Boat: For those who wish for a bigger tug on the line, fishing off the the beaches at Stuart, Jensen Beach, or Fort Pierce will not disappoint you. Both inlets are easily navigable for offshore and flats skiffs alike. The fisherman in the know can get so sick of catching big fish out here that he cuts the hook off his flies. This fishing is done by chumming with live pilchards or mullet. Giant jack crevalle, snook, barracuda, and bonito (little tunny) move into the chum line and will make up the majority of the catch.

Those who don't like chumming can still catch fish (not so many though) around bait pods. Casting into pods of bait can produce some surprising results. Cobia will be found in addition to 'cuda and tarpon. The mackerel and bluefish show up in the fall.

Giant jack crevalle wake the surface in circling pods, many containing 100 fish or more. Tarpon lay up on the surface at sunrise or move lazily in schools not far off the beach. The Spanish mackerel fishing here in the winter is a fly fisher's answered prayer, a fish every cast.

The "Boils," the discharge tube from the power plant north of Stuart, offers permit fishing all summer (along with other species, of course).

For those with big enough boats wishing to venture further offshore you can either chum or look for floating debris. Cobia, kingfish, crevalle, bonito, and dolphin, all that the Gulf Stream has to offer, awaits

Along the Beaches: Again, the fly fisher can have superb angling from the beach. Don't forget a stripping basket! Using the House of Refuge as a starting point, the beach to the north and south is loaded with sub-surface structure, rock reef that can and usually does hold fish most of the spring and summer. Both Martin and St. Lucie counties have purchased beach access. Winter fishing for mackerel and bluefish can be excellent, conditions permitting.

The ambitious angler can walk the mile and a half of beach from Bathtub Reef Park to the north side of the Saint Lucie Inlet. Recent dredging there has created some deep impoundments intended to hold the sands that shoal the inlet every three or four years. Tarpon fishing inside the inlet has shown a marked improvement since the dredging. The snook fishing here has always been excellent.

Normandy Beach, Walton Rocks Beach, and Turtle Beach near the nuclear plant are also hot spots with Walton Rocks leading the way during the fall mullet run. Hooking a tarpon in the hundred pound class from the beach is entirely possible, although landing it is another story altogether. Bring your twelve-weight, try a large black fly, and be sure you've got a stout leader and lots of backing!

Access for fly fishers is also available at Ft. Pierce Inlet. The Hobe Sound National Wildlife Refuge offers six miles of undeveloped beach on the south side of St. Lucie Inlet.

Flies and Techniques

Marcia says, "My favorite patterns are bait fish flies that resemble a pilchard or threadfin herring in the two and a half to three and a half inch size. Of course one should not sacrifice common sense and practicality just to use your favorite pattern. When chasing those giant jacks off the beach a large popper should be close at hand. The days do exist when they are stubborn about poppers and knowing this, a large streamer (bait fish) pattern should work.

"Tarpon can be most stubborn and I like a Black Death better than most standard, long-nosed Tarpon flies. I fall back again on my pilchard pattern if the old standards don't work.

"For flats fishing in the shallower waters I love a red and white spun deer hair bug to push a wake on the surface. I tend to use Clousers most often in the winter months. I personally have come to think that most times something different works better than something akin to 'matching the hatch.' I think that fish key on things that have something different about them, something darker or lighter, something a bit smaller or a bit larger than the bait at hand.

"Use long strips rather than short, and strip faster in summer and very slowly in cold water. Over the past few years I have used a clear intermediate line whenever possible. The advent of clear floating lines increases the angler's advantage.

"I'll use the flies mentioned earlier wherever moving water passes by some type of fish-holding structure, or current brings food to the fish. Whether working a mangrove shoreline, casting along a grass flat, or fishing docks and seawalls, try to let the current carry your fly to where the fish are. You'll catch more and bigger fish this way.

"Along the beach poppers will work when the water is reasonably calm, but if the water is too rough or if the fish aren't coming up for them, bigger flies are needed. Deceivers will usually do the trick, but during the mullet run woolheads and siliclones provide ample size and bulk for the fish to zero in on. As in most beach fishing, use a monocore line for best results."

Access
For Waders- see opportunities for waders.
Along the Beach- it depends which beach you want to fish. For Bathtub Beach and the House of Refuge, take the causeway (SR A1A, East Ocean Blvd.) from Stuart over to Hutchinson Island. Take a right on MacArthur Boulevard. As you head south toward St. Lucie Inlet you will periodically see small parking lots that allow beach access, then the House of Refuge (great place to fish!) and finally the parking lot at Bathtub Beach. From here it's all walking if you want to fish the inlet- this is the southernmost access point on Hutchinson Island.

If you go north on A1A on Hutchinson, you'll find beach access intermittently all the way to the south jetty in Ft. Pierce.

At Fort Pierce Inlet State Park there is beach access on the north side of the inlet.
For Boaters- there are lots of boat ramps in this area. For example:
-Stuart Causeway ramp. This ramp is located on the east side of the Stuart Causeway (SR A1A) and allows access to the grassflats of the Indian River, the St. Lucie River, and St. Lucie Inlet. It is nasty with a south or southeast wind.
-Jensen Causeway ramps. There are ramps on both sides of the Jensen Beach Causeway (SR 732) on the west end. The north facing one is normally the better one to use. If the wind is from the north, though...
-Little Mud Creek. This isn't really a ramp, just a little beach where you can put a small boat in and park the car and trailer. It is the ramp to use though if you want to fish this part of the Indian River, or Big Mud Creek. Coming from Stuart, Little Mud Creek is the third bridge after the power station. The ramp is on the left, just before the bridge.
-Shepard Park in downtown Stuart boasts an excellent ramp, at the intersection of US 1 and West Ocean Boulevard. Access to the north fork of the St. Lucie River.
-In Fort Pierce you can find boat ramps at the both the North and South Causeways.
-In Fort Pierce is Sand Spit Park on Old St. Lucie Blvd, directly west of the Fort Pierce Inlet.
-Port St. Lucie Yacht Club, 500 S.E. Prima Vista Blvd., Port St. Lucie, 772.879.4555.

-Veteran's Memorial Park at Rivergate, 2200 S. E. Midport Road, Port St. Lucie

Fly Shops
-John B's Fly and Light Tackle, 4330 SE Federal Highway, Stuart 34997, 772.287.6535. John B. Sweeney offers complete service for fly and light tackle anglers, as well as rod and reel repair.
-Southern Angler, in Finest Kind Marina on Manatee Pocket, 772.223.1300.

Boat Rentals
-Manatee Marina, 4905 SE Dixie Hwy., Stuart, 772. 288.2888. Powerboat rentals.
-Anchors Aweigh Marine, 2225 NE Indian River Drive, Jensen Beach, 772.334.0936. Powerboat rentals.
-Allied Marine Group, 110 N Dixie Hwy., Stuart, 772.692.1122. Powerboat rentals.
-Dockside-Harborlight Resort, 1160 Seaway Drive, Ft. Pierce, 772.468.3555, 800.286.1745. Powerboat rentals.
-Little Jim's Marina & Fishing Bridge, 601 North Beach Causeway, Ft. Pierce, 772.468.2503. Powerboat rentals.

Guides
-Captain Marcia Foosaner, 772.287.5377. Indian and St. Lucie Rivers, beaches. Marcia loves to wade and is a superb angler.

State Parks and Other Attractions
-Hobe Sound National Wildlife Refuge, c/o US Fish and Wildlife Service, PO Box 645, Hobe Sound 33475-6141. 772.546.2067, http://hobesound.fws.gov. Three miles of beach with reef formations offer excellent fishing for snook and other species during the summer months.
-Fort Pierce Inlet State Recreation Area, four miles east of Ft. Pierce on the Atlantic Ocean. 772.468.3985.
-Jonathan Dickinson State Park is over 10,000 acres on the Loxahatchee River, 12 miles south of Stuart on US 1. There are two camping areas, as well as cabins for rent. Jonathan Dickinson State Park, 16450 SE Federal Highway, Hobe Sound 33455. 772.546.2771.
-St. Lucie Inlet State Park, accessible only by boat. Three miles of beach adjacent to the Hobe Sound National Wildlife Refuge. St. Lucie State Park, c/o Jonathan Dickinson State Park, 772.744.7603.
Information about all state parks can be found online at www.floridastateparks.org.
-South Jetty Park, with its 237-feet of oceanfront, is located on the south side of Ft. Pierce Inlet at the end of Seaway Drive in Fort Pierce. The park offers restrooms, boardwalk, a 1,200-foot fishing jetty (the longest in Florida) and picnic shelters with grills.

Accommodations
-River Palm Cottages and Fish Camp, Indian River Drive, Jensen Beach. 800.305.0511, or locally 772.334.0401; www.riverpalmcottages.com.
-Caribbean Shores, Jensen Beach, 772.334.4759; www.caribbeanshores.com
-The Stuart/Martin County Chamber of Commerce, 800.524.9704.
-The Greater Port St. Lucie Chamber of Commerce can be reached at 772.335.4422.
Or lastly, you can visit www.stuartfla.com.

Jupiter

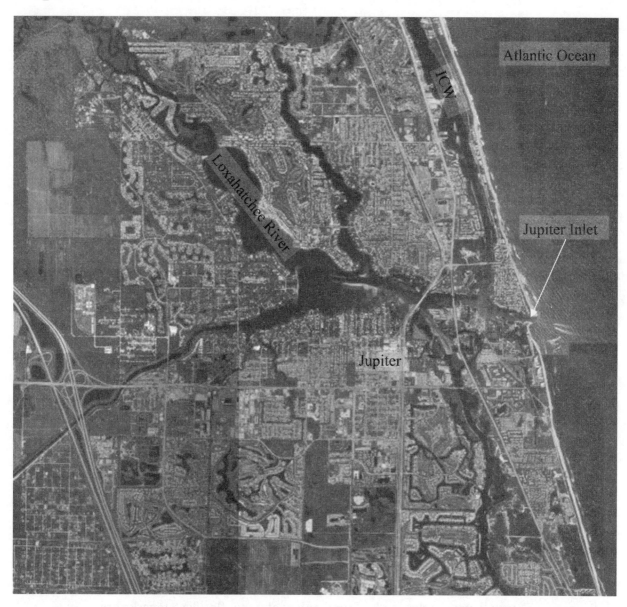

Overview

Jupiter, like the communities of Palm Beach and Fort Lauderdale to the south, is principally an nearhore fishing destination. Approximately twenty species of fly rod targets pass through the area during the course of the year. Little tunny, king and Spanish mackerel, sharks, barracuda, jack crevalle, snook, tarpon, sailfish, and more can be caught in the waters out from Jupiter Inlet. For anglers from the northeast who like fishing for false albacore, the Florida bonito (little tunny) is the same fish. You can very literally get tired of catching them here, as long as they don't destroy all your tackle first. Snook fishing in the vicinity of Jupiter Inlet is as good as it can get anywhere else in the state.

The Intracoastal Waterway does offer fishing, especially for snook, especially after dark. And the Loxahatchee River, while not the fishery it used to be, still provides angling opportunities. Bluefish, crevalle, various types of snapper, and other assorted finned denizens make Jupiter and its environs an excellent place to wet a line.

Opportunities for Do-It-Yourself Fly Fishers

-Inshore Wading: There isn't much access to the ICW for the boatless in this area. North of Jupiter, just south of Jonathan Dickinson State Park, there are excellent wadable flats off of US 1. Fish species are principally snook and seatrout.

-Hand Powered Boat: With a kayak or canoe much more of the ICW is available, even if you want to wade. Small boaters will find fishable areas in the Loxahatchee River as well as in the ICW. One problem with fishing from a hand powered boat here is that the motor vessels tend to be large, and as such throw out large wakes. The Loxahatchee is a federally designated Wild and Scenic River, the only such river in the state of Florida.

-Inshore: Not Jupiter's strong point, inshore fishing here is limited to the ICW and the Loxahatchee River. The Loxahatchee has snook, jacks, bluefish, and ladyfish, and the upper reaches contain Florida's usual freshwater species. Docks and bridges with lights offer night fishing for snook and other species.

-From the Beach: There is good beach access in this region, and many different species of fish. The typical beach fish like whiting and pompano are available on a year round basis. Snook, bluefish, ladyfish, crevalle, Spanish mackerel, and other species could be hooked from the beach at various seasons. Because of the rocks, Blowing Rocks Beach is an excellent place to fish. The rocks at Jupiter Inlet attract fish, but there are usually a lot of bait fishermen here.

-Nearshore: This is Jupiter's strongest point, and it is VERY strong. Capt. George LaBonte says, "Jupiter is home to one of the largest concentrations of trophy snook in the world. This is a very visual experience involving schools of hundreds of fish in crystal clear waters. The fish are easy to coax into eating a fly with a little help from some chumming.

"Tarpon are found here in good numbers from May through August with June and July being the peak months for large numbers of fish. These fish average between 75 and 125 pounds with a handful of larger fish always a possibility. The fish are found cruising in clear water along the beaches where anglers cast flies to them. Then hang on!

"Nowhere in North America offers better action for catching large little tunny (Florida bonito, or false albacore to you Yankees) on fly than Jupiter does. The area from Jupiter south to Palm Beach, also known as the 'Bonito Triangle' is so infested with 10 to 15 pound little tunny that it may be impossible to fish for anything else, since they are so aggressive. We can virtually guarantee you false albacore on the fly-rod during the peak of their run. The fish arrive in April with the first southeast winds, peak in May-July and taper off in September. Plan on leaving the bite when you have caught enough to move on in search of other species. It is a 'slam dunk' for those of you who are tired of chasing them around all day without ever getting to wet your line.

"Other fish available include sailfish, barracuda, dolphin (mahi mahi), king mackerel, and even more. This area is truly an offshore fly fisher's dream come true."

Flies and Techniques

During my own trips to Jupiter the most important factor in having a successful day (besides knowing where the fish live) was a livewell full of live minnows, and I'm talking hundreds if not thousands of them. Pilchards, Spanish sardines, threadfin herring, whatever live bait you can get most easily is what you need. On trips where bait was scarce we have used frozen glass minnows with success, too.

Flies should "match the hatch" (your chum) reasonably closely in both size and color. This means white flies with pearl or silver flash, white and green, white and chartreuse, or white and red are usually good choices. Minnow patterns such as Deceivers (for the traditionalist) or synthetic flies like Puglisi's patterns, Eat'ems, Sexyflies, etc., are all excellent choices. Clouser minnows are good flies to carry. Poppers can provide the most spectacular visuals, too.

When I've had good days off Jupiter (which has been on most summertime trips I've made there) fish were on the chum immediately, literally from the time that the first baits hit the water. Within a few minutes hundreds of fish would be all around the boat– bonito, snook, crevalle, runners, sharks, you never know what will show. Do not exhibit patience, waiting for something to show up. If you don't get immediate gratification, change locations.

Fly Shops
Jupiter doesn't have a fly shop per se; however, information and some fly gear can be had at Fishing Headquarters, 633 N Highway A1A Alt, Jupiter, 561.743.7335

Boat Rentals
-Jupiter Outdoor Center, 18095 Coastal A1A, Jupiter, FL 33477; 877-SIT-ON-TOP, local 561.747.9666; www.jupiteroutdoorcenter.com. They rent canoes and kayaks for use in the ICW and on the Loxahatchee River.
-Jupiter Inlet Boat Rentals, 1095 N. A1A, Jupiter, Florida 33477; 561.741.1212; www.jupiterinletboatrentals.com

Guides
-Capt. George LaBonte, Edge Fishing Charters, 561.746.0032; www.edgesportfishing.com.
-Capt. Scott Hamilton, Hamilton Fly Fishing Charters, 561.439.8592; www.flyfishingextremes.com.

State Parks and Other Attractions
-Jonathan Dickenson State Park, Jupiter, 561.451.1202. 11,000 acres with 135 campsites, fresh and saltwater fishing.
Information about all state parks can be found online at www.floridastateparks.org.

Accommodations
Jupiter lies within Palm Beach County. The Palm Beach CVB is the agency to contact for information, 561.233.3000; www.palmbeachfl.com.

Atlantic Ocean

Lake Worth

West Palm Beach

Palm Beach Inlet

ICW

West Palm Beach

Overview

While this area may lack inshore fishing variety, those willing to look off the beaches can find some superb fly rod action. The Gulf Stream is only a mile or two (it varies) out of Palm Beach Inlet and some great fly fishing is available here.

Inshore fly fishing opportunities definitely do exist for the fly rodder willing to look for them. "Look" is definitely the operative word here. The fishing spots aren't obvious, and sometimes are located in housing developments or other unusual areas.

Following are some widely different perspectives on fishing opportunities around the Palm Beaches.

Opportunities for the Do-It-Yourself Fly Fisher

-Inshore Wading: in North Palm Beach, Lake Worth offers some opportunities, especially at the north end. There's a spillway which attracts the attention of jacks and snook. Get there by taking I-95 to the 10th Avenue exit, then going north on Dixie Highway until you reach the spillway. If you can't find it, ask someone for the locks on the Palm Beach Canal. In downtown Palm Beach the seawalls along Lake Worth attract some huge crevalle, usually in the winter and spring.

-Hand Powered Boat: Kayakers can fish in Lake Worth and also in the canals along the ICW. Munyon Island in the Lake Worth Lagoon is between John D. MacArthur Beach State Park and the village of North Palm Beach. Go east under the bridge into the state park and fish the mangrove-lined lagoon for snook, redfish, and seatrout. Schooling jacks in the 10 pound range have been known to punish fly anglers in December and January. Exercise caution, as there is a lot of motorboat traffic on the lake, especially on weekends.

-Inshore Boat: There is some fishing to be done along the ICW in the Palm Beach area. The water is deep here, but snook, tarpon, big jacks, and barracuda are all possibilities. Night fishing for snook and tarpon around lit docks and bridges can be very entertaining.

The sheltered waters of the Lake Worth lagoon, 20 plus miles in length, also offer angling possibilities, especially when the ocean gets too rough. Jacks to 40 pounds plus cruise the seawalls in downtown Palm Beach sometimes. Places for the fly rodder to try include the flats at the north end of the lake, the tip of Munyon Island on the east side of the lake, Lake Worth Inlet, the discharge pipes from the Florida Power and Light plant, the grassflats just south of the A1A Causeway across the lake in West Palm Beach, the mouths of any canals emptying in on the west side of the lake, the eastern end of the Ocean Avenue Bridge in Lantana, and around the inside of Boynton Inlet. Some surprising catches occur at this location.

107

-Along the Beach: There is plenty of beach access and there are fish to be caught here, but the prevailing winds are from the east. This tends to make fishing tough. Snook are the primary targets, with jacks available anytime and bluefish possible in the fall.

Any of the inlets between Palm Beach and Ft. Lauderdale provide an obvious fish attraction and consequently an angling opportunity for the adventurous fly fisher.

-Nearshore: Off the beach at Palm Beach the Gulf Stream is as close as it gets to land, sometimes less than a mile offshore. The water gets deep very quickly. Pelagic fishes including little tunny, sailfish, mahi mahi, wahoo, and tuna come surprisingly close to land. The run to blue water is very short; the reef being about one mile off the beach. Sharks, snook, king mackerel, Spanish mackerel, and tarpon are other species that are available in season.

See the section on nearshore fishing in Jupiter on p.108 for more information on flies and techniques to use here.

Flies and Techniques

For canal fishing use floating lines combined with streamers, although poppers are useful at times. Flies should be matched to the available baitfish. Below spillways shad imitations work best. At other times flies which imitate the tiny mosquitofish work better. Deerhair minnows often work well if no baitfish concentrations are obvious. Black and yellow are the most frequently preferred colors.

In the Intracoastal, use a #4 Wet-Cel shooting head along with weighted flies. Blanton's Sar-Mul-Mac and a non-buoyant version of the Dahlberg Diver also work well.

It's also possible to fish floating lines in the Intracoastal and still meet with success. The trick? Fish lighted docks, seawalls, or ships at night.

In the shallow area of Lake Worth, you can sometimes sight fish. Floating lines and baitfish imitations work well. In deeper areas sinktips or sinking shooting heads are recommended. Flies should be weighted. You never know what kind of fish you'll come up with in these areas, especially around the inlets.

Fishing along the beach or offshore is done much the same way as described in the section on Jupiter. Please refer to p.108 for details.

Access
For waders/shore fishing- see wading opportunities.
For boaters-
-in Riviera Beach at Phil Foster Park on Blue Heron Boulevard there is an excellent facility on Lake Worth, about one half mile north of Palm Beach Inlet.
-in Boynton Beach at Boat Ramp Park, off of US 1.
-in Lake Worth at Bryant Park, off of Lucerne Avenue.

Fly Shops
-Dewing's Fly and Gun, 123 Datura St, West Palm Beach, 561.655.4434; www.dewings.com. A full service fly (and gun!) shop.
-Fisherman's Center, Blue Heron Blvd, Riviera Beach. 561.735.2149; www.fishermanscenter.com.

Boat Rentals
-Adventure Time Kayaks, 521 Northlake Blvd., North Palm Beach, 888.KAYAK.FL;
www.kayakflausa.com
-Bimini Boat Rentals, Boynton Beach, 561.3865.3355
-Boynton Beach Boat Rentals, Lake Worth, 561.585.6803
-Boynton Beach Boat Rentals, Boynton Beach, 561.735.2149

Guides
-Capt. Scott Hamilton, offshore specialist, 561.439.8592; www.flyfishingextremes.com.
-The Land Captain, Steve Kantner, 954.761.3570.

State Parks and Other Attractions
-John D. MacArthur Beach State Recreation Area, 2.8 miles south of the intersection of US 1
and PGA Boulevard in North Palm Beach, 10900 SR 703, North Palm Beach. 954.624.6095.
Information about all state parks can be found online at www.floridastateparks.org.

Accommodations
The Palm Beach CVB is the agency to contact for information, 561.233.3000,
www.palmbeachfl.com.

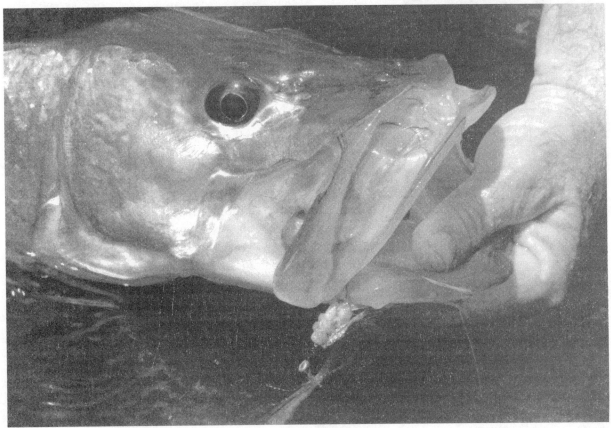

Fort Lauderdale

Overview

Fishing opportunities in the Fort Lauderdale area are much the same as in Palm Beach and Jupiter. In other words, fantastic fishing in the ocean can be had for many species of fish quite close to shore. See those sections for more details on this kind of fishing. There are also some opportunities inshore in the ICW, principally deep water fishing for snook and tarpon, especially after dark around lit docks and bridges. The scenic waterways among south Florida's most elite intracoastal community boast some of the biggest tarpon in south Florida.

In the Fort Lauderdale area, wading opportunities as we usually think of them do not exist. However the entire region is criss-crossed with drainage and flood control canals. Most of these canals hold fish. Some of them hold freshwater species, some hold saltwater species, and some have both.

In the first edition of this book my main information source was the land captain, Steve Kantner. For this printing I also interviewed Capt. Carl Ball.

Opportunities for the Do-It-Yourself Fly Fisher

Inshore Wading: Again, don't expect this to be your usual flats wading scenario. The C-14 canal in Palm Aire Condominium on Powerline Road in Pompano Beach provides fishing, especially at the locks after a rain. Baitfish wash over the locks, and snook, tarpon, and bass (both largemouth and peacock), lurk below waiting for an easy meal. Tarpon merit the most attention, although the peacocks are pursued by some.

A similar situation occurs at the C-13 Canal. Several other easily accessed canals lie along I-75 and SR 84. The Tamiami Trail in Dade and Collier Counties has a canal along its entire length which has been written about for fifty years. It offers sight fishing for snook and tarpon. Griffin Road parallels the C-11 canal down in Davie. You can actually drive along this road on the stretch between SR 441 and Holiday Park and look for rolling tarpon as you go. The best fishing has been east of 90th Avenue or west of Interstate 75.

-Hand Powered Boat: The canals described above can actually be better fished from a canoe or kayak, either of which can be launched almost anywhere you can get access to the water. I once read an article in Florida Sportsman magazine about two crazies who fished for sailfish out of Fort Lauderdale from a canoe, but I cannot in good conscience recommend this technique for small boaters. I don't recollect them being fly casters, either!

John U. Lloyd Beach State Recreation Area offers kayak rentals every day starting at 8 a.m. Paddle down Whiskey Creek where there is no boat traffic.

-Inshore Boat: The ICW here is about it, deep water fishing for snook and tarpon around structures such as docks and bridges, best after dark. If you want classic shallow water fishing

110

you'll need to travel to Miami or Everglades National Park.

The narrow waterways here serve as thoroughfares for the magnificent yachts belonging to the mansions lining the waterway. In this affluent boating paradise hot spots such as the New River, Intracoastal Waterway and Port Everglades hold a bevy of tarpon, snook, barracuda and jack crevalle. They get big. Carl Ball says, "The biggest catch to date on my boat measured out to be 191 pounds. That fish was caught in January 2001 fishing in the New River just past downtown Fort Lauderdale. While there are usually several tarpon over 100 pounds caught each year they typically range in size from 50 to100 pounds." Inshore fishing in Fort Lauderdale is best from January through April, when big tarpon are in abundance. During the summer months, the baby tarpon bite is on, a fly fishers delight.

-From the Beach: There is some beach access here, but beach fishing in this area is nowhere near as good as further north. You cannot fish where bathers are using the beach. The lifeguards will chase you off.

There are still the principal beach targets here, though: snook, pompano, whiting, blue-fish, Spanish mackerel, jack crevalle. There are plenty of barracuda, especially near the inlet. Also near the inlet there's a white marker in the ocean, marking a shallow shoal covered with boulders that extends quite a ways out. The area always holds baitfish, and all kinds of fish can be encountered here. Fishing in the vicinity of the inlet is most likely any visiting angler's best bet. Fishing the inlet itself from the north jetty is possible. You may need a fast sinking shooting head. Fall fishing, during the mullet run, will increase your chances, too.

-Nearshore: Fishing is much the same as in Palm Beach or Jupiter. Again, read those sections (p.108) for information about this type of fishing.

Flies and Techniques

Carl Ball likes Clouser minnows for his lit-dock tarpon fishing, black over white being preferred. For big fish he likes 2/0 and 3/0 hooks, for small summer fish he'll go as small as size two, although the pattern is the same. He says that most of the fish he gets at night are tarpon, with snook being a somewhat unusual catch.

He further says that you can fish the ICW and canals during the day, but it's mostly deep water dredging with sinking lines.

Access

-For Waders: see the section about wading, above.

-For Boaters: In Dania by Port Everglades Inlet there is a ramp just north of John Lloyd State Park, on the east side of the ICW.

Fly Shops

-The Fly Shop of Fort Lauderdale, 5130 North Federal Hwy, Ft. Lauderdale 33308, 954.772.5822; email: flyshopfla@aol.com.

-LMR Custom Rods and Tackle, 1495 SE 17th St., Ft. Lauderdale 33316, 305.525.0728; www.lmrtackle.com.

Boat Rentals

-Club Nautico Powerboat Rentals, 954.799-FUNN; www.fortlauderdaleboatrentals.com

-Thunderboat Rentals, 954.566.3278

Guides
-Capt. Carl Ball, 954.383.0145; www.awolfishingcharters.com.
-Capt. Bob LeMay, 954.435.5666.
-The Land Captain, Steve Kantner, 954.761.3570.

State Parks and Other Attractions
-Hugh Taylor Birch State Recreation Area, 3109 East Sunrise Blvd., Ft. Lauderdale 33304. 954.564.4521. This 180 acre park lies between the beach and the Intracoastal. Canoe rentals available.
-John U. Lloyd State Recreation Area, 6503 N. Ocean Drive, Dania, 33004, 954.923.2833. This park allows fishermen access to both the Atlantic and the Intracoastal. Kayak rentals available.
Information about all state parks can be found online at www.floridastateparks.org.
-The International Game Fish Association's headquarters and museum is in Dania, just off I-95. Their phone/URL is 954.927.2628; www.igfa.org.

Accommodations
The Ft. Lauderdale Convention and Visitors Bureau can be reached at 800.22.SUNNY, 954.765.4466; www.sunny.org.

Buoys like this one are always worth investigating. Cobia, triple-tail, and barracuda commonly set up on these types of structures.

112

MIAMI

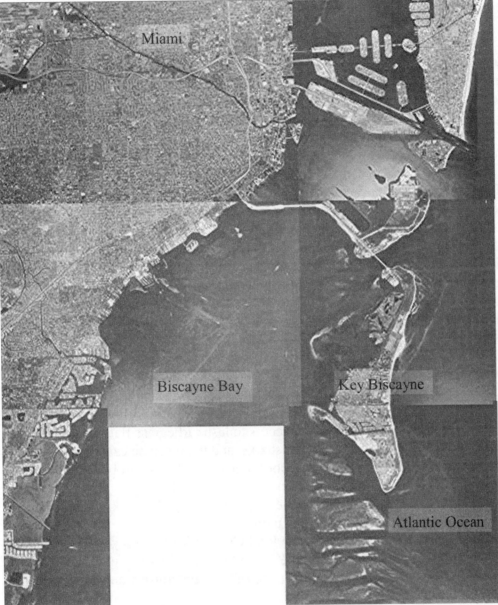

Overview

One thing that makes Miami somewhat unique among America's big cities is the fantastic fishing available almost within the shadows of the skyscrapers. Miami is a great place to fish!

Unfortunately, most of Miami's fishing is available only to those with a boat. But you can find wadable water and it's entirely possible to catch bonefish by wading right off of Key Biscayne.

For those with a boat, bonefish and especially permit fishing is excellent. Tarpon and snook are widely available, and the night time fishing for these species around bridges is often superb. Jack crevalle, seatrout, ladyfish, snapper, and the other usual inshore species fill Biscayne Bay. Barracuda sometimes make nuisances of themselves. A short run offshore can put you in cobia, dolphin, little tunny, mackerel, and several other types of fishes.

Miami boasts many excellent guides who can help the visitor find fish. In the original edition I interviewed two of them, Captain Lee Baker and Captain Jim Weber. Baker, now guiding in Islamorada, was a long time resident of Miami and has been guiding since 1970. Highly respected, he specializes in tarpon, bonefish, and permit fishing. Lee was the featured guide in Billy Pate's "Fly Fishing for Giant Tarpon" video, produced by 3M/Scientific Anglers.

Weber still lives in Miami and still guides there. He has been fishing there for 30 years, guiding for 17. He's been featured in many magazine pieces and on Shaw Grigsby's television show, "One More Cast."

For this edition I updated the information by again interviewing Weber and also Capt. Bob Branham.

Opportunities for the Do-It-Yourself Fly Fisher

-Inshore Wading: As stated above, not much wading is available. On the northeast corner of Key Biscayne are wadable flats where bonefish can often be found tailing. Fishing is usually best early or late in the day. By Matheson Hammock, on the west side of Biscayne Bay south of Miami, bonefish can be caught by wading on lower tide phases. Jim Weber told me there's wading available around the old Cutler Power Plant/Chapman Field Park area south to Chicken Key. And that pretty much wraps it up.

-Hand Powered Boat: If you have your own boat you have a number of options. Some of them lead you into places you really shouldn't be in a hand powered boat. Others will take you to places seldom visited by other boaters, even in the urban sprawl of south Florida.

In North Miami Beach you'll find Oleta River State Park, which provides plenty of options. Paddle amid the mangrove creeks searching for snook and baby tarpon, or paddle up the Intracoastal Waterway about three miles or so into the Oleta River from the west end of the park. The river flows for about six miles from its mouth at the Sunny Isles Bridge through Maule Lake north to Ives Dairy Road. On weekdays, boat traffic is less congested. This trip should take about three hours, not counting fishing time.

Urban Trails Kayaks rents kayaks here and can give you specifics on fishing opportunities between here and Bal Harbor Inlet.

On the southwest side of Biscayne Bay are several places a kayak can be launched as long as the wind is not coming out of the east. Matheson Hammock Park, Chapman Park, and Black Point Park all give the hand powered boater access to lush turtlegrass flats where bonefish are a primary target. Barracuda, snapper, jacks, sharks, and more can be caught here.

-Inshore Boat: The boater has so many different opportunities available it will be hard to decide what to do. Be advised that the list given here is by no means complete.

First of all, the species available include bonefish, permit, tarpon, snook, mutton snapper, sharks, barracuda, seatrout, jacks, ladyfish, and more.

Next, from Key Biscayne south to the Ocean Reef Club on Key Largo you'll find more or less continuous flats covered with lush grassbeds. These flats support vast numbers of large bonefish and seatrout, as well as permit and mutton snapper. Tarpon cruise along the edges of oceanside flats during May and June.

The flat on the southwest side of Key Biscayne often has numbers of large tailing bonefish when a low tide coincides with early morning or late afternoon. These fish average about seven pounds with larger ones being common.

You can find excellent snook and tarpon fishing at night by fishing around lighted docks and bridges. Almost every bridge across the bay offers this kind of action. The 36th Street Causeway offers excellent night fishing. You can actually see the fish cruising along the shadow line, and cast to the ones you want. Many anglers tie up their boats to the bridge, then climb up on the bridge abutments and cast from there.

The oceanside flats of Elliott Key in Biscayne National Park are excellent producers of bonefish and permit when the weather allows. You need to have a west wind to fish here.

Permit love the hard bottom found around the Ragged Keys, also in Biscayne National

114

Park. You'll see bonefish and other species here, too.

-From the Beach: In spite of having a lot of waterfront area, Miami Beach has notoriously little fishing. For a few days or maybe a few weeks during the fall mullet run, the beach will produce fish following the mullet. The rest of the year the beach is best left to vacationers who have activities other than fishing on their minds.

-Nearshore: The Gulf Stream flows just five miles from the beaches of Miami, and is teeming with sailfish, dolphin, kingfish, tuna, and a variety of other species. In addition to kings, Spanish and cero mackerel can be caught. All these fish can be caught by fly rodders, but they usually need to be chummed up. Bouncer Smith and Mark Houghtaling are two guides who will accommodate fly casters.

Flies and Techniques

Lee Baker was rather noncommittal on the topic of favorite flies, saying emphatically that presentation is much more important than the pattern whenever sight fishing. If the presentation is good, and the fish refuses the fly, change flies! He did say that he likes brown epoxy flies in sizes 1 and 2. He likes to use a fly that is big enough for both the fish and the angler to see easily.

Jim Weber likes Bonefish Charlies and other standard bonefish patterns. He likes flies with lead or bead chain eyes when fishing in deeper water (two to three feet), and unweighted flies for tailing fish. Flies with weedguards are an excellent idea. For permit he likes crab flies, with the Merkin being a particularly good one. For Biscayne area tarpon he likes smaller sizes of the standard Keys tarpon streamers, from size 1/0 to 3/0.

Both guides said that they chum bonefish up with live shrimp, especially with first time bonefishermen. The idea is to find a flat with both the wind and current going in the same direction. The boat is staked out 30 feet or so from a white sand patch. A dozen or so live shrimp are cut into pieces and tossed out over the sand. When the bones respond to the chum, they are easily spotted. The angler then presents the fly.

If the wind is blowing the wrong way, or if there are a lot of small chum-stealing types of fish around, they use a chum tube made out of a short section of PVC pipe with a lot of holes drilled in it and a cap at both ends. The shrimp pieces are placed in the tube, and the tube (with a tether attached, of course) is tossed over the sand patch. After that everything else is the same.

Access

For Waders- see above.

For Boaters- you can find boat ramps at the following locations:

-at Oleta River State Park, off of SR 826 in North Miami;

-Crandon Park, at the north end of Key Biscayne;

-Matheson Hammock, off of Old Cutler Road south of Coral Gables;

-at Black Point Park, off of Palm Drive south of Miami, and;

-at Homestead Bayfront Park, off of Canal Drive on the east side of Homestead.

Kayakers and canoeists can use the ramps, or exhibit some creativity as to where they launch their boats.

Fly Shops

-Captain Harry's Fishing Supply has a large selection of fly tackle along with the rest of their inventory. 100 NE 11th St, Miami 33132. 305.374.4661; www.captharry.com.

-Biscayne Bay Fly Shop, 305.669.5851; www.biscaynebayflyshop.com.

Boat Rentals
-Urban Trails Kayak, Haulover Park, North Miami Beach, 305.947.1302 www.urbantrails.com.
-both canoes and kayaks are available for rent at Biscayne National Park.
-Club Nautico, 2560 Bayshore Drive, 305.858.625. Powerboat rentals.

Guides
-Captain Bob Branham, 954.370.1999; phishpeople199@aol.com. Flats fishing on Biscayne Bay and in the Keys.
-Captain Jim Weber, 800.982.3110,;www.captainjimweber.com. Fishing for bonefish, permit, and tarpon in Biscayne Bay, and giant tarpon in Homosassa.
-Captain Bouncer Smith, 305.945.5114; www.captbouncer.com, offshore fly fishing.
-Captain Mark Houghtaling, 305.253.1151; www.magicfin.com, offshore fly fishing.
-There are many, many excellent guides in Miami.

State Parks and Other Attractions
-Biscayne National Park, 305.230.7275, www.nps.gov/bisc. The only national park in the US with most of its acreage under water. Camping is available on Elliott Key.
-Oleta River State Park is located at 3400 NE 163rd St., North Miami. The mailing address is PO Box 601305, North Miami, 33160, 305.947.6357.
-Cape Florida State Recreation Area, at the southern tip of Key Biscayne. 1200 S. Crandon Blvd., Key Biscayne 33149, 305.361.5811.
Information about all state parks can be found online at www.floridastateparks.org.

Accommodations
World class accommodations with world class prices can be found all through Miami. Of course there are lower priced accommodations too. The phone number of the Greater Miami Convention and Visitors Bureau is 888.76.MIAMI, or on the web at www.gmcvb.com/visitors.

An Interview with Capt. Bob Branham
 Bob Branham has been a fixture in Miami's guiding scene for over 25 years. He is what's commonly known as an "acknowledged expert." He prefers fishing for permit, bonefish, and tarpon, during the day when he can see what's going on, and he has strong opinions about the way he does things. Here's what he had to say about his favorite fish species:

 "In Biscayne Bay I don't fish for tailing bonefish very often. I like to start around 8 AM and fish until about 4 PM, so I have fairly good light all day. I fish mostly for mudding fish. We generally have deeper water than in the Keys.
 "In the Keys you can usually find tailing depth water all day long if you keep moving, where Biscayne Bay fills up all at once. In the Bay you might get three hours at low tide where you can fish tailers. After that you either go in, or fish for mudding bonefish or permit.
 "My favorite tides to fish are strong incoming tides in the morning, which are around the full moon and new moon. I like the tide to be high between 10 and 11 AM, and then have falling water the rest of the afternoon. That way you have the sun at your back in the morning and in the afternoon. Those are also the best tides for permit. They seem to school up better

whenthe current runs stronger, and they definitely take better when they're facing you, bringing the fly against the current. I think the neap tides are better for bonefish anyway.

"Permit fishing here is better here than anywhere in the Keys except for the lower Keys. Biscayne Bay has superb permit fishing. For permit I hardly ever use Merkins. I use an epoxy fly that John Emery showed me a long time ago. Harry Spears may have developed it originally. It's like a little tarpon fly with an epoxy head. I like brown, ginger grizzly, or cree colored feathers, tied in and splayed at the back like a tarpon fly with some Palmered hackle around it and then the epoxy head in front of that.

"It's a fairly heavy fly because I like to fish current. I strip it, I don't let it sink. I work the fish almost like a jack. That's what I tell my anglers, 'Bring out the jack in the permit.'

"I use Merkins once in a while. A lot of my anglers have read about them and they bring them, so we try them. When we get refusals we quickly switch. When it's real shallow and quiet and calm and the fish are tailing Merkins seem to work a little better. But in most situations the epoxy fly is definitely my fly of choice.

"I firmly believe stripping the fly is the way to go. You have to strip it properly. It's a real quick strip, it's not a swim, it's a quick hop, and a stop, and the stop is as important as the hop. When you see the fish coming on the fly you strip it. You get him coming a couple of strips, then you skip a strip and he'll overrun the fly. He almost always eats it then.

"The second best scenario is just to bean him when you throw the fly out there and he eats it right away. We have a lot of takes like that. Even when they're tailing this works, we just use a smaller fly.

"I like quite a bit of wind (10 to 15 mph) and a lot of current, and good strong sun. If you're on a big flat with only a little current that's usually not a very good permit spot. They might be there but they're hard to get. The best spots have hard bottom and a lot of current. The epoxy flies I use come up near the surface in the current, especially when they're stripped. Even though the hook point is down they never hang the bottom. I don't even put weedguards on.

"You have to get some shots. Permit fishing is an acquired skill, especially if you use Merkins. They're harder to fish than my fly, because when you throw a Merkin out there you can't move it, you want it just to sit there, especially if it's in the zone.

"If he hasn't seen it you strip it enough to get his attention and then you let it sink. They come over to it. Very often they eat the fly and you won't know it. You'll see them run off and you feel a little 'tink' and it's too late, you missed him. Merkins are hard to fish.

"My fly, you throw it out there, you strip it back fast, you see the fish coming, you see exactly what's happening, you see them eat the fly, it's a great thing. It's a little easier, and I like easier.

"Even when I use a Merkin I like to strip it. I cut the legs off so it doesn't spin. The fish react to the strip and they're easier to catch than most people seem to think. I'm not saying that the 'prescribed' method doesn't work. It does. But when you look at the way I do it there is no comparison. I've gotten permit on everything from tiny little Gotchyas to big tarpon flies and everything in between, in every color combination you can imagine.

"One time I had an English guy who wanted to catch a cuda on fly. He had this big long cuda fly and he's stripping it like crazy and these two permit chased and banged that fly all the way back to the boat. He put on a different fly and threw it out there and stripped it as fast as he could and caught one right away.

"I don't like to strip it that fast all the time, I like to work it, but I do like to strip it fast. Faster is usually better than slower. I've refined it to a real deliberate strip. When you strip it they either come for it or they just keep going. If he doesn't react to the fly you need to pick it up and throw it back to him because he didn't see it.

"You pick it up and put it back in his face real fast. Once you get him following it, then you can work him. You strip, he comes, just when he gets there you pull it away from him, you get them hot and they just eat it.

"You need a lot of shots though, because you're not going to convert them all.

"We have pretty good tarpon fishing. Tarpon used to be my fish of choice, but I'm getting away from them. It's hard for most of my anglers to catch tarpon. They don't bite as readily as they used to. We sometimes find small ones and they still bite good, but the big fish that migrate in the spring are really hard.

"When we see them we throw to them. It's hard to ignore 50 big fish swimming by. But it gets frustrating. You'll get 40 or 50 shots and not get a bite. You have to really be good. You have to know when to strip it, when to leave it, when to wiggle it, and most of all where to throw it. It's hard for me, the guide, to explain quickly exactly where the fly needs to land. I can't will the fly to land in just the right spot. If you miss by just a foot they won't take. It's kind of sad really because they're such great fish.

"Permit bite a lot better than tarpon do. If you had 50 shots at schools of 50 permit you'd probably catch 10 or 12 a day.

"For bonefish my favorite fly is an epoxy fly I call the Razberry, after Raz Reed. It looks like a wiggle jig with a fox squirrel tail. I make them in different weights, real light for tailing fish and heavier for mudders. I like to strip it as well, make it hop a lot.

"I find the mudders in 18 inches to three feet of water, although in the summer they'll be even deeper. The mudding fish are a lot friendlier than tailing fish. They're harder to spook and they're easier to get bites from.

"When it's calm and the fish have their backs out of the water they're almost impossible. They're spookier than permit. The deep water fish are never like that.

"Bonefish really like to eat flies. You can make a permit eat a fly, but bonefish like to eat flies. If you've got the right color and sink rate they'll eat a wide variety of stuff. They're pretty fly friendly.

"I like to start with brown. If they don't like that and the bottom is real light and I'll go to white or a very light tan. If it's real cold and they don't like the brown I'll go to a pink as my second choice. If it's cloudy and brown doesn't work I'll go to yellow or chartreuse. That's my rule of thumb. I try to keep it as simple as possible."

Bob Branham can be reached at 954.370.1999, phishpeople199@aol.com.

Upper Keys
Key Largo to Islamorada

Overview

The Florida Keys hold a long and distinguished history as an angling destination. From Key Largo to Key West, crystal clear water shelters bonefish, tarpon, permit, and many other species of fish. Tackle stores and fly shops abound. Motels and restaurants are plentiful. Sometimes it seems like angling (and diving) is the only reason for the existence of the Keys.

Captain Ben Taylor lives on Plantation Key and trailers his boat all through the upper Keys to fish the Keys waters as well as Florida Bay. He says that "Islamorada offers the world's most consistent fishing for big bonefish and the best shallow water sight fishing for giant tarpon in the world." Ben was kind enough to share the following information.

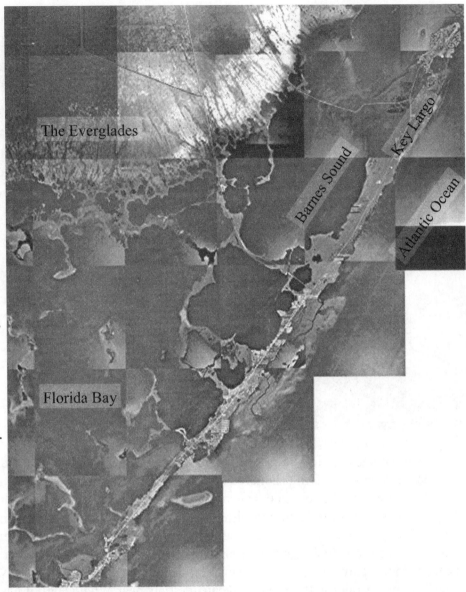

Opportunities for the Do-It-Yourself Fly Fisher

-Inshore Wading: Many ocean side hotels have bonefish on appropriate tides on their beaches. With work, access can be found from Key Largo to Marathon to decent bonefish flats for waders. Good spots with easy access include Harry Harris Park on Key Largo and the oceanside flats at Long Key State Park. County and state parks are surest bets. An open stretch on lower Matecumbe offers good early morning and late evening bonefishing.

-Hand Powered Boat: Canoes and kayaks are available for rent at Pennekamp State Park, giving paddlers access to Largo Sound. I (JK) saw (and hooked!) the first bonefish of my life there from my canoe, way back in the early 80's. You'll find barracuda and snapper as well as bones.

If the weather is nice you can use a hand powered boat along the oceanside flats anywhere in the Keys. Their stealth makes them excellent tools for stalking bonefish.

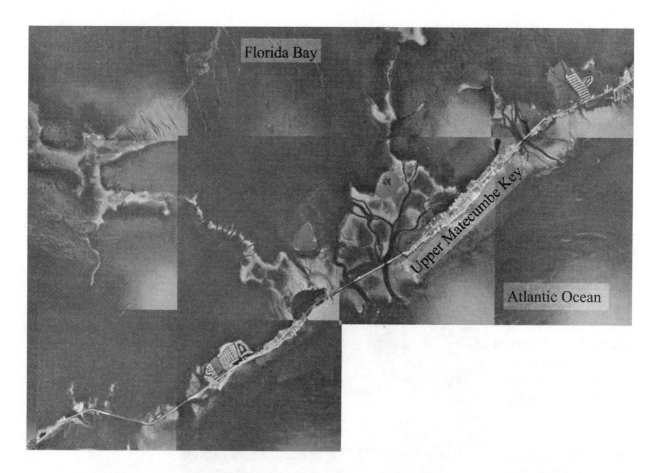

In the back of Key Largo are Barnes Sound, Blackwater Sound, Buttonwood Sound, and other large "ponds" offering sheltered conditions for paddlers. You won't find bones in here, but rather snapper and trout in the sounds and snook and snapper in the connecting creeks.

-Inshore Boat: You can fulfill your life's dreams in the upper Keys for bonefish or tarpon. At Pennekamp State Park both canoes and outboard skiffs are available for rent. With the canoes you can fish for bonefish along the east side of Largo Sound. A motorboat can get you out to the east side of Key Largo to the oceanside flats, which are firm and very wadable. Both bonefish and permit use these flats. Oceanside flats near Whale Harbor Channel and Tavernier Creek by Tavernier Key will produce bonefish. On the bay side, the flats around Cotton Key and the Crane Keys are good.

During the summer and fall every flat on the bay side of the Keys from Plantation Key to Long Key with a direct connection to the populated keys has bonefish and some permit. During the winter the oceanside generally provides better opportunities, weather permitting.

In the Islamorada area try the bridges from Channel Two to Tom's Harbor. Lots of tarpon hang out at Indian Key Channel and Tom's Harbor, while Channel Two is good for snook.

There is excellent fishing for barracuda and sharks all through this area. Additionally, a short trip will put you in excellent position to catch redfish, snook, and an assortment of fun backcountry critters around Flamingo.

-From beach: You won't find many beaches in this area except at hotels where sand has been trucked in.

-Nearshore: Dolphin and kingfish would be the species most available to fly rodders and many Keys charter boats are adept at matching angler to fish. Carysfort and Elbow Reefs are easily

120

accessed from Key Largo, and Tavernier Creek allows access to Molasses and Crocker Reefs.

Flies and Techniques

Captain Ben said this about his favorite flies and when he uses them: "We tend to throw much heavier bonefish flies than anyone else because our fish are big and use more water than most. I fish a lot of size 2 Crazy Charlies for bonefish when they are up on the flats, preferring a copper sparkle braid body and brown bucktail. I am not afraid to use the same fly with lots of weight for spot tailers or edge mudders tied on a 1 with a bunch more weight.

"The Merkin has proved itself for bonefish in appropriate weights and offers the advantage of being the right fly to toss at the occasional permit.

"For tarpon all black early and late in the day and an Apte 2 the rest of the time will feed plenty of fish though they will occasionally get pickier than that."

He suggests that anyone wanting to fish tarpon who doesn't have much experience start early in the day. The fish roll more then and can be seen more easily.

Regardless of where you go, fishing for bonefish, tarpon, and permit on your own often calls for a long hunt and can be quite frustrating. Be prepared to fish for 'cuda, sharks, snapper, jacks, or other species if your primary target plays hard to get.

Access

For Waders- as described earlier. Hand powered boaters can launch at wading access points, or at the boat ramps described below.

For Boaters- On Islamorada try Matecumbe Marina at about mile marker 80 bayside as out of the way and safe. For ocean side fishing in the Key Largo area Harry Harris Park has a nice ramp though it can be hectic on weekends. There is also a ramp in John Pennekamp State Park on Key Largo. Most of the motels have ramps, but you can only use a motel ramp if you're staying there.

Fly Shops

-Florida Keys Outfitters is the shop of choice for up to the minute info. They also run the Florida Keys Fly Fishing School, and have a stable of competent guides. 305.664.5423, www.floridakeysoutfitters.com

-World Wide Sportsman, MM 82.5, Islamorada. 305.664.4615.

Boat Rentals:

-Jeff's Boat Rentals, 888.352.5397. Powerboat rentals.

-Florida Bay Outfitters, Key Largo, 305.451.3018, www.kayakfloridakeys.com

-at Pennekamp State Park a concession has both motor skiffs and paddle boats for rent.

Guides

There are LOADS.

Captain Ben Taylor 305.852.1775; www.bentaylor.com.

Call the Florida Keys Outfitters for other guides.

State Parks and Other Attractions

-John Pennekamp Coral Reef State Park, PO Box 487, Key Largo 33037. 305.451.1202. This park covers over 53,000 acres of water and over 2000 acres of dry land. It is a mecca for both anglers and divers. Canoes and motor skiffs are available for rent, and campsites (bring a good sleeping pad!) are available.

-Lignumvitae Key State Botanical Site, PO Box 1052, Islamorada 33036. 305.664.4815. You need a boat to get out to this wonderful, quiet island. It's a fine place to have a picnic lunch if you're in the area.

-Indian Key State Historic Site, c/o Lignumvitae Key State Botanical Site, PO Box 1052, Islamorada 33036. 305.664.4815. You'll need a boat to get here, but a ferry runs to the key from Indian Fill Key several times on the weekends. As the name implies, lots of history here.

Information about all state parks can be found online at www.floridastateparks.org.

-A highlight is the wild bird hospital on Key Largo just south of the Sheraton or Theater of the Sea. Here non-anglers can view our quarry.

Accommodations

There are a lot of motels. The phone number at the Key Largo Chamber of Commerce is 800.822.1088. At the Islamorada C of C it's 800.FAB.KEYS. Lastly, the phone number for the Florida Keys Visitor's Bureau is 800.FLA.KEYS.Camping available at the Pennekamp and Long Key State Parks. There are also private campgrounds available.

An Interview With Tim Borski

Tim is a native of Wisconsin and was a student at the University of Wisconsin at Stevens Point when it happened. "I was on the way to school one day and as I passed a local bank the outside temperature flashed -14 degrees F." He fled to the Keys and the transition was smooth, like it was meant to be.

The Florida Keys are now Tim's home and in recent years he has kept busy illustrating fine coffee table books such as Flip Pallot's Memories, Mangrove and Magic. He's twice appeared fishing and painting on Pallot's ESPN fishing show, "Walker's Cay Chronicles." More recently, he was filmed for Rick Murphy's show "Sportsman's Adventure," aired in 2004.

Tim's work on paper and canvas over the past decade has drawn a worldwide audience and there are few anglers on the saltwater fly fishing scene today who are not familiar with a number of his fly creations that are as unique and effective as his brush strokes.

When pressed for more personal information Tim admitted to living in a house on a street in the Florida Keys. "Our neighbors have a dog," he says.

Tim's fly patterns are carried by Umpqua Feather Merchants, and his unique art can be viewed online at www.sobaloart.com.

On Tarpon-

"The opportunity to catch tarpon on fly after dark, in the Keys, for your average guy coming down, is very, very high any time of the year. Not many people do this because most are looking for the romance of the sunshine, sight fishing for bonefish in the clear, calm water. In reality the best fishing in the Florida Keys is on bright days when the wind is smoking along at 15 or 20 miles per hour. That's not the image most people have when they think of fishing here though.

"There's a street lamp on the bayside of Indian Key Fill. Three or four of us used to go there after dark on a falling tide. We'd put on guy on a rock we called Todd's Rock, and the rest of us would watch for both tarpon and permit coming along the wall with the falling water. We'd point the fish out to the guy on the rock and when he hooked up then we'd rotate. We'd do this from about 10 PM to 2 AM, but the later it is the better it gets. When the wind is howling out of the north it fishes very well. The fish average 30 to 70 pounds, and sometimes it seems like every permit in the Islamorada area is coming along that wall, too. They take a fly well after dark. I have fished it hundreds of times and have never failed to see fish.

"Another famous place is the Vaca Cut Bridge, or the whole area around the Channel 2 seawalls. After dark there are fish there, lots of fish. You have to know a little bit about what you're doing. You have to fish on the uptide side of the bridge.

"I know guys who fish the west end of the Seven Mile Bridge, or they go to Bahia Honda, or they go down to Spanish Channel, or the Indian Key bridge They go on a full moon or a new moon, and they don't get there until midnight, because that's when the tide is high on that stage of the moon. They fish the falling water until it gets light. One night this past summer they had 88 bites. That's good tarpon fishing. Some of them were little 10 pound fish, but lots of them were between 70 and 90 pounds, good solid fish.

"On slick nights you can go out in your boat and listen for tarpon. You listen for a gulp or a bust or a roll and when you hear one you get uptide of them. Then you start to drift. As soon as you hear one close to the boat you ease an anchor over the side and start fly casting, one guy at each end of the boat. Within five minutes someone is grunting, 'I'm on, I'm on,' and there's a huge fish going off. It's a very surreal kind of fishing, great fun. I'll do that until I die."

On Flies-

"My flies are very impressionistic. They are almost invariably natural colors, which are pleasing to me as well as to the fish. I vary silhouettes to light conditions and sink rates to the depth and speed that the fish are moving at on any given day. I like a fly that's a little bit heavy on my line so I can keep in contact with it and large enough that I can see it given the chance while I see the fish. All my flies represent a little bit of a lot of things as opposed to a lot of one thing.

"My fly box is minimalist right now. If I were going bonefishing this week I'd tie six patterns, two different sizes of each, and that's it, my whole box.

"Back when I was tying all kinds of flies, when I was on my own, when I was fishing 340 days a year, I would catch a fish or two on a fly, take it off, and try something else. It was a matter of trying to find out what I could get them to eat. Now I have a family and responsibilities and I only get to fish two or three days a week. So I would rather spend my time on Maptech looking for new places to get at rather than adding flies to a box that doesn't need any."

The Middle Keys

Islamorada to Marathon

Gulf of Mexico

To Lower Matecumbe

Long Key

To Vaca Key

Atlantic Ocean

Overview

Ranging from Islamorada to Marathon, this area has some of the world's finest fly fishing. Bonefish, permit, tarpon, barracuda, and a host of panfish like snapper are widely available inshore. Dolphin, cobia, and amberjack can be sight fished offshore. Many other species of fish can be found here, too.

Waders can find happiness, and boaters have a wide variety of options. There are many, many motels and a state park with a campground on Long Key. Guiding fishermen is perhaps the number one industry (actually this is an exaggeration, but only a small one) and many good guides are available here.

In the original edition I interviewed Captain Nat Ragland, now retired, a guide who had a reputation for knowledge and innovation unmatched anywhere. Nat was featured as a guide in the video "Fly Fishing for Tarpon," with world record holder Billy Pate, produced and marketed by 3M/Scientific Anglers.

I also interviewed Captain Steve Huff who was widely regarded, even by other Keys guides, as the best damn guide in the Keys. He is semi-retired and living in Chokoloskee now.

For this edition I interviewed Capt. Lee Baker, a veteran guide who started in 1970. He knows the ins and outs of Keys fishing as well as anyone.

Opportunities for the Do-It-Yourself Fly Fisher

-<u>Inshore Wading</u>: There are quite a few opportunities for waders along oceanside flats through this area. Long Key State Park has excellent flats that are easily accessed by private citizens. Although bonefish are the primary species, permit can also be caught out on the deeper part of the flat. I have personally seen big tarpon within easy casting range during tarpon season while I was there wading for bonefish. Other easily waded flats are found on Grassy Key, Missouri Key, and Little Duck Key.

-Hand Powered Boat: When the weather is nice you can use a hand powered boat on many of the flats on both the ocean side and Gulf side of these keys. Oceanside flats tend to be hard, but in the back use discretion before hopping out of your boat. Bonefish, permit, 'cuda, even tarpon, can all be targeted by the fly fishing paddler. The current rips under most of the bridges and through the cuts, so stay away from those kinds of areas.

There's a lagoon inside of Long Key that I've never been in but it looks like an excellent place to explore regardless of the weather. There are flats in Boot Key Harbor on Marathon that sometimes hold bonefish. There are lots of small bays and coves on the Gulfside where you can explore and stay out of the weather.

-Inshore Boat: I was not sure if Nat was being vague or telling the truth when he said "anywhere you can get to by boat is a place you can find some fish!" Steve Huff backed him up when he told me that every piece of water in the Keys which is dry land at low tide gets fish on it at some time or another when the water is up. Nat did specify however that the flat in front of the Seven Mile Bridge oceanside and some Gulf flats in the same area usually hold bonefish.

Oceanside flats in front of many or most of these Keys will produce bonefish. Flats around Lignum Vitae Key, Shell Key, Grassy Key, Fat Deer Key, and Bahia Honda Key, and Gulfside flats behind Little Duck Key will all produce bones.

Lee Baker says that tarpon fishing here during the tarpon run in May and June has gotten tougher over the years. Tarpon live a long time and have seen thousands of flies. Baker says that the oceanside fish frequently completely ignore flies when the water is clear. If the water is discolored they eat much better. Tarpon anglers are advised to try to find fish in the dirtier water in the backcountry whenever possible.

Barracuda are a spectacular wintertime staple, a time of year when other fish may be less than cooperative. A seven weight rod with a brightly colored cuda fly can lead to some memorable fishing.

If you're near Islamorada and the weather isn't conducive to flats fishing you can run across Florida Bay and fish around Flamingo. Lots of the local guides do this.

-From the Beach: There aren't many beaches in this area. You'll find one on Grassy Key where bonefish can be found. Long Key State Park has a beach which is definitely a place to look for bonefish. These beaches are popular with bathers, and need to be fished early or late in the day. Some folks ladder fish in the Grassy Key and Marathon area for tarpon and permit from the

125

shoreline!! Bring binoculars and your own ladder if you want to try this.

-Nearshore Boat: Find weed lines and search them for dolphin. Trolling is another way to find these magnificent fish. Dolphin can range in size from little two and three pound "chickens" that can be taken of little rods like three weights to 40 and 50 pound slammers for which you had better be properly geared up.

Another way to take fish offshore here is to chum over "humps," reefs which rise above the bottom and attract many species of fish, including little tunny, barracuda, amberjack, king mackerel, wahoo, sailfish, and others. This technique has been raised to an art form by several guides working out of Key West, including Jose Wejebe, Ken Harris, and Bob Trosset. Perhaps the most important factor in this type of fishing is a plentiful supply of live baitfish for use as chum. If you can't get these frozen glass minnows will also work, although perhaps not as well. You'll need two or three blocks of these.

Finally, in the Gulf backcountry you can sightfish cobia, amberjack, barracuda, permit, and tripletail around markers or under debris. The fish will also be found over wrecks, if you can locate one.

Flies and Techniques

Which flies are Nat's favorites depends on what he's fishing for. He likes bonefish flies that "breathe", with a bucktail or marabou wing or a combination of these two materials. He also prefers fairly large flies for bonefish (#2), feeling that it's easier for both the fish and the angler to see. He likes these flies in yellow, orange, and brown, or combinations of these colors. Again, the color helps the angler to see the fly.

Steve Huff likes epoxy flies for bones, the MOE style. For tarpon he has gone to a very SIMPLE fly- he simply ties a rabbit strip in at the bend of an appropriately sized hook, and that's that.

Lee Baker has his favorite flies, but was emphatic in his insistence that presentation is more important than pattern. That having been said, for bonefish he likes the MOE flies in tan and brown. If you make a good presentation and the fish snub you, change to something else.

Nat says for tarpon any of the standard Keys style tarpon streamers work well. Actually, any type of saltwater streamer will take Keys tarpon. The Keys style streamer was designed to prevent the fly from fouling on the cast, not because the fish wouldn't eat anything else. Nat has originated several well known tarpon patterns including the Dirty Nellie and the Orange Quindillon. He also likes the Black Death and almost any color combined with grizzly.

Nat was one of the pioneers of permit on fly. He originated one of the first permit patterns, the Puff. Nowadays, crab patterns take fish better than does the Puff. The Merkin is one of the best crab imitations currently available.

Sight fishing for barracuda on the fly is an exciting pastime, especially during the winter months. Long barracuda flies which imitate needlefish are used. These are usually tied with synthetic materials. Needless to say, a short wire trace is needed.

The Keys offer an excellent place to chum for bonefish with shrimp, as was described in the section on Miami. The boat is anchored 30 to 40 feet upcurrent of a white sand patch. Live shrimp are broken or cut up and thrown out over the sand, either by itself or in a PVC chum tube. When bonefish move over the sand, they are easily seen and cast to.

Steve Huff says his most important technique is to keep poling the boat, hunting for fish. He rarely runs his outboard after he reaches the fishing grounds. He believes that if you pole your boat far enough you will find fish, or fish will find you.

126

Access

For Waders- Long Key State Park offers excellent access to excellent, easily wadable oceanside bonefish flats. Others are available on Grassy Key, Missouri Key, and Little Duck Key.

For Boaters- Monroe County maintains many ramps along and off of US 1. See below. Vehicle security is somewhat of a problem in the more secluded areas. Most motels, especially on the Gulfside, have boat ramps. There are also several private ramps whose use if available for a fee.

-MM-79, Indian Key Fill Boat Ramp, access for Lignumvitae and Indian Keys.

-MM-53, Marathon Boat Ramp.

-MM-49, North on 33 St., behind Marathon Yacht Club.

-MM-39, Little Duck Key.

Fly Shops

-Bud 'n' Mary's, Islamorada, 800.742.7945; www.budnmarys.com

-Florida Keys Outfitters, Islamorada, 305.664.5423; www.floridakeysoutfitters.com

-Worldwide Sportsman, Islamorada, 305.664.4615.

-World Class Angler, Marathon 305.743.6139; www.worldclassangler.com.

There are other "tackle" shops all along US 1.

Boat Rental

-Jeff's Boat Rentals, 888.352.5397. Powerboat rentals.

-Marathon Kayak, 305.743.0561; www.marathonkayak.com. Kayak rentals.

-Rainbow Reef Kayak Rentals, Islamorada, 800.457.4354. Kayak rentals.

Guides

Capt. Lee Baker, 305.664.2080, 305.393.0818; www.rnfl.com/captleebaker.

There are loads of guides here. Any of the fly shops listed above can hook you up.

State Parks and Other Attractions

-Long Key State Recreation Area, PO Box 776, Long Key, 33001; 305.664.4815. Swimming and some of the best wade fishing in the Keys are right off of your campsite.

Information about all state parks can be found online at www.floridastateparks.org.

Accommodations

Camping is available on Long Key at the state park. The are also many private campgrounds.

Many, many motels are available. The Marathon Chamber of Commerce phone number is 1-800-842-9580. The Florida Keys Visitor's Bureau number is 1-800-FLA-KEYS, or on line at www.fla-keys.com

Lower Keys
Big Pine to Key West

Gulf of Mexico

Sugarloaf Key

Boca Chica

Key West

Atlantic Ocean

Overview

The Lower Keys, like all the Keys, have some great angling opportunities. However, the area, perhaps more than most others, requires a great deal of "local knowledge". In Stu Apte's book, <u>Fishing the Florida Keys</u> (an indispensable reference, by the way) he says, "THE BACK COUNTRY AREAS OF THE FLORIDA KEYS CAN BE TREACHEROUS TO THE INDIS-CREET ANGLER WHO BELIEVES THAT ALL HE NEEDS IS A CHART AND A BIT OF BOLDNESS."

In the first edition I interviewed Jose Wejebe to fill out this section of the book. He said essentially the same thing. He advises anyone trailering a boat down to this part of Florida to hire a guide for at least one day so you can start to learn your way around. Be sure to tell the guide your intentions so there are no misunderstandings later. Actually, this is excellent advice anywhere you go.

Wejebe shared a wealth of information with me about fishing the Keys from Marathon on down to Key West.

For this edition I spoke with Capt. Dexter Simmons and Capt. Jeffrey Cardenas, both long time Key West anglers. Simon is currently one of the hottest Key West guides, specializing in the pursuit of tarpon, permit, and bonefish with the fly rod. Jeffrey owns The Saltwater Angler Fly Shop in Key West. I also spoke with Capt. Jim Sharpe, an longtime offshore guide and owner of Sea Boots Outfitters on Big Pine Key.

Opportunities for the Do-It-Yourself Fly Fisher

<u>Inshore Wading</u>: Bonefish are the primary species. The best times of year for fishing for bones is between August and November and again between March and June. The best time of day for bones is early and late in the day, especially if the tide is low to mid incoming, or mid outgoing.

Some places to wade for bones include the west end of the Seven Mile Bridge oceanside and the rock bar on the west end of Missouri Key oceanside (permit here, too!). In Bahia Honda State Park you can also bonefish. Take a left when you enter the park and fish on the west side of the point. Fish early, there are a lot of bathers.

Another place to wade for bonefish is on Big Pine Key off of Long Beach Road. When

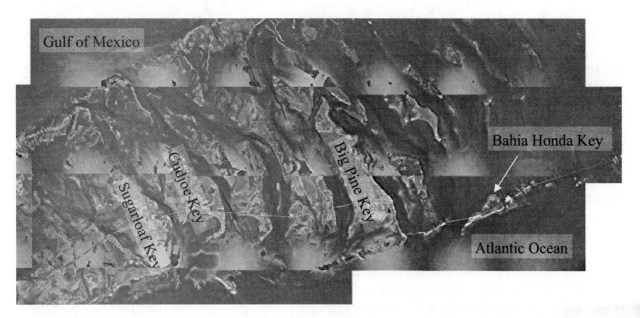

Gulf of Mexico

Bahia Honda Key

Cudjoe Key

Big Pine Key

Sugarloaf Key

Atlantic Ocean

you first drive onto Big Pine from the mainland side, you immediately see Long Beach Road on your left. Take this left and after it makes a sharp bend to the right go to the end of the road. A path leads down near the water. You'll need to traverse a hundred feet of mangrove trees to access the water, but this cuts down the competition, doesn't it? Again, the best times of day are early in the morning and late in the afternoon.

Tarpon can be caught around and off most of the bridges at night between September and November and again during tarpon season, April, May, and June in this part of the Keys. Wejebe said he is continually surprised at the lack of popularity of this fishery. During the fall they are "fun fish", up to about fifty pounds or so. During tarpon season a boat is necessary, not to hook up, but to land them. The fish are too big to be landed from a bridge!

Some of the best bridges to look for these fish include the Seven Mile Bridge, the Spanish Harbor Bridge, and the Bahia Honda Bridge. Wejebe says that by using standard tarpon streamers or especially popping bugs you can have excellent sport on these bridges at night, and few people do it. Give it a try!

Hand Powered Boat: There are flats around most of the lower Keys and channels between all of them. There's enough water here for the most intrepid paddler to spend a long time exploring before he saw the same place twice. Hand powered boats can be launched by many of the bridges here and at many places just alongside US 1.

Paddlers will encounter bonefish, permit, various types of snapper, barracuda, tarpon of all sizes, and sharks of all sizes. Be sure to carry a chart or aerial photo and a compass, and a lot of water before heading off into the backcountry.

Inshore Boat: There are fish everywhere. Stu Apte, in his book Fishing the Florida Keys and Flamingo (sadly now out of print) suggests that the area around the Content Keys may have the best bonefishing in the Keys. Permit and barracuda are other frequent visitors, and tarpon show sometimes, too. Wejebe says (and it's already been mentioned) you will break off your lower unit if you do not know your way around. Extreme care is needed to fish flats in this region. Having said all of that, here are some places to try.

The Bahia Honda Channel loads up with tarpon during season, April, May, and June. The Spanish Harbor Channel also holds tarpon. Another place to fish for tarpon is at the Tarpon Belly Keys, on the gulfside north of Cudjoe Key. Tarpon can be found in most of the channels

129

on the gulfside during tarpon season, and oceanside around all the bridges mentioned earlier, as well as the deeper flats in front of Spanish Harbor Key, Loggerhead Key, Boca Chica Channel, and west of Key West.

Key West Harbor is known for its winter tarpon fishery. Most anglers use bait for these fish. Fly fishers can take them if they run out into the Gulf, find a shrimp boat, load up with chum, and then use the chum to lure the tarpon behind the anchored boat, where they might be convinced to take a fly. Again, most visitors won't know how to do this- a guide will be needed the first time or two.

Bonefish can be found on oceanside flats along literally all of the keys between Bahia Honda and Boca Chica. Big Pine and Saddlebunch Keys have excellent oceanside fishing for bones. On the gulfside, the Content Keys have long been known for producing bonefish and permit. Most of the keys to the southwest of the Contents also produce both bones and permit until you reach the Mud Keys. Bonefishing peters out further to the west.

From the Beach: The only beach anywhere around here is at the state park on Bahia Honda Key on the Oceanside. You can find good bonefishing here.

Nearshore: There can be superb offshore fly fishing for pelagic fishes in the Lower Keys. You usually must chum with live pilchards to see it. Finding the bait takes local knowledge, so again a guide is the best way to go.

The reef is out on the oceanside, and there are a number of wrecks to fish. Over these wrecks all different types of fish can be chummed up, including cudas, amberjack, jack crevalle, and various species of tuna. When I'm down there we usually stay on Big Pine and head south from the Big Pine Fishing Lodge until we find weeds or other flotsam. Dolphin will almost always be around this type of stuff during the spring and summer, into the fall.

Flies and Techniques

Wejebe likes epoxy flies for bonefishing. He says that typically when he bonefishes he looks for tailers and he's only in ankle deep water. The epoxy flies land softly and resist getting hung up. Another important point is that the fish take them quite readily.

Dexter Simmons prefers bonefish flies tied with marabou. He usually uses #4 hooks, going to #2 if the water is deeper. All his flies are tied with weedguards. Simmons says it's important to match the fly color to the bottom color, in other words, green fly over grass, tan fly over sand, etc.

Simmons uses Merkins for permit almost exclusively, #4 and #2. He says, "It's important that you can see the fish. Cast the fly uptide of the fish and let the current take it towards him. Keep the line tight without moving the fly and if it comes tight strip strike."

Standard hackle Keys style tarpon streamers are what Wejebe prefers for tarpon. I had to laugh when he said, "When they're eating they'd hit a piece of s---." He prefers subdued, earth tone colors for both his tarpon flies and his bonefish flies.

Simmons basically agreed, saying black, orange and brown, orange and yellow, the Cockroach, a tan fly he calls the Sand Devil, and a Cockroach-like fly called the Green Hornet were his favorite tarpon flies.

Finally for fishing offshore Wejebe likes large white Deceivers or large poppers. Again, to get the fish offshore to come up near the boat you'll have to chum them up.

Wejebe, along with Ken Harris and Bob Trosset, helped develop the offshore live bait chumming technique which is now becoming so popular all around the state. In order to use it you must know how and where to use a cast net and where the bait is.

130

Access

Access for waders has already been discussed.

Boaters will find ramps at the following places:

-at Bahia Honda State Park, MM-37.

-at the west end of the Seven Mile Bridge on Money Key.

-at the Big Pine Key Fishing Lodge on Big Pine (fee required).

-at the Old Wooden Bridge Fish Camp on Big Pine (fee required).

-at the Sugarloaf Key Marina on Sugarloaf Key (fee required).

-MM-34, Spanish Harbor Wayside Park, on West Summerland Key.

-MM-28, Little Torch Key, go north on old SR 4A.

-MM-11, Shark Key.

-MM-6, Stock Island.

-at the King's Point Marina on the east side of Key West (fee required).

-at the public ramp at Garrison Bight on Key West (fee required).

Fly Shops

-Jeffrey Cardenas' The Saltwater Angler, 800.223.1629; www.saltwaterangler.com , 243 Front Street, Key West. A full service shop with a stable of fine fly fishing guides for flats, inshore, or offshore.

-Sea Boots Outfitters, 800.238.1746; www.seaboots.com, MM 30 on Big Pine Key (next to post office). A full service shop with a stable of fine fly fishing guides for flats, inshore, or offshore.

Boat Rentals

-Blue Planet Kayak Rentals, 305.284.8087; www.blue-planet-kayak.com

-Island Kayaks, 305.292.0059; www.islandkayakkeywest.com

-Mango Pango Boat Rentals, Murray Marina, Key West, 800.342.2001, www.mangopangoboats.com. Powerboat rentals.

-Jay Birds Powerboat Rentals at the Big Pine Key Fishing Lodge, Big Pine Key, 305.872.8500; www.bigpinekeyboatrental.com.

Guides

Many excellent guides are available here. Call the fly shops for others.

-Capt. Dexter Simmons, 305.754.3304; www.keywestflyfishing.com.

-Capt. Bob Trossett 305.294.5801, offshore fly fishing.

-Capt. Michael Vaughn, 305.745.2800; www.heliconfishing.com

-On Big Pine, Capt. Lenny Moffo, 305.872.4683.

-On Big Pine, Capt. Bruce Chard, 888.FLY.FISH.

-On Big Pine, Capt. Jim Sharpe, offshore fly fishing, 800.238.1746; www.seaboots.com.

State Parks and Other Attractions

Key West is an attraction unto itself. Fort Zachary Taylor State Historic Site is on Southard Street on Truman Annex in Key West. 305.292.6713.

-Big Pine Key National Wildlife Refuge is the home of the endangered Key deer. 305.872.0774; http://nationalkeydeer.fws.gov

-Bahia Honda State Recreation Area, Route 1 Box 782, Big Pine Key 33043; 305.872.2353. This park has one of the few natural beaches in the Keys. It also has campsites and cabins for rent, two boat ramps, and great fishing for all of the Keys species close by.

Information about all state parks can be found online at www.floridastateparks.org.

-Dry Tortugas National Historical Monument is fifty miles west of Key West and is accessible only by boat or seaplane. If you go bring everything you need, including water. There's nothing out there. 305-242-7700, http://www.nps.gov/drto

Accommodations
-The Big Pine Key Fishing Lodge on Big Pine has efficiencies, RV sites, and tent sites. Their phone number is 305.872.2351. This is a great place for families. I try to spend a week with my boys here every year.

-The phone number for the Key West Chamber of Commerce is 1-800-LAST-KEY, for the Lower Keys Chamber of Commerce it's 1-800-USA-ESCAPE, and for the Florida Keys Visitors Bureau it's 1-800-FLA-KEYS; www.fla-keys.com

-In Key West The Saltwater Angler provides bed and breakfast accommodations for fly fishers. Their number (again) is 800.223.1629.

An Interview with Jeffrey Cardenas
Capt. Jeffrey Cardenas is the thinking man's consummate angler. His lyrical prose (I can only dream about writing like that) has been captured in several books including Marquesa and Sea Level. Jeffrey guided extensively in the lower Keys before deciding that it was time to turn the reins over to younger, edgier men. He keeps his fingers in it by owning and operating The Saltwater Angler in Key West and fishing several days a week with friends.

"Fishing in the lower Keys is seasonal, which many people don't expect. Our 'glamour fish,' tarpon, bonefish, and permit, are only available when the water temperature is over 70 degrees. When cold fronts start rumbling through in the late fall and the water temperature drops below 70 degrees those fish move out to thermal pockets offshore and their places are taken by what I call 'predator' fish, big barracudas upwards of 30 or even 40 pounds, big roving packs of jack crevalles, big sharks of all kinds, blacktips, bulls, lemons.

"For years and years when those predators would come onto the flats and you told your anglers, 'We're going to fish for barracudas today,' or 'We're going fishing for jack crevalle,' they'd think you were trying to scam them. People get a mindset when they come to the lower Keys that it's always going to be about bonefish, tarpon, and permit. But our wintertime fishing is really spectacular.

"It doesn't last very long. The temperatures get cool around mid-December and start warming up again about mid-February. When the big barracudas come off the reefs and into shallow water sometimes you'll see 60, 80, even 100 big barracudas a day. They take up positions over white spots. They're very aggressive, very predatory. They're there to do one thing, and that's eat. They're feeding on redfin needlefish, and it's a spectacular event, especially with a fly rod.

"You're fishing for 30 pound fish in 18 inches of water. You don't have to perform any physical gymnastics to get them to take a fly. You don't have to put the rod under your arm and strip with two hands. It's a matter of just watching that fish, watching how the pectoral fins quiver. You watch the biological color change that indicates that the fish is ready to eat and that's when you need to make the fly move.

"On the edges of the flats you'll see these roving bands of jack crevalle. They're becoming more and more common in the lower Keys since the net ban has increased the amount of bait we have. We have enormous schools of pilchards. We also have majuga minnows (pronounced ma-HOO-ga, a Cuban name for the dusky anchovy). In the wintertime these baitfish are looking for the warmer water on the flat, and it's not unusual to see many large balls of bait.

"The jacks find those bait balls and it is a spectacular sight, absolute carnage, the majuga minnows flying out of the water, the jacks with their backs out of the water, speed you can't even imagine. When a fly fisher gets in front of a school of jacks like that you wonder why you're even thinking about tarpon, bonefish, or permit. It's tremendously exciting fishing because it's so visual.

"At the far edge of the flat, feeding on the jacks and barracudas when those fish make mistakes, are the sharks. Key West has to be the sharkiest place I've ever been. We're out in the ocean, closer to Havana than Miami. We're right on the seam between the Gulf of Mexico and the Atlantic Ocean. The water is pure, and it's a place that's very attractive to predators.

"When we say sharks I mean blacktips to 70 pounds, bull sharks to 300 pounds, lemon sharks in the 200 pound range. All of these fish are fly fishable, sight fishing catchable. You don't have to put over a half barracuda or bags of chum, buckets of horse blood, or whatever those guys do.

"You can watch these sharks on the flats. They're waiting for a jack or a barracuda to make a mistake. If you put a big fly in front of them you can make them eat it. To hook a 200 pound bull shark on a fly rod, it's going to be something you're going to relish, or maybe have nightmares about, for the rest of your life.

"The winter is a really exciting time to be fishing. That's not to say that during the winter you won't ever see tarpon, bonefish, or permit. All it takes is for the water temperature to inch above 70 degrees. We have resident tarpon that come in after a little burst of warm weather, fish that are 70 to 90 pounds. They don't migrate anywhere except in and out from deeper to shallow water and back again.

"It may be the first weekend in January when we get a little bubble of warm weather and all of a sudden the mature sized tarpon will be in the finger channels. They'll be on the flats. They'll be in the basins. They'll be laid up. They'll be following bait. They'll be warming themselves up. You can catch these fish.

"But that's a bonus. During the winter we're thinking about predatory fish.

"The season changes dramatically around the end of February or beginning of March. The permit come back with a vengeance then. We have hordes of permit that come out of deep water. They get in schools of 40 or 50 fish, big 20 to 30 pound fish that push a standing wake as they move.

"The fishing for the bonefish in the backcountry is spectacular in March. It will generally be windy then, but everything is on the flats. Because of the transition of seasons it's my favorite month to fish. The predatory fish are still there and the glamour fish are coming back in abundance, so you never know what you're going to see.

"A couple of months later as we get into the late spring season the push of migratory tarpon that comes in is spectacular. Big purple clots of fish come out of the Straits of Florida. They seem to make a focal point out of the southwest corner of the Marquesas.

"You see both Atlantic and Gulf fish there all together. They're distinctively different, the Atlantic fish being longer, skinnier, and more silver, and the Gulf fish being shorter and deeper with more of a greenish hue. When they first come in they're mixed together but after three or four days they segregate into Atlantic fish and Gulf fish. I think the Gulf fish end up in Homosassa and Apalachicola, and the Atlantic fish are the mullet eating fish that go all up and down the eastern seaboard.

"In the summertime most of our anglers have left, but that's the season the guides go fishing together. We call it Grand Slam season, when we get most of those tarpon, bonefish, and permit in a single day. The size of the tarpon has slipped down to 50 or 60 pounds, still nice fish, but the bonefish and permit are everywhere especially early or late in the day. Pretty much any backcountry flat will be covered with fish on an incoming tide near sunset. It's a great time of year to fish. You might have the entire flat to yourself.

"Our fall season is wonderful because it's either slick calm with no wind or we're getting our asses blown off the island from tropical weather. It's a great time of year to fish. The fishing is very technical fishing. You have to be very stealthy. You have to use light lines. You have to use long leaders and small flies. It's extremely challenging fishing because of the glassy calm conditions.

"The first fronts start rumbling through in December and the seasons come around again. Key West is thought by a lot of people to be a one season destination but it's radically different as the seasons change. It makes it exciting to be an angler here."

As an aside, what Mr. Cardenas has to say about Key West fishing during the year is also true anywhere else on the Florida peninsula. The species may be different, but the seasonal changes remain the same.

When you visit the Keys there's a good chance it won't be all about bonefish.

Flamingo

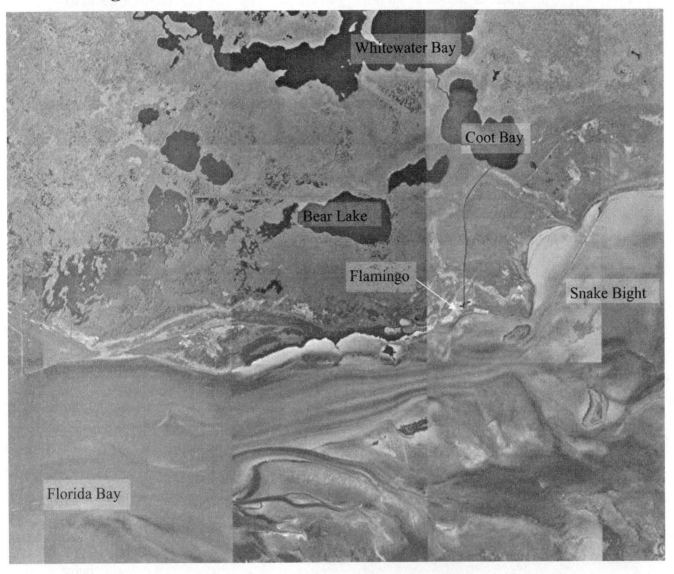

Overview

How can I do justice to Flamingo in just a few pages in this book? For the first edition I put this question to Flip Pallot, one of the best known and most respected names in saltwater fly fishing today. His answers were a little surprising and very insightful. They appear below.

Flamingo allows access to the southern portion of Everglades National Park. There is enough fly fishing here to keep anyone busy for the rest of their lives. Quite frankly, you'd need a lifetime to explore it all and take advantage of it. Most of us just don't have that much time. But even if you only have a few days, most of the time you can find some fish, and you might even catch the fish of a lifetime. They're certainly there.

For the angler hauling a family with non-fishermen, there are plenty of other things to do and see besides fishing. Anyone who loves nature should visit Flamingo before they die!

Opportunities for the Do-It Yourself Fly Fisher

-<u>Inshore Wading</u>: There is absolutely no wading that can be done. Don't even think about it.

-<u>Hand Powered Boat</u>: This may be the best place in the southeastern United States to fish from a hand powered boat. The Wilderness Waterway runs for about 100 miles from Flamingo to Everglades City and allows extensive backcountry trips of up to two weeks. There are numerous other canoe trails such as the Bear Lake Canoe Trail, the West Lake Canoe Trail, and the Hell's Bay Canoe Trail, all of which have excellent fishing for snook, redfish, tarpon, seatrout, crevalle, and more. Closer to the park's entrance several freshwater ponds offer excellent fishing for largemouth bass.

-<u>Inshore Boat</u>: Flip suggested that the first time fly fisher to Flamingo avoid the flats until he learns his way around. You'll find plenty of fishing in channels around Flamingo. You need a Wet-Cel shooting head to maximize your success doing this, either a #2 or #3. You want the fly to be right on the bottom. What can you catch this way? Seatrout, redfish, jack crevalle, lady-fish, snook, tarpon, mangrove snapper and many others.

Why not fish the flats? It's easy to get into trouble on the flats, since you can go from several feet of water to absolutely none in less time than it takes to read this sentence. Also, the flats are large, and many flats are piscatorial deserts. Even productive flats have areas that seldom hold fish. Certainly, anyone wanting to try flats fishing for the first time could work the edges of flats from the safety of deeper waters, learning where it's safe to go and also how to find and see fish.

Why not fish back up in Whitewater Bay and the rest of the backcountry? Backcountry fishing requires knowledge and skill. The area is so large that the chance of just stumbling into fish is unlikely. So Flip recommends the channels and "lakes" in Florida Bay as the best place to start learning your way around.

That being said, on a rising tide it's quite easy to explore the flats in Snake Bight, only a couple minutes east of Flamingo, especially in a jonboat or a canoe. It is NOT a good idea to get way up on this huge flat. The tide or wind or both can push the water out quickly, leaving you high and dry. A strong east wind can keep the water out for days- not a pleasant prospect. Stay close to the edge of the flat, looking for redfish waking or tailing, or moving behind rays.

Another close in and easy place to fish for crevalle, baby tarpon, and seatrout is in

A houseboat lets you sleep where the fish are. Here a crew gets ready for a day's fishing at Ponce de Leon Bay, Everglades National Park.

136

the dredge hole right behind the Flamingo Campground, next to the two spoil banks there. This hole often holds fish and is easy to fish. Again, flats around the hole can be explored from a small boat fairly easily on a rising tide.

-From the Beach: In order to get to the beach, you must have a boat. The beach is out on Cape Sable (about 12 miles west of Flamingo), and is as magnificent a stretch of sand as you will ever see. Snook, jack crevalle, redfish, seatrout, sharks, even tarpon, and other species all come within easy fly rod casting distance of the shoreline out here. Walk the beach on its lee side, up 10 or 15 feet from the water's edge, on a rising tide. Look for snook and redfish cruising along the water's edge, or jacks busting bait, or rolling tarpon.

-Nearshore: Trout, Spanish mackerel, sometimes bluefish, can be found offshore. These latter two species can usually be found by watching birds. Out around the park's boundary markers tripletail and sometimes cobia can be found. Tripletail will also stay under the buoys along the crab trap lines outside of the park boundaries.

Flies and Techniques

Flip's favorite fly is a Clouser minnow. These work especially well on the shooting heads in the channels. Remember to keep the leader short! This channel fishing is essentially blindcasting, although muds, skipping mullet, birds, current rips, and other obvious evidence of fish or locations that attract fish should be thoroughly checked out. Another favorite is a modified Deceiver, used along the beach (and many other places) at Cape Sable. Called a Glades Deceiver, it features a body weighted with fuse wire and covered with silver Mylar, and a grizzly and white hackle tail, and a white kiptail collar. This fly is blindcast along the beach while the angler keeps an alert eye peeled for visible fish.

He also likes a fly called the Prince of Tides, which resembles a cichlid minnow, one of the many exotic species of fish now living in the park. This fly is especially good for snook up in the backcountry, where the majority of these exotic fishes are found.

Access

For Waders- there is none.

For Boaters- there are two ramps in Flamingo. One is on the Buttonwood Canal and gives access to Coot Bay, Whitewater Bay, the Shark River system, and the rest of the Flamingo backcountry. The other is on the small harbor on the Florida Bay side, and gives access to Florida Bay and the Gulf of Mexico.

Folks using canoes can launch at numerous places along the Flamingo Road, including the Bear Lake Canoe Trail, the Hell's Bay Canoe Trail, Coot Bay Pond, West Lake, and more.

Fly Shops

There are none. The Flamingo Marina sells some fishing tackle, but nothing for the fly fisher. The closest fly shop is in Miami.

Boat Rental

The Flamingo Marina rents several different kinds of boats, including canoes, motor skiffs, and houseboats. The houseboat lets boaters camp in comfort in some of the Everglades backcountry. 239.695.3101, 800.600.3813; www.flamingolodge.com

Guides
-Capt. Rick Murphy, 305.242.0069.
-Capt. Eric Herstedt, 954.592.1228; www.floridalighttacklecharters.com/
captains_ericherstedt.htm

State Parks and Other Attractions
Flamingo lies smack dab in the middle of Everglades National Park, the most magnificent wild area east of the Rocky Mountains. What else could you want? The address and phone number for more information is Everglades National Park Information, 305.242.7700, www.nps.gov/ever.

Accommodations
Flamingo Lodge offers both standard motel rooms and efficiency cabins. The phone number at the Lodge is 239.695.3101, 800.600.3813; www.flamingolodge.com
There is also a restaurant, bar, gift shop, and the Marina Store.
The National Park Service operates a campground here. See address and phone number listed just above.

A Conversation with Rick Murphy

We could pile accolades on Capt. Rick Murphy, certainly one of south Florida's most visible guides. His Sportsman's Adventures TV show is watched by millions of anglers. He's on radio, he's a multiple time tournament winner, and much more. But let's see what he has to say about fishing in Flamingo.

"My favorite fishing in Flamingo is for laid up tarpon in the spring time. After a cold winter we have days when it gets slick calm. The 18 inches of water covering the acres and acres of flats warms up in the sun. After an early afternoon high tide, that warmed water starts falling and drains into the channels. The fish pull up to the edges of the flats and the channels to warm up, just laying there in three or four feet of water, often with their tail and dorsal fins out of the water, almost completely motionless. It's just awesome when it happens.

"These laid up fish give the most novice fly caster really good shots at fish that run about 100 pounds, fish that just sit there and let you try over and over again. If the water is below 74 degrees they are real lethargic, almost hibernating. But when it gets above 74 those fish go off and start feeding.

"We generally throw big Deceivers. In dirty water we throw dark brown, dark green, purple, or black. If the water's clear we might throw chartreuse, or tan, something shrimpy looking. Usually the fish are in muddy water, especially mullet muds. The water there tends to be a degree warmer than the surrounding water.

"The fish are doing what they're doing primarily to warm up. Studies done on captive tarpon (small ones) have shown that when the water temperature drops too low you can put their favorite food right in front of them and they ignore it. The colder the water got the more lethargic they got. Their heart rate would go down as low as eight beats per minute. They don't have to eat then, they're not using any calories!

"When the temperature gets into the right range they start moving around, they start using calories, they start eating again. The minimum temperature that this happens is 74 degrees. What I notice when fishing out there is that it can't reach 74 degrees at three or four in the afternoon. After the water hits the right temperature it takes a while for the fish to hit the right temperature. It's best if the water temperature is 76 or 77.

"People coming here for the first time, no matter what they intend to fish for, need to learn the lay of the land before they can really expect to catch anything. Flamingo is complex. Sometimes you can have the right air temperature but the wrong wind direction. Or you can have the right wind conditions but the wrong temperature, so you end up fighting that.

"You need to learn, by asking questions, by using a Top Spot map, by whatever resources you can use. At least a Top Spot map will give you a starting point.

"What makes Flamingo so complex is that there is never the same tide with the same conditions more than one week of the year. Every week is different, 52 different scenarios. It's crazy, but that's how it is. For example, in August you'll typically have slick calm conditions in the morning and a sea breeze in the afternoon. On the full moon in August you'll have high high tides and high low tides. Two weeks later, even though you have the same tides, you'll have low highs and low lows. Even if the wind conditions are the same, the water conditions are not. What happened two weeks ago probably won't happen now.

"If you add wind to it the whole situation changes. The wind could hold the water in, or help blow it out. If you add rain to it, then the salinity levels become a factor. Has it been raining? Is Snake Bight too fresh? Then all the fish are out way off the mainland land mass. Has it been dry? If it hasn't rained, then they're all up near the mainland land mass.

"What people need to understand is that this ecosystem is dynamic. It changes all the time. It's affected by rain, by wind, by temperature, by tide. It can be great one day and horrible for a week afterwards. That's the nature of the place."

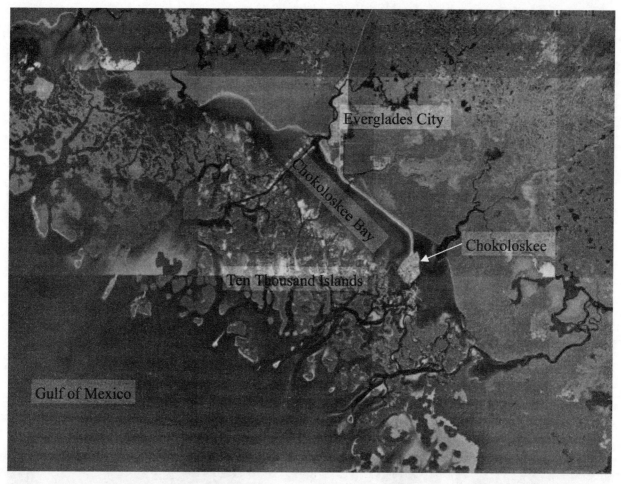

Everglades City

Chokoloskee Bay

Chokoloskee

Ten Thousand Islands

Gulf of Mexico

The Ten Thousand Islands

You can consider the Ten Thousand Islands as the northern gateway to Everglades National Park. This mangrove labyrinth provides excellent angling for snook, redfish, tarpon, seatrout, and many other species, too.

Waders will find themselves out of luck. A boat is mandatory here. You can rent boats, from canoes to motor skiffs, at the Everglades City Ranger Station and on Chokoloskee Island. Many guides also work here, but only a few specialize in fly fishing.

Captain Joe McNichols supplied information for the original edition. Capt. Al Keller supplemented that information for this new edition.

Opportunities for the Do It Yourself Fly Fisher
-Inshore Wading: None available without a boat. Boaters can get out and wade at many of the outside islands, including Rabbit Key, Pavilion and Little Pavilion Keys, and New Turkey Key. Oyster bars at the mouths of the Chatham, Huston, Broad, and Lostman's Rivers offer some difficult but frequently productive wading.

If you want to fish from the shoreline for snook, baby tarpon, or largemouth bass, you can go south of the intersection of US 41 and SR 29, just south of the Visitors Center. There is some shoreline access along the road where you can catch the above species of fish. Another place you can fish is along Sea Grape Drive, right by where the National Park Service has their maintenance buildings. Sea Grape Drive is on the south side of US 41, about two and one half miles east of the intersection of SR 29.

Canals off of US 41 are fishable for snook, mostly little ones, and baby tarpon. This fishing is best in the fall and wintertime, or whenever water is running through the canals towards the Gulf.

-Hand Powered Boat: You had better like paddling, but there is a wide variety of options available to those in canoes or kayaks, ranging from day trips to two week long expeditions. Close to Chokoloskee, in Chokoloskee Bay, the the area around the mouth of the Turner River and north of the mouth of the Baron River offer good fishing. Mud Bay and the Cross Bays off of Hurddles Creek offer fishing for redfish, snook, and blacktip sharks.

Off of Sea Grape Drive (see wading opportunities) there is a marked canoe trail that goes down to Halfway Creek, which goes all the way to Chokoloskee Bay.

-Inshore Boat: The opportunities are limitless. Thousands of miles of mangrove shorelines offer superb fly fishing opportunities for snook, tarpon, redfish, seatrout, sharks, and mangrove snapper. River mouths on the outside (along the Gulf of Mexico) attract tarpon in the spring and early summer and big snook all summer long. Snook move into backcountry bays during the winter and spring months. Shallow flats produce the above species as well as seatrout, sheepshead, and pompano. Redfish could be found anywhere, at any time.

-Along the Beach: with the exception of a few outside islands in the national park there are no beaches available.

-Nearshore Boat: Out beyond the islands and beyond the park boundary you may find tripletail under stone crab trap floats, cobia around the markers or under floating debris, or Spanish mackerel and little tunny busting minnows on the surface. There are a couple of wrecks not too far out (see Rodney Stebbins' Coastal LORAN & GPS Coordinates) with snapper, grouper, pompano, snook, and other species which can be chummed up and enticed to hit a fly.

Flies and Techniques

Joe McNichols's favorite fly is a deerhair popper. He loves tossing a bug with a 1/0 hook and a weedguard up into the mangrove roots for snook. He also loves a chartreuse Deceiver for everything- snook, tarpon, redfish, everything.

As so many other guides have stated, a Clouser minnow is another favorite fly. Joe's favorite colors are white, chartreuse and white, and smoke color (grey) for clear water.

This area provides superb sight fishing for laid-up tarpon in the spring. These fish are just sitting there not moving, very unlike the fishing in the Keys or Homosassa. All the conditions need to be perfect, but when they are... look out!!!

Snook can be sight fished around the mangroves on lower tide phases. Use the chartreuse Deceiver or Clouser minnows for this. On higher tide phases use the deerhair bugs to blindcast in the same locations. Watch out for the heart stopping strikes!

Al Keller says, "A minnow imitation in chartreuse and white is my number one fly, especially in the backcountry. The water in the backcountry is dark, so a brightly colored fly lets the fish see it more easily. I like the flies by Enrico Puglisi. They come equipped with weedguards, a must for any fly you choose to use down here. So much of our fishing is tight against the mangroves, a fly with a weedguard saves you a lot of trips into the trees.

"I like to fish in less than a foot of water, getting in and out again before most people can, so the fish haven't been spooked by anyone else when I get there."

Access

For Waders- none.

For Boaters-You'll find boat ramps in the following places:

-Glades Haven Marina and Campground, across the street from the Ranger Station in Everglades City, 239.695.2746.

-the public boat ramp next to the Outdoor Resort on Chokoloskee Island.

-at the Barron River Marina and Villas & RV in Everglades City, 239.695.3591.

-at the Captain's Table Motel in Everglades City.

Fly Shops

The nearest fly shops are in Naples- the Everglades Angler, 239.262.8228, and Mangrove Outfitters, 239.793.3370.

Guides

-Captain Joe McNichols has apparently retired from guiding in this area. You can try him at 239.262.4132.

-Captain Al Keller works this area, and can be reached at 239.289.4801, or through the Everglades Angler's website at www.evergladesangler.com.

There are quite a few guides working this area. A call to the Everglades Angler or Mangrove Outfitters will put you in touch with others.

Boat Rentals

Everglades Rentals & Eco Adventures/North American Canoe Tours, Inc., 107 Camellia Street, P O Box 5038, Everglades City, FL 34139. 239.695.3299; www.evergladesadventures.com. These folks rent canoes and kayaks and can outfit and shuttle you for a through trip the length of the park.

State Parks and Other Attractions

-Everglades National Park, 2,000,000 acres of mangrove and sawgrass wilderness. For information call 239.695.3311; www.nps.gov/ever. The Gulf Coast Visitor Center is located in Everglades City, in the northwest corner of the park.

-Ten Thousand Islands National Wildlife Refuge, 3860 Tollgate Blvd., Naples, FL 34114, 239.353.8442; http://southeast.fws.gov/TenThousandIsland

Accommodations

Everglades Area Chamber of Commerce 239.695.3941,;www.florida-everglades.com.

Outdoor Resort, Chokoloskee, 239.695.2881.

The Captain's Table, Everglades City, 239.695.4211.

Marco Island and Naples

Naples and Marco Island hold the reputation of being the high rent districts in southwest Florida. Expensive homes face the beach, and line the waterfronts of Naples Bay and Marco Island. The fish care about none of this though.

This area boasts of good fishing opportunities all year 'round. Around Naples proper it's quite possible to catch a dozen or more different species of fish in the Intracoastal Waterway in a single day. In spite of the close proximity to a populated area, anglers can get away from it all and especially on weekdays not see another boat all day.

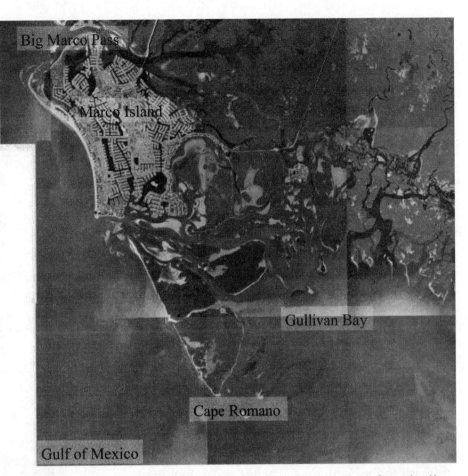

South of Marco you get into the 10,000 Islands National Wildlife Refuge. Fishing here is quite similar to fishing in Everglades National Park. There are lots of mangrove islands, mud and grass flats, channels, and oyster bars, and some beaches along the Gulf side of the islands.

I interviewed Andrew Bostick and Todd Geroy to get my information for this area. Todd has fished Naples and the surrounding backcountry for 28 years. He has been a full-time guide for the past 22 years, starting at the tender age of 18. Andrew's father was a well known guide, and Andrew has been fishing here all his life.

Opportunities for the Do It Yourself Fly Fisher
-Inshore wading: Both guides say in general the bottom here is too soft for wading, and there aren't many wading opportunities available.
-Hand Powered Boat: At the site of the old Briggs Nature Center on Shell Island Road (off of CR 951 on the way from Naples to Marco) there is a launch area that provides access to Rookery Bay. A short paddle places you in a large area (about 12,000 acres) of creeks and bays with very little motor boat traffic. If you have a hand powered boat this is the best place to use it in the vicinity of Naples.

If you continue south on 951 more places to use a hand powered boat present themselves on the north side of Marco Island. Finally, from Goodland you can get access to Goodland Bay, Cape Romano (almost a five mile paddle one way!), and the north end of the 10,000 Island National Wildlife Refuge. There are lots of places to fish here.

Off of CR 92 on the south side of Marco there are many areas where a canoe or kayak could be launched. The primary target species for anyone fishing here include snook, redfish, tarpon (all sizes), and seatrout, with a variety of other species including crevalle, ladyfish, snapper, and more. The canal that runs along this road is a favorite of local fly fishers looking for snook and baby tarpon.

-Inshore boat: Fishing right around Naples, there are 18 species of fish available to fly fishers with boats. Tarpon, snook, seatrout, and redfish are only the most popular fishes available. The Intracoastal Waterway (Naples Bay) behind Naples to the east offers excellent opportunities for all of these species. Night fishing for snook around residential docks in Naples Bay is a summertime institution.

From March through October Gordon Pass is the local snook hotspot. Although most fish are taken with bait, fly fishers can score here by fishing at either end of the day, or by trying it at night. Tarpon also feed at night on the outgoing tide, especially on the full and new moons.

The residential canals north of Gordon Pass hold big tarpon all summer. You'll find these fish very difficult to fool with flies. Try it if you're looking for a challenge.

South of Gordon Pass in Dollar Bay seatrout work the grass flats just to the east of the Intracoastal. Either tide works, especially early in the day. Ladyfish will be found there, too.

Lots of good fishing can be found all along the Intracoastal between Naples and Marco. Those with a taste for adventure will want to explore around Rookery Bay and Johnson Bay.

The many oyster beds in this area will quickly tear up the boat of the incautious navigator, so proceed with caution. The treasure chest of piscatorial rewards available here can definitely make the time and effort involved worthwhile.

Those working from Marco can fish around Cape Romano and the 10,000 Islands all the way down to Chokoloskee. You can fish the outside of the islands if you find the backcountry intimidating, or bolder souls may want to explore in the back. A word of caution– this is not a good place to go charging around at high speed if you're not sure of where you're going.

-From the Beach: jetties and groins right along Naples Beach will attract fish, especially early and late in the day. If you drive north on North Gulf Shore Boulevard towards North Naples you can park your car and hike north a mile or so to Clam Pass, a small unnavigable pass which opens up to a series of brackish lagoons. Snook use the pass and the lagoons, and fly fishing here can be quite rewarding. There's good wading here at low tide, too. Look for fish along the beach as you walk.

South of Gordon Pass, Key Island (Keewaydin Island locally) offers excellent beach fishing for snook from April until October, with 40 fish days possible. This is an essentially un-developed 11 mile stretch of beach. The only problem is you can't drive or walk- you need a boat to get access.

-Nearshore: Todd doesn't go offshore fishing much, but there are fish available. Close to the beach you can find tripletail under crab trap buoys from November until March.

In April the tarpon start showing up. They usually swim in about 15 to 20 feet of water, one half to one mile off the beach. These are big fish averaging over 100 pounds.

Andrew says that mackerel, pompano, jacks, ladyfish, and more are common catches around the passes here, with fish species changing with the seasons.

There are wrecks off of Naples which hold large numbers of barracuda and permit as well as other species all summer long. LORAN/GPS numbers are found in Rodney Stebbins' Coastal LORAN & GPS Coordinates.

Flies and Techniques

Like any experienced angler, Todd has definite preferences when it comes to flies. For snook he likes what's known locally as a mangrove snook fly. This is basically a white Deceiver topped with peacock herl. The whole fly is tied at the bend of the hook like a tarpon fly to pre-vent the wing from fouling. Fitted with a wire weedguard, it eases through the branches without hanging up on those inevitable shots into the trees.

For inshore tarpon Todd prefers a woolhead mullet. The fly has a wool head in grey and white, with big eyes. The tail hackles are natural grizzly. Cast it to rolling, cruising, or laid-up fish, whatever presents itself.

Todd says reds aren't usually very fussy eaters. He prefers fishing them on a low tide when they are more easily sight fished. For this fishing he likes a fly that settles slowly. Seaduc-ers are one of the many patterns that work well.

Finally, in the colder months he likes the Clouser deep minnow, and says they work on everything. Since he fishes in the backcountry a lot this time of the year, and since the water back there is discolored, he prefers darker colors for this pattern. His current favorite is purple.

Capt. Bostick says, "I've been using a lot of Puglisi flies lately. They're inexpensive, effective, and very durable. White Seaducers have been very good for me, especially for snook. For redfish I like small shrimp patterns or crab patterns.

"When we snook fish we just blind cast along mangrove shorelines, or get in very shal-low water and sight fish them. Reds we almost always sight fish in shallow water, looking to see them before we cast.

"We have great fishing for laid up tarpon in the spring time. The fish lie almost mo-tionless just under the water's surface. You have to know where they are in order to have suc-cess, but it is an excellent fishery for fly casters."

Access

-For waders- except as detailed in the section on fishing from the beach, there is no access for waders.

-For boaters- In Naples itself there are two public ramps. The most popular is at Naples Landing on 9th Street, giving access to Naples Bay and the Intracoastal. The other is at Bay View Park on Bay Shore Drive in East Naples. There are several private marinas, all of which have ramps available for a nominal fee.

       South of Naples you can get access to Rookery Bay by using the gravel ramp at Shell Island. Take US 41 south to SR 951, then go west on Shell Island Road. The ramp is at the end of the road. This area is loaded with oysters- be very careful.

       On Marco there's a public ramp on the south side of the island at Caxambas Park. There's also a public ramp in Goodland, on CR 892 off of CR 92.

Fly Shops
-Everglades Angler, 810 12th Avenue South, Naples 33940. 239.262.8228. An Orvis shop. www.evergladesangler.com.
-Mangrove Outfitters, 4111 E. Tamiami Trail, Naples 33962. 239.793.3370; www.mangrove-outfitters.com.
-Sunshine Ace Hardware, 141 9th Street North, Naples, 34102; 239.262.2940.

Guides
-Captain Todd Geroy, 239.793.7141; intowishin@comcast.net.
-Captain Andrew Bostick, 239.394.3010.
-Other fly fishing guides can be recommended by either of the shops listed above.

Boat Rentals
-Extreme Rentals, 239.774.0061. Center consoles and kayaks.
-Powerboat Rentals, 239.774.9100. Powerboats, naturally.
-Capri Fish House Restaurant and Waterfront Chickee Bar & Kayak Rental, 203 Capri Blvd., 239.389.5555. You can eat, drink, and rent a kayak all at the same place.

State Parks and Other Attractions
-Rookery Bay National Estuarine Research Reserve occupies most of the land between Naples and Marco. All kinds of scientific inquiry about estuaries is conducted here.
-Collier Seminole State Park, 20200 E. Tamiami Trail, Naples 33961. 239.394.3397. Over 6000 acres of mangrove swamp. Canoes and kayaks are excellent craft with which to explore and fish. Camping is available.
Information about all state parks can be found online at www.floridastateparks.org.

Accommodations
The Naples Area Chamber of Commerce can be reached at 239.262.6141; www.napleschamber.org. Their address is 3620 Tamiami Trail North, Naples 33940.

Sanibel and Captiva Islands and Pine Island Sound (Fort Myers)

The bodies of water accessible from these communities include Pine Island Sound, Matlacha Pass, San Carlos Bay, the Caloosahatchee River, Estero Bay, and the Gulf of Mexico. Snook, redfish, trout, tarpon, tripletail, cobia, ladyfish, jacks, Spanish mackerel, and little tunny are some of the species available, either year-round or seasonally. Most of the fishing is to a sighted target such as snook on a sand shoreline, redfish tailing on a grass flat, or tarpon daisy chaining off the beach. Blind casting around a pass, a deeper mangrove shoreline or sand-hole, under birds working baitfish, and around oyster bars are some other options.

With the exceptions of the Caloosahatchee River, the west side of Estero Bay, and Captiva Island, most of the mangrove shorelines in this area are intact and hopefully will remain so in the future. Ding Darling National Wildlife Refuge protects the largest part of the eastern shoreline (lower Pine Island Sound side) of Sanibel Island from any development and is a wonderful place for the fisher and non-fishing members of a family to spend time. Pine Island Sound is notable for its miles of clear water grass flats, Matlacha Pass for its seemingly endless sand shorelines, and Estero Bay for it's maze of oyster bars and passes to the Gulf.

Capt. Steve Bailey, well known local guide and fly tyer, was kind enough to supply most of the information on this area.

147

Opportunities for the Do It Yourself Angler

-Inshore Wading: Starting at the south end of Fort Myers Beach you will find Lover's Key State Recreation Area, providing access to both Estero Bay and beach fishing for snook, redfish, trout and numerous other species. Big Carlos, New, and Big Hickory Passes also provide access for the wading angler. Be aware of strong currents in these areas and use caution.

On the way to Sanibel Island on Summerlin Road, look for and turn left on John Morris Road to Bunch Beach, drive to the end, and park. Miles of shallow water wading is available here for any number of fish species. Continuing on towards Sanibel and after passing the toll-booth, the causeway includes two spoil islands with easy wading around both.

On Sanibel, Ding Darling National Wildlife Refuge is a great spot for the non-boater. Besides the usual species, this is an excellent area to look for baby tarpon. A five mile one-way road takes you through the refuge. Fishing from the road and wading is allowed on the right side of the road. No wading or other access is allowed on the left side other than casting from the road.

Continuing north on Sanibel past Ding Darling is Bowman's Beach County Park, which provides access to the gulf beaches. Walk the beach and look for snook cruising in the surf.

-Hand Powered Boat: The Ding Darling National Wildlife Refuge is one of the best places in the state for an angler with a hand powered boat, on par with Everglades National Park or the Merritt Island National Wildlife Refuge. Snook, redfish, seatrout, and baby tarpon are some of the species you may encounter. A maze of islands and channels allow fishing on all but the windiest days, and the bird life will amaze and entertain you. For those without boats, a livery on the south side of Tarpon Bay rents canoes.

There is also a canoe trail, called the Great Calusa Blueway, that runs behind the barrier islands south of Sanibel. The trail runs from roughly Bonito Beach north to Fort Myers Beach, through the Estero Bay Aquatic Reserve. For more information on this resource visit www.greatcalusablueway.com.

-Inshore Boat: There are miles of flats on both sides of Pine Island Sound. Lush grass beds with sand holes, mangrove islands, oyster reefs, sand beaches, and other habitat types support huge numbers of redfish, as well as snook, seatrout, and many other species, depending on the season. The deeper areas outside the bar will hold trout, ladyfish, jacks and seasonally, tarpon. Moving water helps to stimulate better action.

Pine Island Sound and the adjacent Gulf beaches may be the best place in the state for a novice fly fisher to hook a big tarpon (not that it's easy to get a bite, mind you). This fishing peaks during May and June. There is also a spring cobia run. If conditions are perfect the cobia can be sight fished over rays the same way they are fished in Homosassa.

Since the area is so large, it helps to know what to look for. Channels, bars, drop-offs, or similar structures with access to deeper water often have fish near them. Broken bottoms of mixed sand and grass make it easier to find fish. Oyster bars will often attract fish, especially on an incoming tide. Healthy grass in good condition attracts more fish, especially with a current flowing. Redfish and Captiva Passes are obvious fish attractors. Finally, look for activity in the area in the form of stingrays, baitfish, and most importantly birds such as terns or pelicans.

Matlacha Pass separates Pine Island from the mainland, and provides mainly shallow bright sand shoreline fishing with less grass than found in Pine Island Sound, except at the northern end. There's a lot more rock and many more oyster bars than in the Sound. As when operating in any unfamiliar place, go slow and use a good chart. The entire length of Matlacha Pass is a posted manatee zone with speed limits of 25mph in the channel and slow speed from

148

channel to shore. You'll find much the same mix of fish that you find in Pine Island Sound in Matlacha Pass.

Estero Bay, behind Fort Myers Beach, is home to numerous oyster bars with plenty of fish to call them home. Water conditions can be a little cloudy in the summer months, but normally it clears up nicely in the fall and winter.

Night fishing for snook under dock lights is a very popular and productive method of fishing through this entire area. Don't be surprised if a large tarpon eats the fly you used hoping to catch a snook.

-From the Beach: All summer long snook can be caught from around Lovers Key at Fort Myers Beach and the public access points on Sanibel (Bowmans Beach and the Lighthouse at the south end), as well as the Sanibel and Captiva beaches. Get out in the morning as soon as the sun throws enough light to enable you to see into the water. Walk along the beach, taking care to stay out of the water! The snook lie right at the water's edge, and are (sometimes) suckers for a well presented white streamer fly. It's possible to catch snook into double digit weights this way, too. When wind and wave action will allow, these areas can all provide excellent fishing, especially in the May through September time frame. Many of these places are pay parking or fee areas, so keep a roll of quarters in the car. Look for snook right off the beach and fish with a floating line. A spare spool with a full sinking line could be of use to fish away from the beach for pompano.

-Nearshore: If the wind and wave action will allow, the main target on or near the beach in spring is tarpon. Trolling motors are a necessary evil for this fishing as the quickest way to put tarpon down is to run your outboard motor anywhere near them. May through September there are plenty of snook right along the beaches. Look for any downed trees in the water and ease up to them to look for fish. It would not be unusual for redfish, trout or Spanish mackerel to be there as well. In the fall look for flocks of birds to be working over feeding schools of Spanish mackerel and little tunny. Also look at any crab trap float for a tripletail to be floating beside it.

Flies and Techniques

Steve Bailey says, "Personally, I use very few fly patterns in my fishing though I know many more will work. If fishing for redfish, trout, Spanish mackerel, ladyfish, or mangrove snapper, my first choice is a Clouser Minnow in either white and chartreuse or white and tan. For redfish tailing in very shallow water with a lot of grass I carry a heavily hackled Seaducer size 2 in a mixed color of white, grizzly, and yellow.

"When fishing for snook in the Caloosahatchee River, I usually use a Lefty's Deceiver in size 1/0 with my favorite colors being white or white and grizzly. Either way they would both have a chartreuse bucktail-and-peacock herl top. When snook fishing on the beaches any of the above flies, or an all white Clouser with silver flash in the middle, can be productive. If trout, redfish or mackerel show up, they will eat these flies as well. All of the above patterns need the have a weed guard of some kind.

"A large cobia likes a large meal. It's a good idea to keep an extra rod rigged with a large Deceiver or Seaducer in case a cobia shows up.

"Patterns for tarpon can really get out of hand, especially when they are not taking and you are trying to find something they will eat. I suggest this: pick a dark fly, a bright fly and something totally different like a rabbit strip wing or a simple bucktail, and concentrate on presentation. But remember, some days they just don't eat.

"Most of the fishing here is done with floating lines except tarpon fishing where an intermediate or slow sinking line seems to work best. Sink-tips or full sink lines are useful in the passes, covering sand holes on the flats, and fishing the beaches for pompano."

Access
For Waders: Lovers Keys State Park is south of Fort Myers Beach on Estero Boulevard. Carl Johnson Park is also in the same area for bay access.

Bunch Beach at the end of John Morris Road offers access to a large area of easily waded shoreline along Summerlin Road all the way to the Sanibel Causeway.

The Sanibel Causeway's two spoil islands offer plenty of parking and wading access on San Carlos Bay. You may also launch a canoe or car-top boat, but no boat trailers are allowed to park here.

At the south end of Sanibel is the pier. This is a night fishing spot from shore for snook, trout and ladyfish. Driving north on Sanibel you will see the entrance to Ding Darling National Wildlife Refuge and a little further north, the sign for Bowman's Beach

Blind Pass (sadly now filled in) on Sanibel also has access.

For Boaters- Boat ramps are fairly plentiful, and found in the following locations:
-Carl Johnson Park south of Fort Myers Beach on Estero Boulevard, giving access to Estero Bay and through one of the passes to the Gulf.
-in Punta Rassa at the east end of the Sanibel Causeway. Access to the Gulf, San Carlos Bay, Caloosahatchee River, Matlacha Pass and Pine Island Sound.
-For those staying on Sanibel there is a county ramp on the Sanibel side of the causeway.
-Matlacha Park, off of SR78 in the town of Matlacha as you come onto Pine Island. Look for the sign and turn left to the ramp. This ramp is in the middle of Matlacha Pass. A short run north will bring you into lower Charlotte Harbor. Remember, Matlacha Pass is a manatee zone. There are also manatee zones in Estero Bay, the Caloosahatchee River and Pine Island Sound with more likely in the future. Watch for and obey all posted signs.
-at Pineland Marina off of SR 767 toward the northern end of Pine Island ($). Access to Pine Island Sound and the Gulf.
-at the Burnt Store Marina off of SR 765 north of Fort Myers. Access to Charlotte Harbor.
-in downtown Fort Myers between the Edison Bridges. Access to the Caloosahatchee River. Other ramps are available at fish camps and waterfront motels throughout the area.

All of the county ramps listed have a $3.00 charge per day (at present) for parking. Keep that roll of quarters in the car.

Boat Rentals
-Adventures in Paradise, Port Sanibel Marina, 14341 Port Comfort Road, Fort Myers, FL 33908; 239.472.8443; www.adventureinparadiseinc.com. These folks rent both hand powered boats and motor skiffs.
-Jensen's Marina, P.O. Box 191, Captiva Island, FL 33924; 239.472.5800; www.jensen-captiva.com. Motor skiff rentals.
-Tarpon Bay Explorers, 900 Tarpon Bay Road, Sanibel Island FL; 239.472.8900; www.tarponbayexplorers.com. Canoe and kayak rental in the Ding Darling NWR.
-Captiva Kayak Co. & Wildside, 11401 Andy Rosse Lane, Captiva, FL; 239.395.2925; www.captiva-island.com/amrc/kayak.htm

Fly Shops
Lehr's Economy Tackle in Fort Myers carries a full line of fly tackle and has a wide selection of locally tied flies. They also off excellent advice.The phone number there is 239.995.2280. The person to speak with is Dave Westra.
-Lee Island Outfitters, 17699 Summerlin Road, Fort Myers, 239.437.5488, toll free 1.800.294.1659; www.leeislandoutfitters.com.

Guides
-Captain Steve Bailey, 239.489.1379; www.captstevebailey.com.
-Captain Paul Hobby, 239.433.1007; www.fishinghobby.com.
-Captain Rick DePaiva, 239.246.8726; www.saltwaterflyfishing.org.
-Captain Dave Gibson, 239.466.4680; www.sanibelrent.com/about.html.

State Parks and Other Attractions
On Sanibel Island is the Ding Darling National Wildlife Refuge, a bird watcher's paradise. 239.472.1100, http://dingdarling.fws.gov
-Cayo Costa State Park Lies at the northwest end of Pine Island Sound, occupying most of La-Costa Island. This barrier island is accessible only by boat and offers camping on a spectacular Gulf beach. Cayo Costa State Park, 941.964.0375, www.floridaparks.com. Accessible only by passenger ferry or private boat. Reservations are required on the ferry service. Call the Tropic Star of Pine Island at 239.283.0015. Information about all state parks can be found online at www.floridastateparks.org.
-The Great Calusa Blueway, Lee County Parks & Recreation, 239.461.7400, www.leeparks.org.

Accommodations
There are many motels on both Sanibel and Captiva, as well as in Fort Myers. Contact the Lee County Convention & Visitors Bureau at 239.338.3500, 1.800.237.6444, or www.FortMyersSanibel.com.

Seatrout are a popular fish all through Florida, including Pine Island Sound. Here John Thompson shows a nice one.

Boca Grande

Boca Grande Pass holds a national reputation as the world's best tarpon fishing hole. It is a hole, too- about 70 feet deep. Needless to say, with a few exceptions fly fishers aren't terribly welcome in the pass itself, where most tarpon fishermen either use live bait or use heavy jigs.

Tarpon live in many places other than the pass though, and

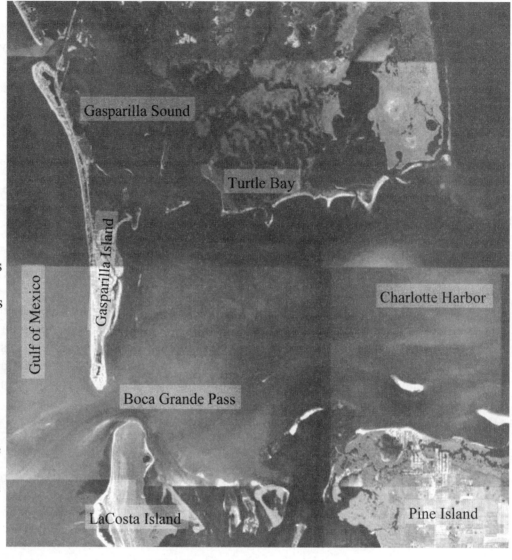

many guides target these fish, especially along the beaches. A number of guides specialize in fly fishing for tarpon during season, mostly during May and June.

When the tarpon leave Boca Grande, lots of other fishing remains. The Peace and My-akka Rivers pour their waters into Charlotte Harbor, creating a huge fishing area. Pine Island Sound stretches off to the south, to San Carlos Bay and the Caloosahatchee River. Countless small islands, a few large ones separated by passes, many smaller bays and rivers, extensive grass flats and oyster reefs, and miles of beach make this as fishy an area as you'll find any-where in Florida.

Some of the state's top guides work this area. Three were interviewed for the informa-tion in this section. Phil O'Bannon has a national reputation for excellence. He grew up in this area in a family that made its living by fishing commercially. Phil knows the area like the back of his hand, and has fished such well-known anglers as former President George Bush.

Zeke Sieglaff caught his first saltwater fish in Boca Grande when he was four years old, and has been fishing there ever since. He owns Boca Grande Outfitters.

Tommy Locke lives on Gasparilla Island and is an excellent, hard working guide.

152

Opportunities for the Do It Yourself Fly Fisher

-<u>Inshore Wading</u>: Although there are literally miles of wadable flats, a boat is needed to reach most of them. However, good opportunities for waders can be found near bridges throughout the area. For example, the SR 775 Causeway out to Gasparilla Island offers waders some access at its northern end. There is some access for waders along the bay side of Gasparilla Island, too. Another place you can wade is at the north end of Pine Island, in Bokeelia. Folks without a boat who want to fish can catch fish along the beach in the summer months. See below.

-<u>Hand Powered Boat</u>: In the vicinity of Boca Grande itself I wouldn't launch a hand powered boat. It's big water, with plenty of large vessels operating at speed, not a safe situation. In the vicinity of nearby Placida, though, you'll find a different situation. By launching your boat here you can explore Gasparilla Sound, Bull Bay, and numerous unnamed creeks and islands, and have a tranquil, undisturbed angling experience, fishing for snook, redfish, seatrout, and more.

-<u>Inshore Boat</u>: The entire area of Charlotte Harbor and Pine Island Sound offers superb opportunities for redfish, snook, and seatrout all year long. Ladyfish, Spanish mackerel, and crevalle jacks are frequent catches. Tarpon are available in season, as are cobia.

The snook here, as well as the rest of southeast Florida, exhibit seasonal movements, moving into the backcountry creeks in the fall and back out through the passes and along the beaches in the late spring.

Miles of grass flats await exploration. Oyster reefs litter the seascape, and mangrove islands dot the area. Large barrier islands are separated from each other by cuts or passes through which enormous volumes of water move as tides change. Small creeks and the large rivers lie off to the east. There's plenty to do!

-<u>From the Beach</u>: All summer long snook patrol the beaches, oftentimes lying right in the wash at the edge of the shore. Sight fish these fish! This fishing starts in April and continues into October, although the best fishing happens during the summer months. Use a white streamer, cast about two feet in front of the fish, and stay out of the water!

Tarpon also work along the beaches during May and June. These fish are usually out of range of an angler standing on the beach, though. During the summer redfish sometimes work along the beach as they go through the passes. This is very much a hit or miss fishery though. Snook provide the most consistent fishing, but trout, jacks, ladyfish, or mackerel could get into the act at anytime.

-<u>Nearshore</u>: Off the beaches tarpon are available in early summer, as mentioned above. Farther out, kings run by every spring (March through May, mostly) and fall (October to mid-December). Using live pilchards you can chum the kings into an absolute frenzy, then easily entice a strike on a fly. Little tunny might appear during the same time frame, easily identifiable by the hordes of diving birds working over them. Cobia remain around markers all year long. Tripletail show during the fall and stay into the spring months. You'll find them if you look under crab buoys, markers, weed lines, and floating debris.

Flies and Techniques

Season has a lot to do with how you fish for some species here. For example, (and as already been mentioned), snook fishing is widely available along the beaches and in the passes during the summer. In the fall those fish start moving into backcountry bays and creeks, where they can be sight fished over white sand holes in grass flats all winter long.

Small schools of reds are here all year long, but the big schools (50-500 fish) arrive in July and are gone by October. Redfish tail more frequently during the winter months. Of course if you see tailers, start casting to them!

The main run of big tarpon begins in April and tapers off by the end of June or beginning of July. These fish are usually fished from skiffs along the beaches. The boat is positioned in front of the school with an electric motor, and then the angler throws a standard tarpon streamer fly in front of them.

Resident tarpon stay in Charlotte Harbor all summer. Smaller fish (and the occasional big one) can be found all year long. These fish frequent the mouths of the Peace and Myakka Rivers and many of the canals on the east side of Charlotte Harbor, where they are easier to catch. A tarpon could turn up anywhere, especially during the summer, so keep your eyes open!

Seatrout have once again become very easy to catch in three to five feet of water over grass flats. There aren't large number of big fish, but fish "in the slot" (15-20 inches) are quite common and a blast to catch on popping bugs.

Kingfish can be taken in 20 to 40 feet of water along the buoy line out of Boca Grande, most easily during the spring run. A livewell full of pilchards is a necessity for this. The fish are chummed up behind the boat and can become so ravenous they will strike anything remotely resembling a pilchard. Not much casting skill is required, since casts are only 30 feet long or so. You'd better have tackle up to the task and adequate fish-fighting skills, though!

Phil and Tommy both like chartreuse Clouser minnows for a lot of their fishing, saying that they are good for all types of fish. They also both like surface strikes, and so like to use poppers. Phil says he loves throwing a big popper in the middle of a school of redfish and watching several fish struggling to eat it before one finally does!

He also likes using a Dahlberg diver type of fly for tailing reds. Finally, since pilchards are such an important baitfish in the area, Deceivers in white or green and white should be carried. This is the fly of choice for beach snook and also for kingfish.

Access
For Waders- Most of this was already discussed in the section on wading opportunities. One thing I didn't mention was the ferry out of Pineland Marina on Pine Island. This ferry carries passengers over to Cayo Costa State Park on La Costa Island. Here anglers can walk the beach while searching for snook. You can camp near the beach, and the park also has some (ugly) cabins for rent which have bunks in them for those allergic to sleeping on the ground. Of course anglers who own boats can also take advantage of this opportunity.

For Boaters- Boat ramps can be found at the following places:
-in Placida, just before the Boca Grande Causeway on CR 775;
-in Englewood off of CR 775;
-at the Pineland Marina on Pine Island, off of SR 767;
-at the Burnt Store Marina, on the east side of Charlotte Harbor, off of SR 765.

Fly Shops
-Boca Grande Outfitters, 941.964.2445, www.bocagrandeoutfitters.com. A full service shop with everything you might need to fish this area.
-Special Effects and Fishing Unlimited, an Orvis shop on Boca Grande, 941.964.0907, 431 Park Avenue, Boca Grande, www.4tarpon.com.

Guides
There a lot of good guides in this area; however, not all of them fly fish or understand fly fishing. Here is a list of a few who do:
-Captain Phil O'Bannon, 941.964.0359.
-Captain Tommy Locke, 941.766.9070.
-Capt. Zeke Sieglaff, 941.964.2245; www.bocagrandeoutfitters.com.
-Captain Pete Greenan, 941.923.6095; www.floridaflyfishing.com.

Boat Rentals
-Gasparilla Marina, 800.541.4441; www.gasparillamarina.com. Powerboat rentals.
-Boca Boat Rentals, 941.964.1333; www.bocaboat.com. Powerboat and kayak rentals.
-Grande Tours, 941.697.8825; www.gulftobay.com/grande. Kayak rentals.

State Parks and Other Attractions
-Cayo Costa State Park, PO Box 1150, Boca Grande, 33921; 941.964.0375. Accessible only by boat, but a ferry runs out to the island from the Pineland Marina. Camping right on the Gulf of Mexico is the main attraction here. Fishing is literally at your doorstep.
-Gasparilla Island State Recreation Area, c/o Cayo Costa State Park. Access is via the Boca Grande Causeway (CR775).
Information about all state parks can be found online at www.floridastateparks.org.
-There is a restaurant on Cabbage Key in Pine Island Sound which is famous for its excellent lunches, and which, legend has it, was the inspiration for the Jimmy Buffet song, "Hamburger in Paradise". It's an unusual and interesting place which is worth a visit.
-The beaches in this area are famous for their shelling opportunities.

Accommodations
Charlotte County Convention &Visitor Bureau, 941.743.1900; www.pureflorida.com.

A Conversation with Zeke Sieglaff
    Capt. Zeke Sieglaff owns and guides from Boca Grande Outfitters. Zeke has fished extensively throughout the Florida Keys, the Marquesas, the Tortugas, and the Bahamas, but he prefers his home waters of Charlotte Harbor and Pine Island Sound. He is an innovative fly tyer and fisherman who has created several unique flies that have become standards for the waters of Boca Grande. Zeke caught his first saltwater fish in Boca Grande when he was four years old, and has been fishing there ever since.
    Zeke launched right into our conversation with a discussion of flies, and went on in a stream of consciousness from there:
    "In terms of flies, in the past I would throw bendbacks, or a small crab pattern, to tailing redfish. I've mostly gone to baitfish patterns, especially the Enrico Puglisi flies, in that situation. It's just a lot easier to show a redfish this fly because it pushes a lot more water. It's a lot easier to get a client to show that fly to a fish than it would be to show a thumbnail sized mud crab or a shrimp. In spite of the fact that the crabs and shrimp are what they're feeding on while they tail, they seem to respond very well to the baitfish flies. There are times when I'll go back to the old standards, but the baitfish flies definitely bring more fish to the boat, for myself and my customers.

"A lot of people don't associate cold, windy winter weather with good fishing, but I've found those kinds of days to be some of my best. When the temperature drops the snook are heading towards creeks that have deeper bends. The creeks in the vicinity of Boca Grande tend to have dark bottoms and deeper holes on the bends, and you can find enormous numbers of fish in these areas. I've had some great days when my anglers would say, 'Let's not go today, it's too cold and windy,' and that's exactly the kinds of days when these fish get in there.

"The new generation skiffs let us get back there in these creeks so you don't have to walk very far. It's been fantastic for my business. It's pretty much all sight fishing. If you're not finding them, sometimes you'll come to a bend with a deeper bottom. You find huge numbers of snook there, where the whole bottom moves. You think it's dark bottom and then you realize there's a hundred fish in there. It's pretty much all sight fishing.

"Sometimes you'll find a place where it's too deep to see, and then there is some blind casting. Those are good places to bring someone who may not have a deep background in saltwater fly fishing and is looking to get his confidence up.

"But when the water is shallow and the sun comes up and warms up the water just a little bit, even on a cold day, that's when you find the snook cruising around with his back out of the water looking for minnows. In my opinion they become real opportunists at that point. It requires a long accurate cast but they will generally oblige a good cast. It's cold and there's not a lot of food around, so if you put that baitfish fly in front of them they will usually eat it.

"In addition to the Puglisi flies I really like Borski's Haystack. It has a lot of motion with minimum forward motion so you can suspend it and keep it in the strike zone a longer time without having to move it. The fly 'breathes' very well in the water.

"Bunny flies [the Haystack is a bunny fly– Ed] are very effective in these situations. Cold water, sleeping snook, just the slightest bump and the fly jumps to life, just the slightest water movement and the fly comes alive. It's a very neutrally buoyant fly, it doesn't sink fast. Tim's a fantastic tyer, and that Haystack in tan, gray, black, those and the Enrico flies are my two wintertime go-to snook flies. You can keep them in the strike zone. They stay high in the water, and we all know a snook's never going to go down to feed.

"From the perspective of fishing for snook, obviously from what I just said we focus on creeks during the winter. As the water warms up in the spring and baitfish flood up onto the flats the fish start their migration out of the creeks toward the passes and beaches. That's when I focus on more areas outside of the creeks. We still go into creeks but you don't go as far back. There's no need to.

"Shallow little mangrove bays allow snook to ambush bait very effectively. Around islands in Bull Bay and Turtle Bay, Catfish Creek, during the spring these are definitely areas I focus on. I go to almost all Enrico patterns this time of year. I also start fishing a lot of topwaters like gurglers and Hot Lips.

"By May and June the beaches are absolutely loaded with snook. This is a great do-it-yourself time of year. There are only a couple of flies that you need for this, with one in particular being the DT Special. Basically it's a small, Keys style, all white tarpon fly, a number 1. It's got two hackles on either side, splayed out, with a tiny bit of bucktail between them, and Mylar eyes, and an epoxy head. It imitates a small baitfish in the surf.

"Your opportunities are great when just walking down the beach. Anybody can do it. Just figure out which way they're moving and go towards them. The biggest mistake I see people making is they get into the water. You want to stay well above where the water meets the sand.

156

"You definitely have to lead them. These fish are often quite spooky. Some days you can catch a bunch, other days they're hard to catch. Either way, the shots are amazing, you're getting tons of shots.

"You want to get out there about 8 o'clock. If you get out any earlier you don't have enough light to see them. It stays good until about 1 o'clock, when the sea breeze kicks up, which makes it very difficult to sight fish them. This puts you into a blind casting situation, which can be effective, particularly on an outgoing tide around the passes. You can hook some bigger fish doing that.

"In the fall the snook start heading back into the bays and creeks, and the whole cycle starts all over again.

"When it comes to tarpon fishing, there's a lot more people fishing now, both along the beach and in the backcountry. The biggest change I've seen in about thirteen years by the fish in response to this is that the schools are a lot smaller. There are just as many fish, but they're not in the huge schools that they used to be because there's more pressure on the fish.

"So long as you approach the fish quietly and fish them properly, generally speaking you're rewarded with great results. Even with the increase in traffic, I still think it's one of the greatest places on earth to catch a tarpon on a fly, just from the sheer number of opportunities and strikes you get. My numbers certainly are not going down. We're just not fishing the giant schools that used to come through, but you've got the same number of fish in smaller groups.

"Given that backcountry spots are pretty closely guarded, there are great opportunities throughout Charlotte Harbor and Pine Island Sound for laid-up, rolling, and cruising tarpon in three to six foot water depths, particularly in late April and early May. I focus a lot on the backcountry, casting to a lot of laid up and slowly cruising fish.

"The beach always has fish on it from Fort Myers to Sarasota, and those fish always come back to Boca Grande Pass because of the tremendous amount of food that gets washed into and out of that pass on the change of each tide. It amounts to a giant cafeteria for them.

"We use all twelve weight rods. While a lot of guys use intermediate lines I've gone to sink-tips in the past few years. It's a lot easier to adjust a cast that you're not happy with because you can pick it up.

"From a fly perspective we use a lot of Enrico's tarpon patterns, the peanut butter patterns in 3/0, lots of black and purple, browns, oranges. It's a bigger fly that pushes a lot of water and is easy for the tarpon to pick up. A lot of the beach fish feed on threadfin herring and these tarpon patterns create a great threadfin silhouette.

"Crab flies with heads of spun deer hair are also very effective, especially as you get to the hill tides on the full and new moons. Tremendous number of crabs get flushed out of Pine Island Sound and Charlotte Harbor. The tarpon come out of Boca Grande Pass and up into the harbor to feed on them. Everybody knows about it, it's like the wild, wild west, but you can sure put a lot of tarpon into the air during those tides. It's a lot of fun because you can use a floating line and a floating fly. We actually Gink them (the flies) up so they float better. You can get some great surface strikes. It's pretty exciting when you can get a 120 pound tarpon to eat something off the top.

"Our tarpon season generally starts around mid-April and it runs through the summer. After the big migratory schools have left there are still plenty of resident fish up in Charlotte Harbor. There are also fish along the beaches and in Pine Island Sound in relatively fishable numbers through September. Last year we caught our last fish on October 15. They'll stick around a lot longer than most people think."

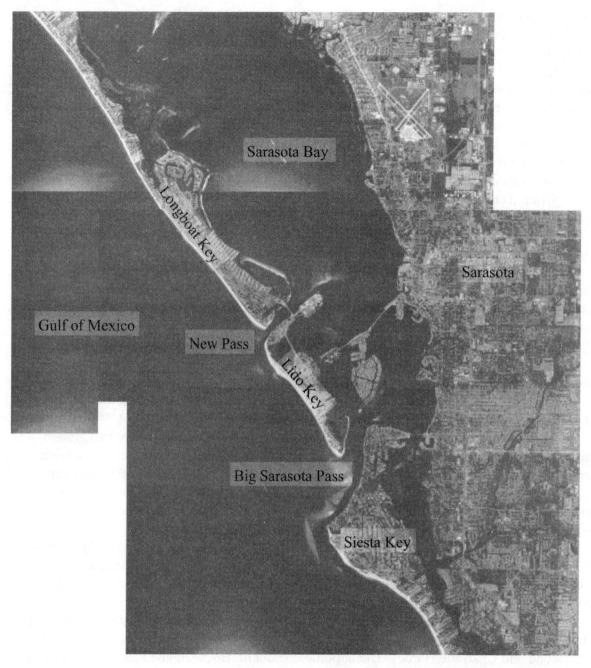

Sarasota

Sarasota Bay also offers good fishing in its passes, Longboat Pass, New Pass, and Big Pass, for pompano, bluefish, and Spanish mackerel during spring and fall. Fishing along the beaches for tarpon is excellent from mid May through June. Spring and fall offer great coastal gulf fishing for king and Spanish mackerel, cobia, tripletail and little tunny. Numerous canals along Longboat Key are good wintertime areas for snook, trout and redfish. Little Sarasota Bay is also a good wintertime area for trout, ladyfish, jack crevalle, redfish and snook. It is mainly a mud and shell bottom, which holds heat during cool winter days. The ICW in Venice, locally known as "snook alley", is one of the top snook fishing areas in the state.

Pete Greenan and Rick Grassett graciously supplied the information for this section.

Opportunities for the Inshore Fly Fisher
-Inshore Wading: Many opportunities await waders in Sarasota, Bradenton, and Venice. Side roads west of US 41 invite exploration.

In north Sarasota Bay, off US 41 at Whitfield Ave, there is a flat that runs along the east side of Sarasota Bay. The same flat can be accessed further south, just north of the Ringling Museum and New College.

Along the bay front near downtown Sarasota is a good wading spot near Selby Gardens.

The Ringling Causeway, SR 789, connects Sarasota to Lido Key. Between the twin bridges a flat on the north side of the causeway produces redfish, seatrout, and snook. The best times to fish are early in the morning and late in the evening.

On Lido Key go south until you run out of beach. A long grass flat extends out to the left, into the bay, and often produces excellent angling for the above named species.

Siesta Drive intersects US 41 on the south side of Sarasota and leads out to Siesta Key. On the southeast side of the Siesta Drive Causeway a flat produces (on occasion) excellent fishing for snook, reds, and seatrout. On the northeast corner of the Siesta Drive Bridge, there is a sand bar and flat that extends to the north which can be waded.

Out on Siesta Key you'll find beach access on Midnight Pass Road (SR 72), with good fishing along the beach during the summer for snook, especially around the Point O' Rocks.

On US 41 south of Sarasota look for the Sarasota Square Mall. Across US 41 from the mall you'll see Vamo Road. Take Vamo Road to Vamo Drive, then go right. You can park at the end of Vamo Drive, and the oyster bars and islands on the flat before you usually hold snook and redfish, especially on the higher tide phases.
At the south end of Lido Key, there is a canoe/kayak launching area that has a wadeable flat, which faces Bird Key.
-Hand Powered Boat There are several places that paddlers can fish in Sarasota. Near the downtown area, a canoe or kayak could be dropped off the seawall at the south end of Island Park. Fish the sand bar that parallels the seawall beginning at Selby Gardens and running south. This is a good area for snook and reds. The deep grass outside the bar is good for trout.

Or, cross the Ringling Causeway to Lido Key. Go south to South Lido Park. There is a canoe and kayak launch area on the left just before you get to the main entrance, and a trail through the mangroves with a nice flat. This area is a good snook and redfish flat. It also gives easy access to Big Pass where you can fish for pompano, bluefish, and Spanish mackerel.

If you head north out of St. Armands Circle on Lido Key and turn right on City Island, just before the New Pass bridge, a paddler can launch at the tip of City Island and fish the Radio Tower flat on the south side of City Island or the Middle Ground flat on the north side of the New Pass channel. Both areas are good for trout, pompano, bluefish, Spanish mackerel, cobia.

If you go back to US 41 (Tamiami Trail) and head north about five miles, there is access to the east side of the bay at Edwards Drive where it intersects with Uplands Drive, just north of New College, and further north another two miles at Whitfield Avenue. This is a nice flat for reds and snook, or trout on the outer edge.

Head south about seven miles from the downtown area on US 41 and turn right on Vamo Road, then turn right again on Vamo Way to get access to Little Sarasota Bay. This is a good cooler weather spot for snook, reds and trout. If you head further south three or four miles to Osprey and turn right on Blackburn Point Road. and then cross the swing bridge, there is a county park on the right side that gives access to a good area of Little Sarasota Bay.

At the south end of Siesta Key, there is a public launch at Turtle Beach which gives access to Little Sarasota Bay and the Jim Neville Marine Preserve, another good cool weather area.

-Inshore Boat: Sarasota Bay is a wide, open bay with a sand bar that runs around much of its perimeter. There are good flats at Buttonwood Harbor and at various places along Longboat Key. Long Bar is a popular spot on the east side of Sarasota Bay. Just inside New Pass and Big Pass are deep grass flats that are good areas for trout, ladyfish, pompano or bluefish depending on the season. Little Sarasota Bay is narrow and has good flats, particularly for winter fishing. It is mostly a mud and shell bottom, which holds more heat in the winter.

The flats and oyster bars at the north end of Sarasota Bay in the vicinity of Longboat Pass provide excellent fishing for redfish and seatrout, along with the occasional snook. Between Stickney Point and Point Crisp is another good area to try.

The keys along the west side of the bay, especially Whale Key and White Key, usually attract and hold fish.

Down in the south bay, the grass flats between markers 5 and 7 consistently produce excellent fishing for jack crevalle, ladyfish, and seatrout.

During the winter months, Zwick's Channel and the adjacent boat turning basins provide a deep thermal refuge for many species of fish, including snook, black drum, seatrout, jacks, and others. This channel runs from just inside of New Pass north almost the entire length of Longboat Key, ending between Buttonwood Harbor and Longboat Pass. Fish with a sinktip or sinking shooting head with fast sinking flies.

When the current is flowing over or past them, the oyster bars and the docks along the shoreline of Roberts Bay are consistent producers, too.

-From the Beach: You can find good action along beaches from Longboat Key to Gasparilla Island, particularly from spring through fall. Snook lay along the trough of the beach all summer. Cast a white streamer, such as Deceiver, making sure that you do not walk in the water and spook the fish. Additionally, sometimes schools of redfish work along the beach. One of these schools may appear at in front of the fly fisher any time. Other species available include ladyfish, jack crevalle, Spanish mackerel, whiting, and pompano.

Casey Key is only accessible from the north end by walking south from Turtle Beach, at the south end of Siesta Key, or at the south end by walking north from Nokomis Beach. There is limited access to the beaches of Longboat Key and Manasota Key since these areas are largely residential.

-Nearshore: Beach fishing for tarpon gets more popular every year. Electric motors put the fly fisher in front of a cruising string of fish, and when the fish are in range, you deliver the fly. If things go according to plan, the fireworks start immediately after this. This fishing begins around the end of April and lasts into early July.

Off Sarasota beaches there is good seasonal activity available to the small boater for Spanish mackerel, king mackerel, cobia, tripletail, and little tunny. Tripletail and cobia can be found around markers, and cobia can also be chummed in close to the boat. Artificial reefs in the inshore range (one to three miles) and mid range (seven to ten miles) are abundant. Published lists of reef sites and their coordinates are available at most tackle shops or locations where fishing licenses are sold.

Flies and Techniques

Pete Greenan supplied the following list of fly patterns for specific types of fish, and hook sizes:

Tarpon: Black Death.... AM #4/0
                Cockroach.......AM #4/0
                Orange/ Grizzly. AM #4/0
                Blue/Grizzly Gold. .All day #4/0
                Chartreuse/yellow.......Back country #1/0
                Purple/Black....Back country #1/0

Snook: Red/White finger mullet #1/0
                Greenback finger mullet #1/0
                Greenback Deceiver (no weed guard for beach) #1
                Chartreuse/White or Yellow deceiver (tannic water)
                Clouser (grey, chartreuse, pink, etc.)
                Pearl Glass minnow #2 (under lights)

Reds: Greenan Redfish #1
                Popper (red/white) #1
                Clouser (Chartreuse, Black, Grey)
                Brown/ Olive crab #1
                Tan shrimp #1

Trout: Purple/black Clouser (grey, Chartreuse, Pink)
Jacks: anything
Ladyfish: anything

Use a weed guard for back country fish and around mangroves. Seatrout don't usually require one, though. Baby tarpon are in canals and boat basins with at least 6 feet of water and access to a river, the Intracoastal Waterway or other egress. You must be able to adjust and adapt to rapidly changing conditions!

Rick Grassett had this to say: "Clousers and baitfish patterns such as Deceivers and synthetic fiber flies are very effective here. Clousers can be tied in various sizes and of various materials depending on depth of water and species targeted. Clousers for redfish on #4 hooks with extra small lead eyes will fish well in shallow water. For other species in deeper water, a #2 hook will work better.

"When ladyfish, bluefish, or Spanish mackerel are possibilities, tie flies with Ultra Hair and epoxy the head of the fly to make it more durable. Bend backs and spoon flies are other good shallow water flies for reds, snook and trout. Poppers can work well, too.

"Night snook flies are usually small (an inch and a half long) glass minnow or shrimp patterns tied on # 4 or #6 hooks. Popular local patterns are Grassett's Grass Minnow and the String Bean. Larger baitfish patterns will work during summer and early fall.

"For the coastal gulf waters, glass minnow patterns and small Clousers work well for Spanish mackerel and little tunny. Crease flies are a must for little tunny and Spanish mackerel when they are breaking. An olive bendback fished on a floating line has been an effective tripletail fly, and for cobia use a large Deceiver or synthetic fiber baitfish pattern.

"Floating lines are a must for wading or fishing shallow water (twelve inches or less) from a boat. Intermediate or intermediate sink-tip fly lines are good choices for deep grass flats and the coastal gulf waters."

Access
For Waders: see above information about wading opportunities.
For Boaters: Boat ramps are available at the following locations:
-on 10th Street in Sarasota (Centennial Park).
-at City Island on Lido Key.
-at Turtle Beach on Siesta Key.
-at Blackman Point in Nokomis.
Public ramps in the Venice area are at Albee Road and Higel Park, near the south jetty. The Higel Park ramp is a marine park with restrooms.

There are a couple of dirt ramps where small boats, canoes or kayaks can be launched at Bishop Harbor and along US 19 near the Crab Trap Restaurant. There's a public ramp off Manatee Avenue at 59th St., which is the Warner's Bayou ramp. Further to the west off Manatee Avenue is the Kingfisher Boat Ramp just west of the Manatee Avenue Bridge.

Boat Rentals
-C.B's Saltwater Outfitters, 941.349.4400; www.cbsoutfitters.com. Powerboat rentals.
-Economy Tackle / Dolphin Dive & Kayak, 941.922-9671; www.floridakayak.com. Hand powered boats.
-Sarasota Boat Rental, 941-951-0550; www.sarasotaboatrental.com. Powerboat rentals.

Fly Shops
-Discount Tackle, 3113 1st St. E., Bradenton, FL. 941.746.6020.
-CB's Saltwater Outfitters, 941.349.4400; www.cbsoutfitters.com. An Orvis Outfitter.
-Economy Tackle, 941.922.9671.

Guides
-Capt. Rick Grassett, 941.923.7799; www.snookfin-addict.com or www.flyfishingflorida.net, offers bay, backcountry, night snook, tarpon and coastal gulf fly fishing. A Federation of Fly Fishers Certified Fly Casting Instructor, and Orvis endorsed guide.
-Captain Pete Greenan, 941.923.6095; www.floridaflyfishing.com. A Federation of Fly Fishers Certified Fly Casting Instructor.

State Parks and Other Attractions
-Myakka River State Park, 13207 State Rd. 72, Sarasota, FL, 941.361.6511.
-Oscar Scherer State Park, 1843 Tamiami Tr. S., Osprey, FL, 941.483.5956.
Both parks have campsites available.
Information about all state parks can be found online at www.floridastateparks.org.

Accommodations
-Holiday Inn Express, Siesta Key, 941.924.4900 is convenient to the area covered in this segment and is reasonably priced.
-The Calais Motel, 941.921.5797, a clean, comfortable, mom and pop type motel with efficiency units.
-Sarasota Visitor and Convention Bureau, 941.957.1877; www.visitsarasota.net.

Tampa/ St. Petersburg

The Tampa/ St. Pete area again offers anglers one of those delightful paradoxes- a major metropolitan area surrounded by clean water full of fish. What more could a fisherman want?

Tampa Bay extends inland for over 30 miles, all the way up into Lake Tarpon in Tarpon Springs. The Bay is Florida's largest open-water estuary, covering an area of 398 square miles at high tide. Popular for sports and recreation, the bay also supports one of the world's most productive natural ecosystems.

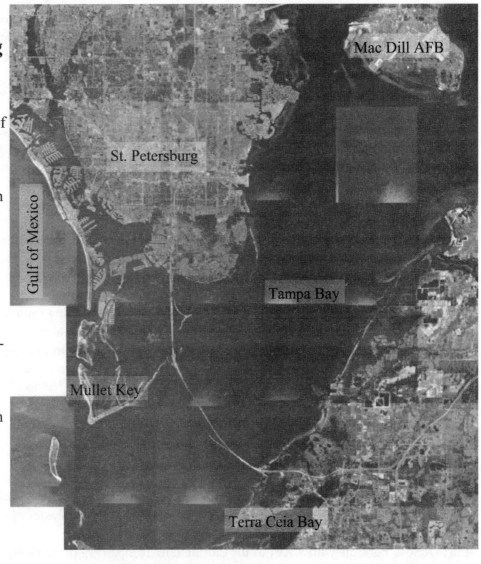

Wildlife abounds along the shores of Tampa Bay. As many as 50,000 pairs of birds, from brown pelican to the colorful roseate spoonbill, nest in Tampa Bay every year. Many other species, like the white pelicans and the sandpipers, are seasonal visitors.

A series of barrier islands stretch down the coast from Honeymoon Island off of Dunedin south to Anna Marie Island off of Bradenton and beyond, offering beach anglers countless opportunities. Pass after pass cut through the barriers, offering fish and fishermen easy access from the Intracoastal Waterway out to the Gulf of Mexico. Literally thousands upon thousands of acres of fishable water await the visiting angler.

Many rivers enter Tampa Bay, including the Hillsborough, Alafia, Little Manatee, and Big Manatee. You'll find good fishing around all of these river mouths, as well as around the docks and seawalls in downtown Tampa. Obtaining a copy of the Top Spot Fishing Chart #N 202 for Tampa Bay is highly recommended. See the catalog at back of this book to order.

Tampa Bay consists of four distinct areas; the Gulf, the upper bay, the middle bay, and the lower bay. At the mouth of Tampa Bay, Fort De Soto Park to the north and Terra Ceia Bay to the south are both aquatic preserves with no-motor zones. These are some of the best wading flats in Florida and large schools of redfish, seatrout and jack crevalle are common. Since the adoption of the net ban, it's not uncommon to see tailing permit on these flats. All fish coming into Tampa Bay must pass by one of these two flats. Tailing redfish in these areas rate as the most sought after fly rod challenge.

The middle bay is bounded by Pinellas Point and Weedon Island to west and the Cockroach Bay Aquatic Preserve to the east. This section of the bay has two of greater Tampa's largest power plants, one on each side of the bay. In the winter, these plants produce a warm water outflow which attracts large schools of jack crevalle, tarpon, ladyfish, and offers some of the best cobia fishing in Florida. To some extent, this is somewhat like fishing in a fish bowl! During the warmer months, these same fish move out onto the flats, where they are great targets for sight fishing.

The upper part of the bay is probably the least fished. Water clarity can be a problem in the summer because of the influx of silt from the rivers during the frequent rainstorms. Visibility improves during the winter, but wade fishing is difficult because of the soft bottom. Nevertheless, there are plenty of fish in this section year-round for those willing to do lots of blind casting. This is one of the best areas in Tampa Bay to catch large snook.

The Gulf coast region is a mecca for the fly-fisherman seeking multiple species from a boat. Large schools of king mackerel, little tunny, Spanish mackerel, and redfish abound nearshore. Early morning shoreline wading for snook is a popular pastime for the fly-fisherman, during the summer when these superb game fish are in their spawning season. Tarpon fishing along the beach during May and June ranks with the best the state has to offer.

My information for this area originally came from Paul Hawkins. Dan Malzone supplied lots of new information, with some also coming from Rick Grassett.

Opportunities for the Do It Yourself Fly Fisher
Inshore wading: The entire perimeter of Tampa Bay is ringed with flats, the only exception being the dredge and fill areas. All these flats are wadable, and if there's seagrass and/or mangroves there will be fish there at one time or another. Some of the easier places to get access include (but are not limited to):
-Fort DeSoto Park on Mullet Key at the entrance to Tampa Bay offers both beach fishing and wading off Anderson Boulevard;
-either end of the Sunshine Skyway at the fishing piers;
-Pinellas Point, at the north end of 4th Street in St. Pete, just before I-275. Potholes in grass flats offer targets for the wading fly fisher. Also, some deep dredge holes in this areas will hold fish during winter's cold snaps;
-North Shore Park;
-Weedon Island Park, on the east side of St. Pete just south of the Gandy Causeway, offers miles of grass flats interspersed with oyster beds;
-at both ends of the Gandy Bridge waders can get access to good flats;
-Picnic Island Park, south of Port Tampa of the west side of the Interbay Peninsula;
-Ballast Point Park on the east side of the Interbay peninsula;
-north of the Howard Frankland Bridge on the Tampa end;
-Courtney Campbell Causeway has some nice flats east of the boat ramp;
-the American Legion flats off Westshore Boulevard in Port Tampa has excellent wade fishing.

The flats to the north of Port Manatee in lower Tampa Bay are good flats to wade for reds, trout and snook. At the southeast end of the Manatee Avenue Bridge there is a good wading flat that extends to the south all the way to Price's Key.

Hand Powered Boat: There are many opportunities for folks in canoes or kayaks in the Tampa Bay area, including the no motors areas around Weedon Island on the east side of the Pinellas peninsula, or in Cockroach Bay on the south side of Tampa Bay. Both of these areas have excellent fishing, and receive less angling pressure because of the use restriction.

Three more popular and productive destinations for fly anglers are the Double Branch in upper Tampa Bay, from fall through early spring; Fort Desoto Park, any season; and Allen's Creek in Clearwater, at the mouth and on the adjoining flat, late fall through early spring. These all have good launch facilities, an easy paddle to the fish, and some interesting and varied scenarios for the neophyte to advanced angler. Osprey Bay Kayaks (727.524.9670) can give detailed information about this area.

For the fly caster looking for more adventure there is a great, late summer fishery in Clearwater for blacktip sharks as well.

-Inshore boat: the opportunities are truly unlimited. Boaters can fish most of the same areas that waders can, and have so many more options. They can sightfish for reds, trout, and snook along the relatively undeveloped south shoreline of the bay where waders have very little access. Obvious places to try are grass flats, bars, points, mangrove shorelines, and creek or river mouths.

The area of lower Tampa Bay from Terra Ceia Bay to Cockroach Bay contains lush grass flats, sand and oyster bars and mangrove islands and is largely undeveloped. Included in the area are also several smaller bays, Bishop Harbor, Joe Bay, and Miguel Bay.

There is a sand bar that runs along the edge of the bay with shallow flats between the bar and shoreline. Caution should be used when running inside the bar. At low tide, there are many spots to run aground and the area is dotted with numerous oyster bars. The same is true with the waters inside Bishop Harbor, Joe Bay, and Miguel Bay.

Boaters can fish for tarpon all summer long on deeper flats (from three to ten feet deep) and the edges of those flats. Sight fishing for tarpon in Tampa Bay isn't as publicized as it is in other parts of the state, but it's done the same way and it's just as good.

Channel markers along the main shipping channel in the bay offer the investigative angler shots at cobia and tripletail. Kingfish also hang around these buoys and can be chummed up and caught on flies. Spanish mackerel, little tunny, crevalle jacks, and bluefish are other species which could show up at any time, depending on the season. Look for surface activity or working birds in the open waters of the bay.

All the lighted bridges provide good fishing at night. During the summer you can have heart-attack fishing for tarpon here.

-From the beach: the beach runs from Honeymoon Island all the way down to Mullet Key. Jacks, bluefish, Spanish mackerel, pompano, seatrout, snook (summertime), and various other species can all be caught from the beach. Structure along the beaches always attracts fish, and it's no different here. Jetties and passes are the two most obvious places to check. Some of the better known passes, from north to south, are Hurricane Pass, Dunedin Pass, Clearwater Pass, Johns Pass, Blind Pass, and Pass-a-Grille. Possibly the prime beach fishing site in the entire metro area is Fort DeSoto Park on the tip of Mullet Key.

If you've read about beach fishing in the previous few sections, especially for snook (see the "Conversation with Zeke Sieglaff," p. 155), it's done the same way here.

-Nearshore: There are plenty of tarpon along the beach in the early summer. The buoy line marking the channel out of the bay attracts the same species as it does in the bay itself- cobia and tripletail on top and kingfish down below. You can sightfish the first two species, but kings will usually need to be chummed up. There are wrecks off the coast over which, in addition to the cobia and king mackerel, amberjack, and barracuda will also be found.

While nearshore fishing off St. Pete and Clearwater beaches is similar to what's available farther south, Pinellas County Utilities has twelve artificial reef sites, from three to 38 miles offshore, in the Gulf of Mexico. Each reef's individual design has different sized openings for different sized fish. These openings attract bottom dwellers like grouper, snapper, and grunt. The height of the structures attracts migratory species like mackerel, amberjack, cobia, barracuda, and baitfish. The reef sites can have a base diameter of up to 100 feet and reach up to half the water's depth. Additionally, Pinellas County Coastal Management maintains nine more artificial reefs. Live bait chumming over any of these structures could provide for a very memorable day's fishing.

Flies and Techniques

The standard fly-fishing outfit for Tampa Bay is a nine foot, seven-weight to nine weight rod. Weight forward, floating line are usually best, although clear sink tips can often be useful for deeper runs. Tapered leaders, eight to 12 feet long with 10 to 15 pound tippets will cover most circumstances. If pursuing tarpon, 12- to 13-weight outfits are needed, as well as 60 pound (or more) shock tippets and high quality reels with considerable backing capacity. Most flies are tied on size 2, 1, or 1/0 hooks. Popular fly patterns are crabs, woolhead mullet, Deceivers, and Clouser minnows.

The flies to use depend on what species you're targeting. Paul Hawkins is fond of the bonefish fly known as the Crazy Charlie, which has an inverted hair wing with bead chain eyes. He ties these on number 1 and 1/0 hooks for use on the bay's seatrout, redfish, and snook. He likes red and white or brown and orange color combinations.

The Clouser deep minnow is a favorite all along Florida's coast.

Merkins are an excellent pattern for permit anywhere you can find them in the bay.

For fishing the bay's abundant tarpon Paul Hawkins uses the standard Keys-style tarpon streamer. His favorite colors are orange and grizzly (good anywhere tarpon swim, by the way) and black. These are tied on 2/0 or 3/0 hooks.

As far as techniques go, Paul greatly prefers hunting, stalking, and casting to fish on the flats above all else. He looks for an area with clean water, healthy grass, and bait or other signs of life, and then starts hunting. When the fish are spotted then the stalk begins, which culminates in the cast and presentation. Hopefully the fish eats and a hookup results!

Putting the fly where it needs to be is <u>much</u> more important than pattern.

In dark water or deeper areas the best thing to do is to blind-cast, working the shoreline or structure in the water.

Access

For waders- as described earlier.

For boaters- The metro Tampa area has a lot of good boat ramps.

In the St. Petersburg area:

-Fort DeSoto Park ramp, 3500 Pinellas Bayway South.

-Maximo Park boat ramp at 34th Street. S. and Pinellas Point Drive.

-Bay Vista, at 4th St. and Pinellas Point Dr. S.

-at 1st St. and 31st Ave., NE.

Access, con't.
-at Poplar St. and 35th Ave. NE.
-at Bayshore Dr. and 2nd Ave. S.
-6th St. and 39th Ave.
-Park St. and Elbow Lane N.
-Pinellas Point Dr. and 34th Dr. S.
-and at Sunlit Cove Dr. and Bay St. NE.
In Tampa, boat ramps will be found at:
-Ballast Point on Bayshore Boulevard.
-Marjorie Park, on Davis Island Boulevard.
-on Picnic Island.
Elsewhere in the Tampa Bay region you will find ramps at:
-Baycrest, on Baycrest Boulevard off Memorial Highway.
-Cockroach Bay, on Cockroach Bay Road, east of US 41.
-Courtney Campbell, on the north side of the Courtney Campbell Causeway.
-on Davis Island, on the south end of Davis Island Boulevard.
-Domino, on the south end of 22nd Avenue and 8th Avenue in Ruskin.
-E.G. Simmons, 2401 19th Avenue NW, two miles west of US 41.
-Ruskin Commongood, 121st Street and 2nd Street, Ruskin.
-Salty Sol Fleishman, on Gandy Boulevard west of Tampa.
-Williams, 6401 Riverview Drive, west of US 41.

There is an excellent system of boat ramps in this area. Two on-line sites that give a more complete listing than is possible here are www.tampabayangler.com/BOATRAMPS.htm and www.boatclix.com/links/boatramps.html.

Fly Shops
-Bill Jackson, 9501 US 19, N. Pinellas Park, St. Petersburg, 727.576.4169; www.billjacksons.com.
-The Saltwater Fly Fisherman, 2219 S. Dale Mabry Hwy, Tampa 33629. 727.443.5000; www.fly-fisher.com.
-Tampa Bay Outfitters, 701 South Howard #102, Tampa, 813.254.2445; www.tampabayoutfitters.com.

Boat Rentals
-Tierra Verde Boat Rentals, 727.867.0077, http://tvboatrentals.com. Powerboat rentals near St. Petersburg Beach.
-Frenchy's Boat Rentals, 727.360.8669, www.frenchysjetski.com. Powerboat and kayak rentals near St. Petersburg Beach.
-Osprey Bay Kayaks, 17910 US Hwy 19, N.Clearwater, 727.524.9670, www.ospreybay.com. These folks have guided kayak fishing trips as well as kayak rentals.

Guides
Capt. Dan Malzone, 813.831.4052, capt.dan.malzone@worldnet.att.net. Dan has been fly fishing for nearly 40 years, is a two time IGFA world record holder for tarpon on fly and has also guided his anglers to new IGFA world records for tarpon on fly. He's Orvis endorsed.

-Capt. Russ Shirley, Salty Fly Charters, 727.343.1957; www.captruss.com.
-Capt. Paul Hawkins, 727.560.6762; www.flatsguy.com.
-Capt. Ray Markham, 941.723.2655; e-mail flatback@infi.net

State Parks and Other Attractions

-Weedon Island State Preserve, 1500 Weedon Island Drive, St. Petersburg 33702; 813.570.5146. This preserve has 1250 acres for hiking, picnicking, and fishing, The waters around Weedon Island are a no motors allowed zone.
-Little Manatee River State Recreation Area, 215 Lightfoot Road, Wimauma, 33598. 813.634.4781. This park, over 1600 acres, allows canoeing and fishing among the recreational opportunities offered. The Little Manatee River, which flows for four and one-half miles through this park, is a designated Outstanding Florida Waterway and is part of the Cockroach Bay Aquatic Preserve.
-Honeymoon Island State Recreation Area, #1 Causeway Boulevard, Dunedin 34698; 813.734.4255. Beach fishing here can be awesome, especially during the summer when snook prowl the near-shore waters. A ferry here takes visitors to Caladesi Island, another state park which is not accessible by road.
-Caledesi Island State Park, #1 Causeway Boulevard, Dunedin 34698; 813.443.5903. One of the last undeveloped islands on the Gulf Coast of Florida, it offers the same fishing opportunities as Honeymoon Island.

Information about all state parks can be found online at www.floridastateparks.org.

Of course you can always visit Busch Gardens, and probably should if you've never done that sort of thing before. If you have, once is probably enough. Let's face it- the fish need catching!

Accommodations

A huge number of accommodations are available all through the metro Tampa area. Dan Malzone recommends the following:
-Holiday Inn Marina, St. Petersburg, 800.227.8045 or 727.867.1151.
-Tahitian Inn, Tampa , 800.876.1397 or 813.877.6721.

The Tampa Bay Convention and Visitors Bureau can be reached at 813.223.1111 or at www.visittampabay.com.

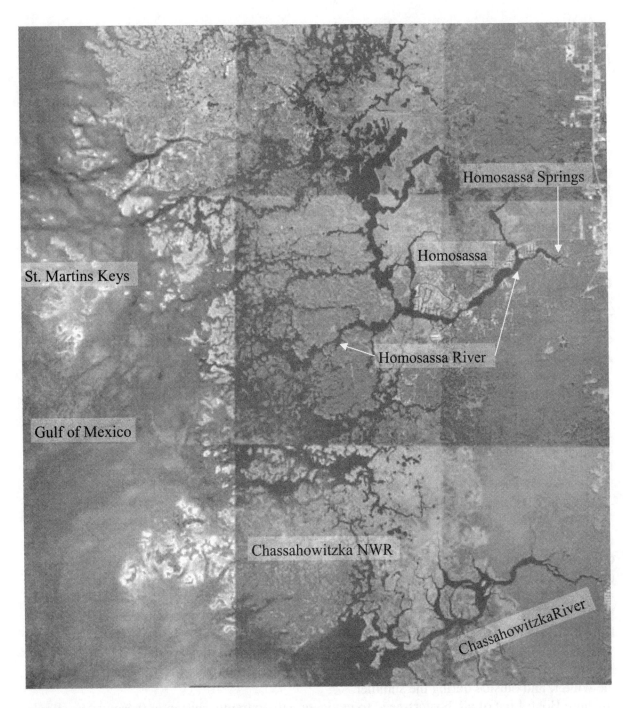

Homosassa Springs

Homosassa

St. Martins Keys

Homosassa River

Gulf of Mexico

Chassahowitzka NWR

ChassahowitzkaRiver

Homosassa/Crystal River

Florida's coastline is somewhat arbitrarily divided into sections. There's the First Coast, the Space Coast, the Gold Coast, and others. Homosassa and Crystal River sit smack dab in the center of what's called the Nature Coast. With extensive salt marshes and very little shoreline development, the coastline here is as beautiful and wild as any coastline anywhere, with lots of birds and other wildlife.

The widest Continental Shelf on the Gulf Coast lies off of this region. This wide shelf makes for extensive shallow flats. Lush grass beds, which anchor the bottom sediments and quickly trap any suspended material, cover the bottom. As a result, the water here is as clear as what you are used to drinking, adding to the aesthetics of fishing here. Those extensive grass beds support one of the finest redfish fisheries on Florida's west coast.

Homosassa/Crystal River has lots to offer besides redfish, too. Cobia and seatrout are other well known fisheries. Spanish mackerel and bluefish are available, and large jack crevalle and ladyfish live in the headwaters of the rivers during the winter months. But what Homosassa is best known for, and what draws fly fishermen here in droves year after year after year, are the giant tarpon that come through early each summer, giant fish in shallow, crystalline waters, fish that make your heart quake, your knees shake, and your breath come hard. Homosassa is the Holy Land for fly fishing tarpon anglers.

Mike Locklear grew up in Homosassa. He's fished it all his life, and has been guiding for a good portion of it. I've fished with him several times, and we spent a lot of time on the phone, while he related the following information to me.

Opportunities for the Do It Yourself Fly Fisher
-Inshore Wading: There isn't a great deal of wading here, but you can find some quality fishing. Taking it from the north to the south, in Crystal River SR 44 goes literally right to the water's edge, ending in a boat ramp at Fort Island Gulf Beach. Wade here for redfish and seatrout. Jacks and ladyfish will sometimes show up.

South of Crystal River, SR 494 leads off to the west of SR 19, heading to Ozello. Waders can fish back in the salt marsh in the St. Martin's Aquatic Preserve, again mostly for redfish and seatrout.

South of Homosassa a ride along SR 50 west will bring you to several wading opportunities. If you take SR 595 north, you'll find extensive grass flats off the beach at Pine Island. Fishing is also possible out at Cooglers Beach. And lastly, you can park at the county park in Bayport and wade fish. In all three places the primary target will be redfish.
-Hand Powered Boat: Literally thousands of miles of shoreline await the intrepid paddler here, an enormous maze of islands and waterways, much of it the Chassahowitzka National Wildlife Refuge. Before venturing off into the great unknown you had better have a recent nautical chart or aerial photo and a compass, with the knowledge to use both. Of course you can launch your boat at the above mentioned wading spots.

A fifteen mile long, marked canoe trail winds its way between Homosassa and Crystal River. While fifteen miles is a long trip for a single day's fishing, you can work a portion of it from either end and use the markers to easily find your way back.

The waterways between all these islands tend to be shallow. Any deep spot is likely to load up with trout and redfish during cold snaps. In general the fishing is better inside during the winter, and outside during the summer.
-Inshore Boat: First of all, boaters need to navigate with extreme caution in these waters. Rocks are frequently seen, and sometimes not until after they've smashed some part of the boat. Local knowledge is very important here, and even the locals hit rocks sometimes. The wise angler uses an aluminum boat.

Several seasonal fisheries exist off the Nature Coast. By the end of February cobia start following stingrays around on flats in about three to four feet of water. Active rays will often have cobia, and sometimes big cobia, shadowing them. These ling take a well presented fly, and put up a whale of a fight in the shallow water. This fishing ends around the beginning of May.

When May comes, though, people start thinking about tarpon. Several fly rod world records have been caught here and every season all of the biggest names in saltwater fly fishing congregate in Homosassa for eight tough weeks of searching for the Big Mamoo. This is not a type of fishing for the first-time do-it-yourselfer, due to the tackle and knowledge you need. There is no more exciting fly fishing anywhere, though. Every serious saltwater fly fisher should try this fishing at least once!

Redfish are available most of the year. Without going out into the Gulf, redfish can be found in all of the creeks feeding the Homosassa River all year long. Mason's Creek is one good one to try. All of the others are worth exploring, too.

If you want to try the Gulf for reds, the areas of the coast to the north and south of the Homosassa River offer almost unlimited opportunities. Mike says that summer (particularly July and August) provides some of the best fishing of the year for reds, but they feed all year long IF the water stays over 70 degrees. In January and February the water often becomes colder than that, though.

Anyone who cares to tow the boat up to Crystal River can be in redfish less than a mile from the boat ramp at Fort Island Gulf Beach at the end of SR 44. Oyster bars in this area a most always attract and hold redfish, and seatrout too. Once again, take care in navigating. Oysters are unforgiving creatures when you run a lower unit into them.

Trout fishing off the Nature Coast has recovered well since the first edition of this book came out. Depending on the season (think outside during the summer and inside during the winter) some areas which can usually be counted on to produce a few fish include the Ship Rock grass flats, north and west of channel markers 26 and 24 out of the Homosassa River, around any oyster reefs, the Mangrove Point grass flats, in Dixie Bay, and in Pea Pass and Fish Creek.
-Along the Beach: there are no beaches to speak of along this stretch of coast.
-Nearshore: Mike told me about a fly fishing opportunity off Homosassa of which I had never even heard, but would love to try- shallow water grouper. I mentioned above that there were rock piles which required the boater to proceed with caution. These rocks hold grouper, and are shallow enough that the fish can be reached with a fly. These rocks can be found visually just by looking, or with a LORAN unit. The numbers are published in a book called Coastal LORAN & GPS Coordinates, by Captain Rodney Stebbins.

Cobia hold around the markers for most of the summer, sometimes in gangs. My guess is that they would also be around the same rock piles that the grouper are. Some of these fish get to be well over 50 pounds. It's quite difficult getting them away from the marker after the hookup. It sure is fun trying, though!

Sea bass can be caught on flies over deeper grass flats. The bottom here drops only one foot per mile, so you could be ten miles offshore in only ten feet of water. The clear water allows the seagrass to grow, and catching seabass with a fly rod in this situation is easy.

During the fall and winter months Spanish mackerel can come through in miles-across schools, dimpling the surface as they feed on glass minnows and driving the birds nuts. Fly fishers can catch fish until they're sick of it. Although less likely, kingfish are another possibility, especially over the artificial reefs. The location of these reefs is again found in Stebbins' LORAN & GPS book.

Flies and Techniques

Mike Locklear is yet another fan of fly rod poppers. He likes them for both seatrout and redfish.

Deceivers work well on everything.

He likes the Merkin for redfish, especially on an incoming tide. The fish often tail then, digging for crabs. A well placed cast is almost a sure hookup.

Mike told me of a fly I hadn't heard of, the Wakulla Wobbler, originally designed by Ted Forsgren. This "fly" is actually a gold colored spoon made from epoxy. Mike said he thought this fly would soon be marketed by Orvis. Evidently it is deadly on reds.

Large weighted flies are used over stingrays for spring cobia, especially around the markers of the Chassahowitzka National Wildlife Refuge. Eelworms and tarpon bunnies in dark colors are good. These need to be fished on a nine- or ten weight rod equipped with a monocore line. If the fish appear to be selective, or are out of range, they can be teased up with a six inch black or brown plastic worm on a 1/4 ounce jig head. Cut the hook off the jig. The cobia will strike and follow the worm right into range of the fly rodder.

For tarpon Mike keeps his fly selection simple. He wants his fly to have color contrast with the bottom. Over light sand bottom he likes purple, brown, or black. Over dark grass bottom he likes red and white or yellow and orange. Depending on the depth of the water a floating or intermediate line is used.

Most Homosassa tarpon fishermen use twelve-weight tackle. Big fish are the rule rather than the exception. Eighty and 100 pound fish are called rats and the truly serious world record seekers just break them off so when a big fish comes by the angler will be ready! Most fly fishers appreciate the lively battle provided by these smaller fish, however. Heavy tackle is needed to take the fight to the fish and whip it so it can be released in good shape.

If you're fortunate enough to hook one of these fish, fight it hard. No fish should be fought for over an hour, as doing so makes the chances for post-release survival very slim. Sharks love to eat tarpon! Do not remove it from the water- get your photos from the boat or get into the water to hold it if necessary. Let the fish give someone else the same thrill it gave you!

Access
For waders- as detailed above.

For boaters- boat ramps can be found in the following places:

-MacRae's, on the Homosassa River. Use of this ramp is free, but parking is along the road and it does get crowded.

-River Haven Marina, on the Homosassa River. There is a $5.00 charge to use this ramp, but it's the best on the river and there's plenty of room to park.

-Tradewinds Motel has a ramp on the Homosassa River. They charge $2.00 to use it.

-In Bayport on the west end of SR 50 there is a county park with a boat ramp. There is no charge to use this ramp.

-In Crystal River there is a ramp at the west end of SR 44 at Fort Island Gulf Beach. There is no charge.

Fly Shops
-Nature Coast Fly Shop in Crystal River, the only game in town. 352.795-3156; www.naturecoastflyshop.com.

Boat Rentals
-River Safaris, Homosassa, 352.628.5222, 800.758.FISH; www.naturecoast.com/river/. Power-boat rentals.

-Homosassa Riverside Resort, 800.442.2040; www.homosassariverside.com. Jonboat, kayak, and canoe rentals.

-Riversport Kayaks, Homosassa, 352.621.4972 or 877.660.0929; www.flakayak.com.

-Crystal River Watersports Rental, 352.302.0757, 877.352.7667; www.visitcrystalriver.com/watersports.html. Canoe, kayak, and powerboat rentals.

-Aardvark's Florida Kayak Company, Crystal River, 352.795.5650; www.floridakayakcompany.com. This website is an excellent resource for paddlers.

Guides

Oh yes, there are a lot. Many guides work here seasonally during the tarpon run.

Captain Mike Locklear, 352.6284207,www.homosassafishing.com

Visit the website of the Homosassa Guides Association for other options; www.homosassaguidesassociation.com, or call the Nature Coast Fly Shop.

State Parks and Other Attractions

-Crystal River NWR, 352.563.2088; http://crystalriver.fws.gov. This 46 acre refuge provides a wintering area for manatees.

-Chassahowitzka NWR, 352.563.7961; http://chassahowitzka.fws.gov. The refuge consists of coastal saltmarsh, shallow bays, tidal streams, and rivers, mangrove islands, and coastal maritime hammock.

-Homosassa Springs State Wildlife Park, 9225 West Fish Bowl Drive, Homosassa 32646. 352.628.5354. See manatees, bears, bobcats, fish of all kinds, and other wildlife displays.

Accommodations

-McRae's of Homosassa, 352.628.2602.

-Riverside Inn, 352.628.2474.

-Homosassa Springs Area Chamber of Commerce, 352.628.4615; http://homosassaspringsareachamberofcommerce.visualnet.com/.

-Citrus County Chamber of Commerce, 352.795.3149; www.citruscountychamber.com.

Cedar Key

Many folks would argue that Cedar Key is one of the most beautiful areas in Florida. A quaint small town with a lot of artists, historic buildings, and old time Florida charm, the area around this key also attracts a lot of birds and wildlife, fishermen, and other lovers of the outdoors.

Jim Dupre, famous for the Dupre Spoon Fly, answered my questions about the fly fishing opportunities in this area in the original edition. Much of his commentary still remains valid, and is included. Tommy Thompson, a fly guide who fishes much of the Nature Coast, rounded out the current edition.

Opportunities for the Do It Yourself Fly Fisher

-<u>Inshore wading</u>: Wading is not recommended in most of the Cedar Key region because of the soft, marshy bottom.
-<u>Hand Powered Boat</u>: If you use a canoe or kayak you can access the numerous oyster bars in the backcountry, from which it is

Gulf of Mexico

Cedar Key

Seahorse Key

possible to fish on foot. By fishing the backcountry areas around Cedar Key you can target seatrout, redfish, and in the spring and summer, big black drum. You can launch at either the SR 24 ramp by the bridge out to Cedar Key, or at the end of CR 326. You'll find lots of rocks and oyster bars in both places and the water tends to be murky.

Tommy Thompson says it's possible to paddle to two islands out off of Cedar Key. The closer of the two is Atsena Otie Key. On the southeast side of this island are flats that are wadable, or you might sight fish from your boat.

The longer trip is out to Seahorse Key, about two miles out in the Gulf, a pretty good ride. There are beaches and bars, both of which can be fished on foot. Redfish move along both these keys in small schools on a rising tide, especially on the south sides. You can walk and look for them, or just stake out and wait.
-<u>Inshore boat</u>: You can also fish the backcountry out of a motor skiff. It's an easy place to bang up a motor skiff- most folks use aluminum boats. Look for moving water around the oyster bars

and you're much more likely to find fish. Although you should cast to any fish you see, you'll usually blindcast around here.

On a rising tide take your skiff to the outside islands, North Key, Seahorse Key, or Snake Key. Plenty of grass flats with clean water over them allow for excellent sightfishing opportunities for seatrout, or you may stalk tailing or waking redfish.

-<u>Along the beach</u>: there are no beaches for fishermen here.

-<u>Nearshore</u>: You will find Spanish and king mackerel, ladyfish, little tunny, bluefish, tripletail, grouper (over rock piles), sea bass, jack crevalle, and sometimes amberjack and sharks in the near shore Gulf waters. There are always bait pods during the summer, they usually have Spanish mackerel around them. You can look for diving birds, or set up a chum line and wait to see what shows up. Cobia can frequently be found around the channel markers. There is a small group of offshore fly fishers from the North Florida Fly Fishers Club who fish out of Cedar Key. Most of the time they use chum to entice mackerel, kingfish, and little tunny into range.

Flies and Techniques

Dupre has developed a couple of patterns for fishing in this area which are becoming quite well known. The most famous is probably Dupre's Spoonfly, an epoxy spoon resembling a small, lightweight Johnson Minnow. He says the flash and vibrations this lure makes enables the fish to find it from quite a distance away, even in the murky backcountry waters.

Jim uses another epoxy fly, simply a larger version of the MOE flies bonefishermen use in the Florida Keys. Dupre's version of this fly is about three inches long.

Another favorite is the seaducer in red and white or red and yellow, but Jim prefers his with lead eyes. He strongly believes redfish like picking up their meals from the bottom. The lead eyes sink the fly into the strike zone quickly, and produce an up-and-down motion when stripped that the fish find appealing.

He says folks fishing the oysters in the backcountry should blind-cast with flies that bump the bottom like the Clouser minnow, or the Spoonfly fished on a sinking line.

During the winter months try to find deep holes in the backcountry areas. These deep spots act as thermal refuges and they will quite literally fill up with fish. Use a weighted fly, such as the Clouser deep minnow.

Eight months of the year you can find reds, sometimes in big schools, waking and tailing over the grass flats on the outside. You must find clear water in order to do this, most easily done around the outside islands mentioned earlier. At lower tide phases it's quite possible to get out of the boat and wade, always an excellent strategy when the fish are spooky. Don't expect a firm bottom- you'll sink in a little.

Tommy Thompson says, "I like to keep it simple. For redfish a chartreuse Clouser minnow is my personal favorite, with a black Clouser minnow a close second. Out on the mackerel grounds a chartreuse Clouser minnow is absolutely number one. Back inshore, I'll use Redfish Candy sometimes, or the Dupre Spoon Fly.

"Redfish will eat anything you put in front of them if they're hungry. The big trick for a lot of people is getting it in front of them."

Access

For waders: there is almost none. During the winter you can walk out on bars at low tide from the CR 326 ramp at the Shell Mound. Cast into holes and flowing current around the ends of oyster bars for trout and reds.

-For boaters: The crude ramp on CR 326 north of Cedar Key is usable only by small boats. You can of course launch your canoe/kayak there. Another small ramp suitable for canoes/kayaks is at the first bridge going out to Cedar Key. There are loads of oysters, and fish, in this area. Dupre suggests trying in the #4 channel. The first bridge from the mainland going out to Cedar Key crosses this channel.

In Cedar Key itself you'll easily find a good ramp at the boat basin since much of the town is built around it. Put in here to fish either outside or in the backcountry.

Fly Shops
-Nature Coast Fly Shop in Crystal River, 352.795.3171; www.naturecoastflyshop.com.
-The Tackle Box in Gainesville, 352.372.1791; www.tackleboxfishingteam.com.

Guides
Not many work out of Cedar Key. Jim Dupre is semi-retired.
-Capt. Tommy Thompson, 888.843.9949; www.twotree.net/tommy.

Boat Rentals
-Cedar Key Island Hopper Boat Rentals, 352;949;0200; www.cedarkeyislandhopper.com/rentals/rentals.html. Powerboat rentals.
-Adventure Outpost, 815 NW Santa Fe Blvd (Hwy 441), High Springs, 32643, 386.454.0611; www.adventureoutpost.net. These folks are about an hour's drive from Cedar Key, renting both canoes and kayaks.

State Parks and Other Attractions
Cedar Key is an attraction in itself. The Cedar Key State Museum is off SR 24 on Museum Drive. Visit the official Cedar Key website (www.cedarkey.org) for more information on what to see and do there
-Waccasassa Bay State Preserve and the adjoining Cedar Key Scrub State Preserve account for almost 35,000 of wild lands, including extensive areas of salt marshes and tidal creeks. A primitive campsite is accessible only by canoe/kayak. This area lies nine miles east of Cedar Key on SR 24. The phone number: Waccasassa Bay State Preserve/Cedar Key Scrub State Reserve, 352.543.5567.
Information about all state parks can be found online at www.floridastateparks.org.

Accommodations
Contact the Cedar Key Chamber of Commerce, PO Box 610, Cedar Key 32625, 352.543.5600; www.cedarkey.org.

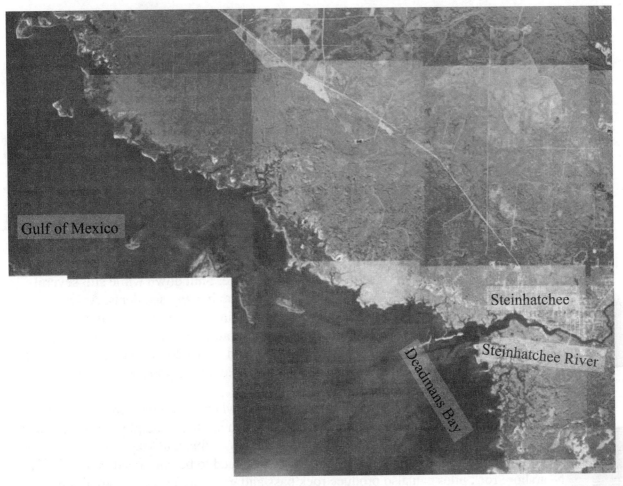

Gulf of Mexico

Steinhatchee

Steinhatchee River

Deadmans Bay

Steinhatchee

Steinhatchee might have the least developed fishery in Florida. "Steinhatchee is one of the last undeveloped clods of dirt in Florida," says local guide Sam LeNeave. "Fishing here is as pristine as you will find in this state." If you look at the photo above it is quite clear that there are miles upon miles of undeveloped shorelines. All these miles of undeveloped coastline offer the angler lots of places to explore where most of the time he is unlikely to see another angler. There are lots of rocks in the shallows here, offering the fish a haven and the unwary fisherman an accident if he fails to exercise due caution, or if his luck is bad.

Fish species here are similar to the areas north and south: reds and trout inshore, tarpon in season, cobia, blues, mackerel, ladyfish, grouper, and more farther out into the Gulf. There's a lot of open water and you may make a lot of blind casts, but when conditions are good sight fishing for redfish here is as good as or better than anywhere else in the state.

Opportunities for the Do It Yourself Fly Fisher
-<u>Wading</u>: If you don't have a boat there isn't any wading available. Kayak rentals are available.
-<u>Hand Powered Boat</u>: Many fine opportunities await the paddler. Lots of creeks enter the Gulf along this shoreline. Paddlers can catch reds and trout to the north of the mouth of the Stein-hatchee River where there is a mass of oyster reefs. If the weather allows you can paddle along the Gulf shore to either the north or south of the river's mouth. Dallas Creek and Hagan's Cove

177

lie north of Steinhatchee. Rocky Creek and Cow Creek, south of the river mouth by Pepperfish Key, are other good areas to try. The "Road to Nowhere" gives easy access to these areas. All of these areas are productive. The bottom in all of these areas is hard, even though the grass is lush, and once you reach the fishing area it is very easy to wade should you so desire.

For the truly motivated there is a paddling trail that runs for about 100 miles along the coast from St. Marks to the Suwannee River. Visit www.florida-outdoors.com/bigbend.htm for more information.

-Inshore Boat: For boaters the opportunities inshore are unlimited. You can go in either direction. You must exercise caution as there are uncharted rock piles all through the shallows. Sam LeNeave says, "I've been fishing Steinhatchee for 17 years and I still find rocks I didn't know were there. Boaters should run out of the river following the channel markers to marker two or three before turning either north (0 degree compass heading) or south (180 degree compass heading).

"The depth of the water increases at a very modest foot per mile here. Run as far as you intend to and then start to head due east, but slow down to idle. Shut down while still several hundred yards off the shoreline. It's best to pole in to avoid having any accidents. At low tide on a spring tide the bottom will be exposed out off the shoreline for 200 or 300 yards."

The principle fish species will be redfish, but trout of all sizes will also be found. From March into June cobia will follow active stingrays. You could find a 20 or 30 pound fish in 18 inches of water, its tail sticking up out of the water. Actually any time you see an active ray there could be fish on it, if not cobia then reds or trout.

-Nearshore: Nearshore fishing here is much the same as elsewhere along this stretch of coast. Spanish mackerel, ladyfish, little tunny, crevalle, and bluefish are the principle species, most easily found under diving birds. They can all be chummed up. Cobia and king mackerel will be encountered sometimes, although kings will almost always need to be chummed up.

Nearshore rock piles can also produce rock bass and grouper. These fish are quite aggressive, so if you can find a rock in eight or ten feet of water, especially during the cooler months, some blind casting around it may produce a very tasty surprise or two.

-Along the Beach: There are no beaches here.

Flies and Techniques

Sam likes the Dupre Spoon Fly. "I am sold on this product. It's well made and it works extremely well," he says. "My favorite color is gold, it seems to outfish all of the others.

"East Cut Flies, a Texas company, makes a small gold colored popper that the reds and trout just love. Deceivers, Seaducers, bunker patterns, all of them work, but only in natural colors. Nothing flashy, no pinks, no limes. Browns, blacks, dark greens, they all work well.

"I mostly look for water movement, something contrary to what all of the other water is doing at the time. You have to learn to identify your target, to differentiate the reds from the much more numerous mullet. The reds come in groups of all different sizes, from singles to small groups to schools with 200 or 300 fish. The reds here are not spooky at all, you can fish a school for hours sometimes. There's so little fishing pressure here the fish haven't learned what boats are.

"When you find a big school like this the best fly to use is a Clouser Minnow in a natural color combination, tan and cream, brown and tan, something like that.

"The redfish range in size from about four pounds at the low end to 10 or 12 pounds at the upper end. The quantity of fish has been climbing steadily too, and we're seeing more schools than we ever used to. Trout come in all sizes, and trout over 25 inches are becoming much more common.

"I like to catch a low spring tide in the morning. If I could pick any day to fish I'd get out there about 7:00 am for a low tide of 9:00 am. I'd fish the falling water until slack tide, when there's not much activity, and then would push back in with the fish with the rising water.

"At high tide you need to get right up against the shoreline and work creek mouths and rocky points. There's a lot of blind casting then, but it can still be productive. That when I really like Dupre's Spoon Fly or the East Cut popper."

Access
For waders: none available.
For boaters:
-Steinhatchee Boat Ramp, Valentine Road and CR358 on the Steinhatchee River.
-Sea Hag Marina. They will launch your boat with a fork lift, for a fee. Recommended by Sam LeNeave.

Fly Shops
-Nature Coast Fly Shop in Crystal River, 352.795.3171; www.naturecoastflyshop.com.
-The Tackle Box in Gainesville, 352.372.1791; www.tackleboxfishingteam.com.

Guides
-Capt. Sam LeNeave, 352.374.4003; www.flyfisherfla.com.
-Capt. Tommy Thompson, 888.843.9949; www.twotree.net/tommy.

Boat Rentals
-Wood's Gulf Breeze Marina, 352.498.3948. Powerboat rentals.
-Ideal Marina, 498.3877. Powerboat rentals.
-River Haven Marina, 352.498.0709. Powerboat and kayak rentals. Damon will give kayakers shuttles to productive fishing areas. They also offer pontoon/kayak fishing trips on the flats.
-Pace's Cottages, 352.498.0061. Powerboat rentals.
-Sea Hag Marina, 352.498.3008. Powerboat rentals.
-Westwind Fish Camp 352.498.5254. Powerboat rentals.
-Steinhatchee Outpost, 800-589-1541; www.steinhatcheeoutpost.com. Canoe and kayak rentals and more.

State Parks and Other Attractions
While there are several state wildlife management areas in the vicinity, there are no state parks in the immediate area.

Accommodations
-The Steinhatchee Network has accommodation information online at http://steinhatcheenetwork.com.
-Another website with Steinhatchee accommodation information is www.steinhatchee.biz.
-The Steinhatchee Landing Resort is by far the nicest place to stay in town, 352.498.3513; www.steinhatcheelanding.com.

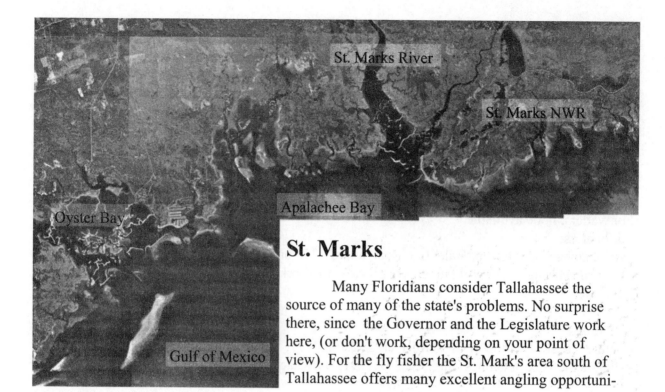

St. Marks

Many Floridians consider Tallahassee the source of many of the state's problems. No surprise there, since the Governor and the Legislature work here, (or don't work, depending on your point of view). For the fly fisher the St. Mark's area south of Tallahassee offers many excellent angling opportuni-

ties far removed from the halls of the Legislature, if not by actual distance then certainly by their laid back southern ambiance.

The St. Marks National Wildlife Refuge contains a good portion of this coast. The Refuge faces out onto Apalachee Bay and the Gulf of Mexico. The rest of the coast in this area looks as if it were part of the refuge- very little coastal development has occurred anywhere along here. Extensive *Spartina* grass marshes with points and bays, tidal creeks and oysters, rock piles and grass flats, and the open Gulf, all beckon the fly fisher. It's a good area. Capt. Dave Lear supplied the information for this edition.

Opportunities for the Do It Yourself Fly Fisher

-Inshore Wading: There aren't a great many areas for the non-boater to gain access around these parts. Wakulla Beach is one. Trout, redfish, and occasional Spanish mackerel and bluefish can be found over the grass flats here. Another wade area lies off of Lighthouse Point at the mouth of the St. Marks River, where the same species are available. One caveat– there are a lot of alligators in the St. Marks National Wildlife Refuge, so be careful.

-Hand Powered Boat: There are lots of opportunities for folks with hand powered boats. Even a boat as simple as a canoe will give you a lot more flexibility to fish in the creeks, sloughs, and bayous in the refuge for redfish and trout. Certainly the numerous oyster bars at the mouth of the St. Marks River usually hold fish.

It should be obvious from the above photo that there are a lot of protected areas for a hand powered boat to work in effectively. The habitat is principally *Spartina* grass salt marsh with numerous rocks and oyster reefs. The bottom is usually hard, making for good wading should that be desired. Principle fish species will be seatrout and redfish, with flounder, bluefish, jack crevalle, ladyfish, black drum, and other species on occasion. You of course have the same access that the waders do, as well as the boat ramps. Remember the alligators!

-Inshore boat: With a power boat, even more choices await. Nine miles of grass flats extend to the east of Coast Guard Light at the mouth of the St. Marks. These are known locally as the East Flats. Five miles of flats extend to the west, known as the West Flats. On these flats, depending on the time of year, you may find any or all of the following species- cobia, redfish, seatrout, Spanish mackerel, bluefish, and some large tarpon.

Evidently the Air Force used the West Flats as a bombing target during World War ll. The craters the bombs made are still there, sandy depressions in an otherwise lush bed of grass. These craters often hold both reds and trout.

There are many rock piles in the area. THESE PRESENT A HAZARD TO NAVIGATION! Keep your eyes open and speed to a minimum until you learn your way around. Most rocks are within a mile and a half of shore. The rocks attract fish of course. Gray Mare Rock (LORAN 14507.1, 46435.2) is found about halfway between the St. Marks and Aucilla River mouths, on the east flats. This rock clears the water surface at half tide or lower.

Another well-known rock on east flat is Blacks Rock (LORAN 14496.3, 46444.5), found about four miles east of St. Marks. Although this rock has a sand patch around it, the surrounding area is all grass. This is a good one to find, because to the north of it is the Rock Garden (LORAN 14459.0, 46443.2), a number of rocks sticking up from the grass beds.

The area of Deep Creek and Palmetto Island produces a good number of redfish. Slough Island and Stoney Bayou also produce. Use caution, there are numerous rocks, with many just below the surface of the water. This area produces best in the early morning on a moving tide. For those able to access the real skinny water, try Stony Bayou Pool and East River Pool

Lighthouse Point produces good catches of trout and redfish, with an occasional flounder. In mid to late spring fish this area for cobia. Those mariners new to the area should do their exploring on low tide. This helps reveal the area's underwater obstructions that you wouldn't otherwise see and gives the added assistance of the incoming tide should you get stuck.
-From the Beach: except for the areas mentioned in the wading section there are no beaches in this area. If you want to fish from the beach the best place locally is St. George Island.
-Nearshore: Two miles out from the light at the St. Marks River mouth is the Bird Tower. This piece of structure often attracts and holds fish, especially cobia.

Straight out from the mouth of the Aucilla River two miles lie Cobbs Rocks (LORAN 14505.7, 46414.5). Like all the rock piles, the crabs and other creatures living on and around the rocks attract gamefish looking for a meal.

The St. Marks area has the same types of offshore fishing as other areas in the Panhandle, although you need to go out farther to find it. There are a series of 100 foot tall towers out from the lighthouse at St. Marks, the K (26 miles out, LORAN 14368.0, 46346.6), S, and O towers. These structures attract fish, including kings, cobia, barracuda, and some blackfin tuna. Small chicken dolphin will also show, especially when grass floats into the area.

At Pass Buoy #24 (12 miles south of the light house, LORAN 14443.3, 46361.8) look for balled up bait. If it's there you won't need to go any farther. The LORAN/GPS coordinates of all these structures will be found in Stebbins' book, Coastal LORAN & GPS Coordinates.

There are also numerous artificial reefs in this area. Their coordinates can be found at the following web address: www.fishingtip.com/Florida%20Stuff/Florida%20Reefs3.htm.

You can chum these areas with ground pogies or cat food for king and Spanish mackerel, and little tunny. Chumming works well. Over the reefs you never know what might show up, with grouper, snapper, and other reef fishes being a distinct possibility. In this area live bait chumming is a lot more trouble and only is slightly more effective than using a chum "soup" containing cat food, ground up bait fish, and/or frozen chum.

Flies and Techniques

Dave Lear likes the Dupre Spoonfly for redfish, especially for dark or turbid water, in gold or red. The flash attracts the fish from a distance, and the lure is quite weedless.

Another effective fly in this region is a yellow epoxy minnow with doll eyes, designed by Ed Arrington, and known locally as Mr. Ed's Minnow. This fly accounts for many big seatrout, usually when retrieved quickly.

Poppers are good for all species which will take surface lures, primarily jacks, seatrout, and redfish. Dahlberg divers and deerhair sliders are also effective.

Everyone likes the Clouser deep minnow, and Dave Lear is no exception. He prefers this fly in grey and white when fishing for mackerel of any kind.

Dave also likes deceivers, in various color combinations containing white, saying they work well for most species of fish.

He also like shrimp patterns, especially for trout. Borski's Slider is a particular favorite.

Those looking for redfish are advised to start at low tide. Slowly motor inshore until you can't go any more. The fish will work in with the rising tide. Wait until you see tailing fish and work in along with them. You can do this from your boat, or you could get out and wade, as you prefer.

In the event that the reds don't show, find a rock pile and blind-cast around it with a popper. Remember to approach these rocks quietly or you'll spook all the fish before you ever get a chance to cast.

Should this not work either, try drifting and blindcasting across the west flats. Work the potholes well. You should catch some trout this way, and possibly other species as well.

Dave says that during the winter time the fish tend to be up in the creeks and rivers. As the weather warms, the outside areas are more productive. Nearshore fishing is best during the spring and fall months, when the mackerel, jacks, and little tunny are most numerous.

During the spring and early summer more and more cobia are showing up on the flats. Due to the dark bottom these fish are hard to target; however, it would behoove anyone fishing here at this time of year to keep a cobia rod rigged.

Lear further says that the rocks from Stoney Bayou east are bad, with rock many piles not shown on the charts. He advises that anyone not familiar with these waters not run on plane here until they learn their way around, which may take quite a while.

Fish, trout, redfish, and cobia, are found around all of these rocks. Work this area with a pushpole or trolling motor.

Access

For waders: Wakulla Beach is reached by taking SR 363 south from Tallahassee, then heading west on US 98-30. After crossing the bridge over the Wakulla River take the first road on the left. Follow this road to the beach.

To reach the lighthouse, take SR 363 south from Tallahassee, but head east on 98-30. Go south on CR 59 all the way to the end. There's a charge to get in.

For boaters: canoes can be launched in many different places around here, including those locations listed above for waders. Consult DeLorme's Florida Atlas and Gazetteer for details.

You can find boat ramps at the following places:

-on the Aucilla River. SMALL BOATS ONLY. Take US 98 and take a right about a mile and a half east of the bridge over the Aucilla River, then follow the signs. This river is difficult and dangerous to run because of all the rocks and oysters.

-there is a ramp for small boats at the St. Marks Refuge on CR 59.

-in St. Marks there are three ramps. One is at Shields Marina, where fuel, rest rooms, and a marina store will be found. ($)

Another ramp is at Shell Island Marina, which has similar facilities. ($)

Lastly in St. Marks you can find a ramp without facilities at San Marcos de Appalache. Keep in mind that the Wakulla River and the area around Shell Island are manatee zones- slow speed only.

Fly Shops

Kevin's Fine Outdoor Gear and Apparel, Tallahassee, 850.386.5544; www.kevinscatalog.com. The Fly Shop of Tallahassee, 850.386.3474; www.flyshoponline.com.

Boat Rentals

-Lighthouse Central Canoe and Bait, SR 98, Newport, 850.925.9904. Canoe, kayak, and power-boat rentals.

-Riverside Café and Recreational Rentals, 69 Riverside Drive, St. Marks, 850.925.5668. Canoe rentals Monday through Friday 10 am to 10 pm.

Guides

Capt. Dave Lear, 850.216.1951. Dave had been guiding here for nine years, and is an editor at large for Salt Water Sportsman magazine.

State Parks and Other Attractions

-St. Marks National Wildlife Refuge, 850.925.6121; http://saintmarks.fws.gov. Over 65,000 acres of wild lands, including extensive salt and brackish marshes.

-Apalachicola National Forest, 850.942.9300. Over 500,000 acres south and west of Tallahassee. Someplace to explore when you get sick of catching fish. Includes the Leon Sinks Geological Area, where there are more than a dozen different sinkholes. Don't fall in!

-Wakulla Springs State Park, Wakulla Springs, 850.922.3632. Wakulla Springs is one of the world's largest, deepest, and clearest springs. This place is definitely worth a visit, especially for a refreshing swim after a hot day in the boat.

Information about all state parks can be found online at www.floridastateparks.org.

Accommodations

The Leon County Tourist Development Council can be reached at 850.413.9200 or 800.628.2866; www.co.leon.fl.us/visitors.

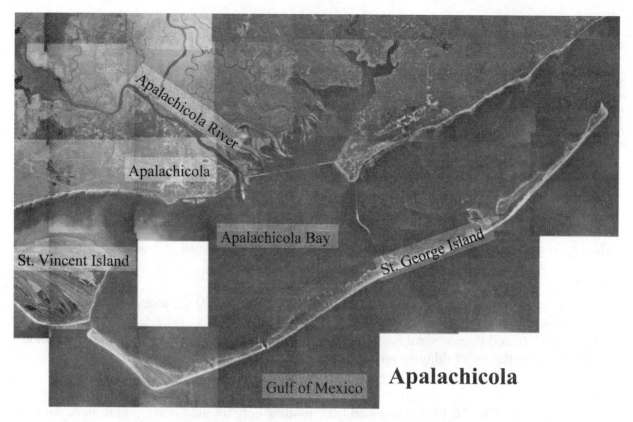

Apalachicola

No matter what style of saltwater fly fishing you prefer, it's likely available in the Apalachicola area, known as the Forgotten Coast. Tidal rivers, salt marsh, plentiful oyster bars (Apalachicola oysters are famous for their size and sweetness), flats, beaches, the bay, and the open Gulf are all here. Fish species are the same as along the rest of Florida's Panhandle Gulf coast. Inshore, redfish and trout are targeted all year long. Pompano, flounder, black drum, bluefish, crevalle jacks, Spanish mackerel, and tarpon appear seasonally. Gulfside, Spanish and king mackerel, cobia, tripletail, crevalle, little tunny, and again tarpon, show up at various times throughout the year. Striped bass are available in the Apalachicola River during the winter.

Speaking of the river, it delivers a steady stream of nutrients into Apalachicola Bay, making it one of the most productive estuaries in Florida.

Capt. Chris Robinson and Cathy Robinson, owner of Robinson Brothers Guide Service, were kind enough to share the following information.

Opportunities for the Do It Yourself Fly Angler

-<u>Wading</u>: Anywhere along US 98 you can stop and park, from Shell Point by St. Marks to Mexico Beach, is a place you can wade fish. The bottom is usually hard, making for easy walking. As long as you are not in the immediate vicinity of the Apalachicola River mouth the water is usually clear. Good areas to try include inside of Lighthouse Point and between Carrabelle Beach and Yent's Bayou.

Additionally, there are wadable flats along the causeway to St. George Island, and along the mainland sides of St. George Island and Dog Island (you need a boat to get here). The Rattlesnake Cove and East Cove areas in St. George Island State Park are good places to try. Principle fish species will be trout and redfish, with flounder, jacks, pompano, bluefish, and other species showing up depending on how good your luck is.

184

-Hand Powered Boat: If you bring a kayak or canoe here you might think you've gone to heaven. There are lots of places to use a hand powered boat, beginning with all the places just mentioned in the wading section. You have the bay, around all of the islands (which are particularly good), the Apalachicola River, the Carrabelle River, the New River, all the associated salt marshes, and you should be getting the idea. There are lots of places to paddle.

The truly motivated can paddle all the way from Apalachicola to Panama City through the Intracoastal Waterway.

-Inshore Boat: Good access is available for the boater, and there's a lot of variety. Cathy Robinson told me that you could spend seven days here and have seven completely different fishing trips, never fishing the same water twice. You can fish in either the river mouth, East Bay, St. George Sound, Apalachicola Bay, inside the islands, or the Indian Pass area. Her guides fish 120 miles of coastline. Where do you start?

Weather has something to do with where you fish, as does the season. In general, points, passes, and the smaller river mouths are all good places to try. Oyster bars frequently produce fish if water is flowing over them. The inside of St. George and Dog Islands can also be good, especially with a south wind.

Birds will indicate the presence of mackerel, bluefish, ladyfish, and crevalle, usually in the open bay. Reds, trout, and pompano will usually be close to the shoreline.

-Nearshore: On the Gulf side of the islands there are shoals, wrecks, and artificial reefs, as well as the passes between the islands. Like everywhere else along the Panhandle coast, chumming over one of these structures will pull fish up to the boat where you can cast flies to them. The fish include snapper, grouper, amberjack, dolphin, and of course king and Spanish mackerel, and little tunny. Where are these structures? A visit to www.neilbranch.com/reef.htm will list some of the bottom structure off of St. George Island. As always, Stebbins's Coastal LORAN and GPS Coordinates will have a complete list.

During the late spring and early summer the cobia come through on their annual westward migration. The fish are heading west, and could be right against the beach or out a half mile to a mile. Large, heavy, hard to cast flies are used for this work. Minimum rod size is a ten-weight.

Apalachicola has a directed tarpon fly fishery. There are enough fish here all summer long to target them with a better than reasonable prospect of success. While some of the fish are in the bay, others work along the beaches, similar to what's available from Tampa south. Minimum rod size is a twelve-weight.

In the spring and fall there's a run of bull redfish along the beaches.

-Along the Beach: You can drive out to St. George Island. The beaches here offer excellent surf fishing, best on a north wind. The entire east end of the island is in the state park. There are always whiting here. Pompano are best in the spring and fall. Reds, trout, bluefish, mackerel, and the usual cast of characters may appear. If the wind is down and the water is clear sight fishing is your best approach. With a south wind and dirty water you're probably better off fishing the bay side.

The other islands also offer excellent beach fishing, but if you don't have a boat you won't be going there.

Flies and Techniques

Chris Robinson had this to say about the flies he likes and how he uses them: "We have redfish year-round. In the springtime we get runs of pompano, Spanish mackerel, cobia, big 20 to 30 pound jack crevalle. The tripletail come in a little later, early in the summer.

"In the bay we're fishing around oyster bars, and on turtle grass or shoal grass flats. Our basic patterns for redfish include Clouser Minnows, Dupre Spoon Flies if we're fishing in heavy grass, and poppers sometimes. We fish in water depths ranging from inches of water, tailing water, five or six inches deep, up to water that's two or three feet deep. The best all around fly for redfish here is definitely the Clouser. Use the size lead eyes you need to get it down, depending on water depth and current.

"You can't forget about bendbacks either. When the fish are up real shallow you need something that's not going to spook them when it lands, something you can slide right through the grass until you get it in front of them.

"If the water is real clear I like chartreuse and white or garnet and gold. In dark water I like dark browns or black. On the beach side of the barrier islands we get a lot of reds, and they tend to be big ones. They eat almost anything that will get down to them, color doesn't seem to matter very much. Crabs like the Merkin are good, and so are big Clousers. In the spring and fall they get in close to the beach. They'll be in three to eight feet of water, but the bottom is light and the water is clear and you can see them. They're schooled up, big fish, 15 to 40 pounds, just kind of milling around. You just run into them sometimes.

"We get a lot of trout in the spring and fall. The big trout come up shallow on the sand flats during the spring. Big streamer flies like Deceivers or Seaducers seem to work best, but a slider is a killer sometimes. Any chunky flies that look like a good meal will work.

"When those big trout get up shallow they're very tough. Wading is probably the best way to get them if you can find a concentration.

"The schoolie trout get up on the grass flats and you can get a bunch throwing Clouser Minnows on an intermediate or sink-tip line.

"For pompano little crab patterns or Clouser Minnows trimmed short work best. Pompano like those small flies. They can be sight fished at times when the sun is right, if you get a good incoming tide.

"I don't go out into the Gulf much more than a mile, and usually only when I see birds diving. They could be over mackerel, or bluefish, or little tunny. They'll be feeding on glass minnows or bay anchovies. You want to match the hatch, especially size-wise. Any little fly will work. This usually happens in the fall and spring.

"When I'm fishing in the bay, sight fishing, I like the last couple hours of the falling tide and the start of the rise, for about two hours into the rise. On the high tide we just blind cast and tell jokes! Actually the reds will get up into the Spartina grass on a good high tide and you can see them and cast spoon flies at them.

"We get tarpon in the bay in the summer time. We fish them mostly with a floating line. When they get into the passes then we go to a fast sinking line, 450 or 500 grain shooting heads. We use the standard tarpon patterns, the Cockroach, Black Death, black and purple. We mostly cast to rolling fish or fish crashing bait.

"The tarpon come in after menhaden schools. We get out away from the pogie schools and wait for the tarpon, trying to intercept them before they reach the bait. Once they get into the bait there's so much mud, so much commotion, and so much competition, that you can fish them there but it just won't work. There's so much activity with the sharks, sailcats, and everything else, getting a tarpon bite is like picking a winning Lotto number.

"The water clarity varies. We like stained water because the fish eat better. As long as it's clear enough to see them that's good. When it gets too clear they get lockjaw and it's hard to get a bite. We have clear water beach fishing for tarpon and it's definitely tougher fishing.

"We get stripers in the winter, a pretty good fishery. They're not huge, but there are a lot of them. They run from about three pounds to 10 or 12. It's a lot of fun, they take care of the wintertime blues, when it's too cold to do anything else."

Access
-For Waders: much has already been discussed, but various access points are available along US 89, along the St. George Island Causeway, and on St. George Island. Hand powered boaters can use most of these same access points.
-For Boaters: Boat ramps are available at the following locations:
-Alligator Point Campground, SR 370, Alligator Point.
-County Boat Ramp, SR 370, Alligator Point.
-Alligator Point Marina, SR 370, Alligator Point.
-Battery Park & Marina, Market St. & Bay Ave. on Apalachicola Bay, Apalachicola.
-Bay City Marina & Lodge, Bay City Rd., on Apalachicola River, Apalachicola.
-Scipio Creek Marina, Market St., Apalachicola.
-C. Quarters Marina, Hwy 98 on Carrabelle River, Carrabelle.
-Carrabelle City Ramp, 4th St. W & US 98, Carrabelle.
-Carrabelle Marina, Hwy. 98 on the Carrabelle River, Carrabelle.
-City Waterfront Area, Marine St. & Kelsey Ct., Carrabelle.
-The Moorings, 1000 US 98, Carrabelle.
-Ferry Dock Ramp, SR 65 on East Bay, Eastpoint.
-Sportsman's Lodge & Marina, off US 98 on East Bay, Eastpoint.
-County Boat Ramp, Corner G1A & SR 300, St. George Island.
-Dr. Julian G. Bruce, St. George Island State Park, St. George Island.
-St. Theresa Wayside Park & Boat Ramp, off US.98, St. Theresa.

Boat Rentals
-Jeanni's Journeys, St. George Island, 850.927.3259; www.sgislandjourneys.com. Canoe and kayak rentals.
-Island Outfitters, St. George Island, 850.927.2604; www.bayboatrental.com. Powerboat rentals.

Fly Shops
Forgotten Coast Outfitters, 94 Market Street, Apalachicola 32329; 850.653.9669.

Guides
Robinson Brothers Guide Service, 850.653.8896; www.flaredfish.com.

State Parks and Other Attractions
-St. Vincent National Wildlife Refuge, 850.653.8808 ; http://southeast.fws.gov/StVincent.
-St. George Island State Park, 850.670.2111, nine miles of undeveloped beach. Camping available. Information about all state parks can be found online at www.floridastateparks.org.

Accommodations
Apalachicola Bay Chamber of Commerce, 850.653.9419; www.apalachicolabay.org.

St. Joseph Bay

St. Joseph Bay lies along the edge of the Florida panhandle in a lightly populated area of the state between Panama City and Apalachicola. No freshwater rivers enter the bay, so it receives very little runoff from the land. The north end of the bay is wide open to the Gulf of Mexico, so it "flushes" extremely well. As a result, the water is extremely clear. This just may be the most pristine bay in Florida.

St. Joseph Bay has other unique features. Of all the bays in the panhandle, only this one runs north and south. You can usually find a fishing spot protected from the prevailing winds. St. Joe Bay is deep- over 30 feet in places. It attracts and holds big fish as a result. Rich grass flats line the entire periphery of the bay, supporting an excellent shallow water fishery. Primary targets will usually be seatrout and redfish, but flounder, Spanish mackerel, bluefish, ladyfish, jack crevalle, sometimes tarpon and more will all be available.

Captain John Guinta provided the information in the original edition. For this version, Capt. Trey Landry shared his knowledge.

Opportunities for the Do It Yourself Fly Fisher

-Inshore Wading: You can wade on both sides of the bay, and there is a lot of wading area. The bottom tends to be hard, until you get down near the south end of the bay, where more sediment has collected, making the bottom softer.

From the boat ramp in Port St. Joe south for about three miles lush grass beds parallel the easy access from SR 30. The bottom has a series of troughs which run parallel to the shore

188

line, and which stair-step out into deeper water. Because of the deep water access it's possible to wade fish for cobia here! Redfish and seatrout will be the usual targets, however. Some truly big sharks work this shoreline, and there are plenty of stingrays (which many species of gamefish will follow). Keep your eyes open and keep those feet shuffling.

North of Port St. Joe there is some wading access off of SR 30, best with an east wind.

Along the west side of the bay there are seven miles of wadable flats, accessible through St. Joseph Peninsula State Park. In order to get to most of the fishing spots you'll have to be willing to hike a while. Access here requires more effort.

-Hand Powered Boat: You can drop a canoe or a kayak into any of the wading areas just mentioned. With an east wind fish the east side of the bay to get a protected shoreline.

Before you get to the state park on the St. Joseph Peninsula there is a BP gasoline station on the right hand side. You can get access to the south end of the bay here. If you call Happy Ours Kayak at 850.229.1991, they can give you tips for other access points at the south end of the bay.

In the state park itself there is a boat ramp. With a west wind the entire shoreline along the bay in the state park is very protected. The water is clear and beautiful.

-Inshore boat: Many different species are available. Spanish and king mackerel, cobia, bluefish, sharks of all kinds, redfish, seatrout, flounder, jack crevalle, and tarpon (sometimes) all show up either on the flats or in the hole at St. Joseph's Point.

As has already been stated, grass flats 1/4 to 3/4 of a mile wide surround the entire bay. Sandy potholes in these flats attract trout and reds and while over the sand they can easily be seen, stalked, and cast to.

The islands at the south end of the bay sit in clear shallow water with thick grass beds carpeting the bottom. Reds and trout love this area and you can fish here on the windiest days.

A deep hole and strong currents at St. Joseph Point act as a natural fish magnet. If fish aren't seen on the surface you can often chum them up. Mackerel, bluefish, and cobia will ordinarily appear in the chum, but sharks are always a possibility. If you get bored with the everyday ordinary kinds of fish, use a few ladyfish to try chumming up sharks.

-Along the Beach: Along the peninsula beach you'll find good fishing for pompano, whiting, and flounder. Redfish show up sometimes. All the fish found in the bay work along the beach out toward the end of the point. With calm conditions this is all sight fishing. Use a mostly white Clouser minnow and walk along the beach, looking for fish.

You can drive out on Cape San Blas at the south end of the peninsula. Folks frequently fish for sharks out here along the sand bar which extends for miles out into the Gulf. They use a steel cable attached to a winch on the front of their four wheel drive trucks to pull the 600-700 pound brutes in. Fly fishers will have to settle for smaller quarry, such as pompano or redfish.

Also, the stretch of sand between St. Joe Beach and Mexico Beach on the mainland side offers similar opportunities.

-Nearshore: Like elsewhere in the Panhandle, king and Spanish mackerel are common all summer long. Little tunny, crevalle, and ladyfish are other common species. Tarpon put in seasonal appearances. Look for breaking fish, or use chum to lure them in.

The buoy line running out of the bay into the Gulf is a natural fish attractor. Cobia are sometimes seen swimming around the buoys, and they are excellent places to set up a chum line. Another resource are the artificial reefs set up north of St. Joseph Peninsula. Visit the website of the Mexico Beach Artificial Reef association at www.mbara.org for coordinates.

Flies and Techniques

John Guinta preferred to use poppers of any kind for as much fishing as possible-seatrout, reds, jacks, and anything else that will hit them. For subsurface work, he liked the following patterns:

-Whitlock's Baitfish in green and gray or chartreuse.

-Clouser deep minnows.

-crab patterns for redfish, especially the Merkin.

He said that in the clear water of this bay a poling tower gives a huge advantage, allowing the anglers to spot fish from quite a distance. He liked to fish the east side of the bay in the morning, and the west side in the afternoon. This allowed him to use the sun to his advantage as he tried to spot the fish.

He also said that when the stingrays are active you should work them, as redfish, cobia, and even big seatrout will cruise over them looking for an easy meal.

John said that the seatrout here are the largest found in this part of the state, often reaching five and six pounds and sometimes reaching eight or nine.

Trey Landry says, "The fly of choice in this light colored water is a light colored Clouser Minnow. White with either a little chartreuse or a little brown thrown in will catch most of the fish we have here, pompano, flounder, trout, redfish, just about everything. The Clousers work both in the bay and along the beaches.

"The Dahlberg Diver is real nice. I also like saltwater Muddlers on anything in the bay. I like them in fairly dark colors. I tie a lot of mine with a three inch bunny tail, it looks like an injured baitfish swimming along the top. Tarpon like to eat these.

"Other effective tarpon flies here include the Black Death and the Cockroach. It gets endless with the flies if you let it.

"The Dupre Spoon Fly is a great go to fly in the bay, especially on the redfish."

Access

For Waders- as described earlier.

For Boaters- You can find three boat ramps on the bay:

-In Port St. Joe there a ramp downtown, just south of the old paper mill.

-Six miles south of town there's a ramp at Presnel's Fish Camp, on SR 30. ($)

-On the west side of the bay there's a ramp it St. Joseph Peninsula State Park.

There is also a ramp up in Mexico Beach at Marquardt's Marine. This isn't convenient to the bay, but does give access to the Gulf.

Fly Shops

-Half Hitch Tackle, 850.227.7100.

-Blue Water Outriggers, 850.229.1100; www.bluewateroutriggers.com.

Boat Rentals

-Seahorse Water Safaris, Inc, Port St. Joe. 850.227.1099; www.seahorsewatersafaris.com. Powerboat and kayak rentals.

-Happy Ours Kayak and Canoe Rentals, 775 Cape San Blas Road, Cape San Blas, 850.229.1991; www.happyourskayak.com.

Guides

Capt. Trey Landry, 850.227.9393; www.captaintrey.com

State Parks and Other Attractions

St. Joseph Peninsula State Park, 850.227.1327. This park has 2,516 acres surrounded by the Gulf of Mexico and St. Joe Bay. The highest sand dunes in the state are found here along the miles of beach. Camping is available, and there are cabins for rent and a boat ramp here. Information about all state parks can be found online at www.floridastateparks.org.

Accommodations

The Gulf County Chamber of Commerce can be reached at 850.227.1223; www.gulfchamberofcommerce.com.

It's entirely possible to stand up and fish from a canoe. Here a pair of anglers prepares to cast to shallow water a redfish.

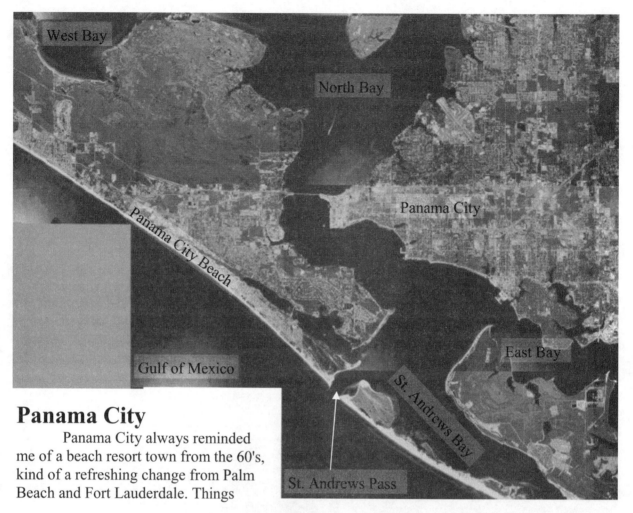

Map labels: West Bay, North Bay, Panama City, Panama City Beach, Gulf of Mexico, East Bay, St. Andrews Bay, St. Andrews Pass

Panama City

Panama City always reminded me of a beach resort town from the 60's, kind of a refreshing change from Palm Beach and Fort Lauderdale. Things moved slowly here, and the people were friendlier, and there was little traffic and congestion. It was nice! My understanding is that the face of Panama City is now changing rapidly though, going from a Mom and Pop feeling to that of condos and big hotels.

Panama City boasts of lots of attractions for the angler. The St. Andrew Bay system is an extensive, sprawling body of water which reaches well inland, and exceeds 30 miles from east to west. Panama City Beach faces the Gulf of Mexico, with all of its piscatorial attractions. Plenty of places to stay, and eat, and lots to do make it a great place to visit for any non-anglers in the family. The beaches are among the finest in Florida.

My informant for this section in the original edition was "Captain Blood"- the late Mike Ware. For this edition I interviewed Capt. Buddy Dortch, who's been fishing this area for over 30 years.

Opportunities for the Do It Yourself Fly Fisher

-Inshore Wading: Much of the extensive shoreline of St. Andrew Bay is wadable and accessible. Most of the bay has a hard bottom, which waders always like. Some easy places for wader access to the bay include Carbury Park; along Beach Drive (US BR 98) on the south side of Panama City proper (several parking/access places here); at the flats on both sides of the north end of the Hathaway Bridge (US 98); and at the north end of the Dupont Bridge (US 98) across East Bay. You can also drive to St. Andrews State Recreation Area to wade in the Grand Lagoon and fish the Bay Point side, casting for trout and reds. In the St. Andrews State Recreation Area you can walk out to Deepwater Point to try for some Spanish mackerel. This particular fishing is best in the spring.

-Hand Powered Boat: At any of the areas just mentioned (with the exception of Deepwater Point in the state park) you can launch a hand powered boat, giving you access to more water. Additionally, any of the boat ramps in the area will give you access to other areas in the bayous, the upper bay, etc. SR 79 gives access to the west end of West Bay. CR 2321 gives access to the north end of North Bay and Deer Point Lake. These areas are particularly good in the winter for trout and reds. See the section on access.

-Inshore Boat: The large and fairly deep bay has no dangerous shoals, making it an excellent place to explore. Exploration is heartily recommended. It's divided somewhat arbitrarily into sections- St. Andrew Bay, West Bay, East Bay, and North Bay. Salt marshes and bayous surround every section of the system. These and the numerous points of land are good places to look for fish. Healthy beds of grass surround the edges of the bay, and these are good places to look for trout and reds.

Another place to look includes any structure you find. Bridges, docks, pilings, etc. will all hold both reds, trout, and you never know what else.

During the spring and fall large schools of Spanish mackerel, ladyfish, and jacks will be in the bay system. These fish tend to hold in deeper water, often near the edges of the grass flats. Look for them (or diving birds) working schools of bait.

On the southeast side of St. Andrew Bay, directly south of Panama City, the bay extends out to the Gulf behind Shell Island. This old St. Andrew Pass (now locally known as Old Pass), used before the present pass was dredged out, still allows Gulf access for shallow draft boats. You'll find many sandy shoals here, excellent places to fish for cobia, jack crevalle, redfish, seatrout, bonito, sharks, and many other species. Camelback Shoal, located about five miles northwest of the old pass, is the first of these. Located in the middle of the southern side of St. Andrew Bay between Shell Island and the main shipping channel, the water surrounding this shoal is 25 to 30 feet deep and attracts bluefish, ladyfish, Spanish mackerel, and sharks.

-From the Beach: From St. Andrews State Park west there is almost unlimited beach access all the way to Phillips Inlet and beyond. You'll find all the typical beach species available during the warmer months- pompano, whiting, Spanish mackerel, ladyfish, bluefish, jack crevalle, redfish sometimes, and blacktips and other species of sharks. The water typically is so clear that this is pure sight fishing- you walk along the beach looking for fish and do not cast until you spot them.

Another excellent trip possibility is to take the ferry boat from St. Andrews State Park over to Shell Island. Use the same technique- sight fishing from the beach. There are a lot fewer people over there so the chance of hooking up with Charles Atlas or his girlfriend is much less than it might be on Panama City Beach.

-Nearshore: Nearshore in Panama City during the spring means one thing- COBIA! Not just any cobia, either- BIG COBIA! No one around here raises an eyebrow at a 50 pound fish and triple digit specimens are caught every year. Again, most fish are caught with conventional tackle only because a directed fly rod fishery is so small.

These cobia always head west, sometimes traveling just yards off the beach in two to twenty feet of water. Keep the sun at your back when looking for these fish.

You frequently find BIG jack crevalle cruising along the coast at this time of year.

During the summer months cobia will still use flotsam and weed lines, markers and buoys, or the artificial reefs. Many other fish make the reefs their home, too. Chum, either dead or alive, will pull these reef dwellers up to the surface where the fly rodder can tangle with them. Small 20 to 30 inch amberjack in particular are plentiful and aggressive. Kingfish and little tunny are other common catches. Schoolie dolphin may show up in a chum line at any time from June on through September.

During the late summer and into the fall bull reds show up at the passes. Fishing for these fish is at its most fly rod friendly on an outgoing tide near sunset. You'll need a sinking line (400 to 600 grains) in order to be successful at this.

Flies and Techniques

Clouser deep minnows in chartreuse and white work for much inshore fishing, although when bluefish are found switch to a pink and chartreuse deep minnow. Small versions of the Keys-style tarpon streamer for seatrout work in various color combinations.

When fishing offshore a white Deceiver with either a green or blue back is a good choice, although for fishing for dolphin along the Sargassum weed use yellow and brown flies that match the color of the baitfish and crabs found in the weed.

Mike used to sight fish the shallow areas in the bay for redfish. Jack crevalle were also sight fished, primarily while churning into baitfish. They're not terribly difficult to find then! Jacks school according to size, and many of these flats jacks run 25 to 30 pounds. A large noisy popper can work well, but if it doesn't try the bait and switch technique with a large, hookless popping plug.

Anchoring in the bay and chumming often proves effective for Spanish mackerel and bluefish. Mike liked menhaden (pogies to you Northerners), either fresh or frozen. Most of these will be ground up, but he would throw chunks in too. He would anchor off of points, or over shoals, or by drop-offs or channels and try to chum the fish in close. Visit Half Hitch Tackle and ask where the fish have been holding recently before wasting time chumming where no fish are present.

Chumming over wrecks and artificial reefs offshore is a great way to have plenty of action. While the best chum is undoubtedly live baitfish, oftentimes the fish aren't very fussy. Ground chum or frozen minnows often work just as well.

Capt. Buddy Dortch says, "While I use Deceivers, Seaducers, and other standard saltwater patterns, in the bay system the best fly for all around use is a Clouser minnow."

While redfishing in West Bay with Steve Bachman we would use lightly weighted Clouser minnows, often doing well on tailing fish. Off the beaches the Puglisi series of flies was very effective for us. We'd fish under diving birds for jacks, ladyfish, and little tunny.

Access

For waders- as described above.

For boaters- in Panama City proper the Municipal Marina is on Harrison Avenue (US 231), downtown behind the Civic Center.

-at Carl Gray Park on the east side of the Hathaway Bridge.

-at St. Andrews State Recreation Area (closest ramp to the pass).

-in Calloway Bayou on East Bay by the Calloway Men's Club.

-on US 98 at the north end of the Dupont Bridge (under the old bridge).

-on SR 77 at the Bailey Bridge, on the south side of North Bay.

-on SR 79 over the Intracoastal Waterway on West Bay.

-at the Bayside Trailer Park off Wildwood Road on the west side of the Hathaway Bridge ($).
-on Dolphin Drive, on the south side of Grand Lagoon.
-on the west side of Pretty Bayou on Danley Avenue (turn right off of Michigan Avenue).
-for military personnel only, on Tyndal AFB.

Fly Shops
-Half Hitch Tackle, 2206 Thomas Drive, 850.234.2621; www.halfhitch.com.

Guides
-Captain Buddy Dortch, 850.896.8371.
-Capt. Marc St. Angelo, 850.896.1201.

State Parks and Other Attractions
St. Andrews State Recreation Area, 850.234.2522. The park is right on St. Andrews Pass and offers waterfront campsites, a boat ramp, two fishing piers, and a jetty.
Information about all state parks can be found online at www.floridastateparks.org.

Accommodations
There are loads of motels in Panama City and on Panama City Beach. The phone number at the Panama City Convention and Visitors Bureau is 1-800-PCBEACH or locally 850.233.5070; www.thebeachloversbeach.com

One of Enrico Puglisi's creations was the ticket for this little tunny, a.k.a. Florida bonito.

Choctawhatchee Bay

Fort Walton Beach

East Pass

Destin

Santa Rosa Island

Gulf of Mexico

Destin/ Fort Walton Beach

East Pass, an inlet that slices Santa Rosa Island from Moreno Point, separates the towns of Destin and Ft. Walton Beach. To the north lies Choctawhatchee Bay, to the south the Gulf of Mexico. Miles of white, sugar sand beaches line the Gulf, arguably the finest beaches in Florida. It's a beautiful area with friendly people, competitive prices, and a family orientation.

Why should an angler care about all that? Unique in Florida, a quarter mile off the beach the water is 40 feet deep. You can catch redfish, flounder, and seatrout in the bay, and dolphin, cobia, and bonito in the Gulf, within minutes of each other by boat. It's not easy finding these shallow water and deep water species so close together anywhere else in Florida.

The near shore fishery has vastly improved since the net ban went into effect (about the time the original edition of this book came out). "Every year it gets exponentially better," says local guide Gordie Hinds. "We've had little tunny in every day, from February until now" (I interviewed Gordie in mid-August). "We can catch 15 big, ten pound plus little tunny every day. There a lot more king mackerel, and a lot more and a lot bigger Spanish mackerel. My son got a Spanish last month that weighed 11 pounds, a giant Spanish mackerel."

Paul Darby is a long time Ft. Walton Beach resident, known for his fine custom rods. Paul owns and operates Quality Reel Repair at the Shalimar Yacht Basin. Gordie Hines was one of the first fly fishing guides on the Emerald Coast. Both of these men shared the following information with me.

Opportunities for the Do It Yourself Fly Fisher
-Inshore Wading: You'll find wading opportunities in the bay for redfish from March through November. During the winter reds slow down to almost nothing; however seatrout, both spotted and white, can be caught all year. Jacks are also present all year, and catching one less than ten

196

pounds is unusual. Other species available include ladyfish, sheepshead (a real challenge for the fly fisher!), Spanish mackerel, and sometimes bluefish.

One of the better bay areas with easy access for waders is Elliott Point, east of the SR 98-30 bridge on the north side of the Intracoastal Waterway in Ft. Walton Beach. A huge, lush grass bed here supports a lot seatrout and sometimes reds. Spanish mackerel, ladyfish, big jack crevalle, and bluefish all come through this area sometimes, too.

Another good wading area is White Point, on the north side of the bay. Access is south off of SR 20, and public facilities here make this spot quite popular. Another large and healthy grass bed attracts the same species as mentioned in the previous paragraph. One can wade the grass flat looking for trout and reds, or try blind casting along the drop-off on the west side of the point.

Wading is also possible near the Mid Bay Bridge by Legendary Marine, at Regatta Bay, at the Coast Guard station north of the pass, and at the park at Okaloosa Island.

-Hand Powered Boat: You can do a lot. Point Washington gives access to the ICW and the mouth of the Choctowhatchee River. The river mouth is a maze of islands and channels, lots of marsh, very fishy looking.

The SR 331 bridge offers structure for fish, which attracts quite a few species. Not terribly aesthetic perhaps, but if a school of 15 pound jacks is there your attention probably won't be on the cars whizzing by.

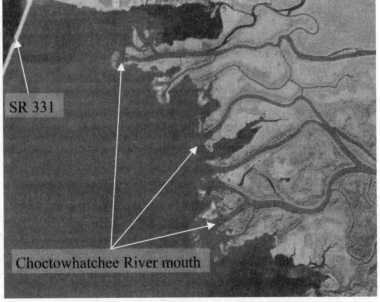

SR 331

Choctowhatchee River mouth

The bayous on the south side of the bay offer fishing on a south wind (accessible from Joe's Bayou), and some of the bayous on the north side are accessible from the SR 331 bridge.

Fish species anywhere in this area would include redfish, seatrout, bluefish, ladyfish, Spanish mackerel, and jack crevalle. These jacks are the bad boys of the bay. Gordie Hinds says they are seldom less than 15 pounds. He also says that you could also have your fill of gafftopsail catfish (always a popular fly rod target!).

-Inshore Boat: Even anglers with small boats can use them in the bay, being mindful of the weather of course. The same species are available to boaters as to waders. Boaters have more flexibility in where they fish, obviously. There are few flats here. The fishing tends to be in deeper water. You can sightfish for reds up close to the shoreline, but these tend to be smaller fish.

There are several bayous off of the main bay. In the Ft. Walton Beach area Chico Bayou and Grande Bayou provide good fishing even on the windiest days. You can fish under dock lights at night in these two bayous, too, and expect to find good concentrations of seatrout.

North of Destin are two other bayous, Boggy Bayou and Rocky Bayou. Again, these bodies of water provide good fishing for trout and reds. You'll also run into the occasional striped bass in this area, some of which hit 20 pounds. To the east you will find several other bayous. All invite exploration. Fishing the mouth of any of the bayous early in the day is always a good idea.

As mentioned in the hand powered boats section, the bridges all provide structure, and structure attracts the bait that attracts the fish, even tarpon.

There are a couple of wrecks that are in the bay, the best known of which is a Liberty ship wreck in about 28 feet of water off of Four Mile Point. The top of this wreck is within six feet of the surface, meaning a sinking line is not a necessity. Crevalle, tarpon, good sized trout, redfish, sheepshead, bluefish, and more can all be found here. It's probably the most consistent place in the bay. You'll lose a lot of flies here, and it's easy to lose an anchor, too.

Lastly, at the extreme east end of the bay you'll find an extensive system of creeks and islands where the Choctawhatchee River enters the bay. This pristine area provides excellent fishing all summer long, and being the farthest distance from Destin and Ft. Walton, gets little fishing pressure.

-<u>From the Beach</u>: Fishing from the beach here is as good as it is anywhere. Gordie Hinds said, "Fly casters have to realize that if you fish from the beach here you're regarded as somewhat of a novelty. Tourists will get right behind you to watch, wondering what you're doing, so you have to be careful you don't hook anyone."

Pompano and whiting are the most popular beach fish. Sinking lines with small crab imitations will take pompano, which can be sight fished, as well as whiting. Clouser minnows will also work for both species.

There are two sandbars that run parallel to the beach. Fishing in between them, or if you can get out to the second sand bar at low tide, you can also take ladyfish, crevalle jacks, bluefish, and Spanish mackerel. King mackerel come in close sometimes. There are a lot of sharks. Cobia and tarpon sometimes show up. You don't even need a sinking line, although a monocore sink-tip does come in handy. Small, white flies work well, especially if you keep them moving right along.

Near the Coast Guard station on the west side of the pass is a large rock jetty. Adventurous fly fishers can scramble out here and cast off of the rocks. A stripping basket is a necessity!

-<u>Nearshore</u>: As already mentioned, the nearshore fishing is consistently spectacular. In addition to the little tunny and mackerel, crevalle, ladyfish, bluefish, pompano, even redfish are catches on a daily basis. By chumming over wrecks amberjack, king mackerel, grouper, snapper, and the occasional wahoo will all take flies. It's good. Where else in Florida can you catch dolphin from a johnboat? Offshore in Destin is only a long cast from the beach.

The cobia run along this part of the Florida coast is legendary. Cobia reaching triple digit weights cruise off the beaches, following rays, turtles, or just free swimming from March through May. These fish are sight-fished. You'll need serious tackle- these fish are BIG. Many hundred plus pound fish are caught (on conventional tackle) every year. The only reason a fly fisher hasn't caught one yet is because so few folks fly fish up this way. As Paul Darby put it, "Fly fishing is just exploding onto our fishing scene and lots of folks are getting involved- it's only a matter of time before fly rod world records for cobia are broken."

During the summer you can also catch little tunny, big jack crevalle, amberjacks, kingfish, dolphin, and more within a mile of the beach, especially if Sargassum weed comes in.

Gordie Hinds says that any time after March the jacks are a possibility. Look for them up on top, sometimes daisy chaining. Again, these are big, strong fish.

If you can find ladyfish it's almost a sure thing that bluefish and Spanish mackerel will be around them. Sometimes you'll see birds working, but a lot of times you just see the delicate

198

breaking of ladyfish striking glass minnows on the surface. In the fall, anytime you find the ladyfish, if you can get a fly down through them there will be little tunny and sometimes black-fin tuna underneath.

Paul and Gordie all say they and their friends sometimes catch both black and red snapper and grouper on flies, difficult to do in most other parts of the state. Chum gets the fish up near the surface where they can see and hit the flies. Once you get the snapper and grouper up there might also be triggerfish, cobia, amberjack, king mackerel, and other species, a regular smorgasbord for you. Both agree that you had better be ready for a tough fight if you hook a ten pound snapper on a fly. You'd better be properly geared up and ready for a _very_ tough fight if you tangle with an 80 or 90 pound cobia or a big amberjack!

Flies and Techniques

Mr. Darby has very definite opinions about fly selection. He likes the Clouser deep min-now in both chartreuse and white and in gray and white with blue crystal flash. He especially likes this color combination at night. He also likes glass minnow imitations. He often ties these on long shank hooks (Mustad 34011 or equivalent) leaving the front 2/3rds of the shank bare. He then uses these flies for bluefish and Spanish mackerel. Lastly, he likes a shrimp imitation developed by Vance Cook of Pensacola, called the Cook's Critter. Darby prefers this fly to have a tan body and a gray squirrel hair wing.

Darby prefers to find his bay fish in shallower areas so he can see them before casting to them. For this work he uses a floating line.

For the cobia run use big squid flies, or big Deceivers, or other large, light colored patterns. The drill is to cruise slowly along the beach until you spot some fish in the clear water, then position the boat for a good, head-on cast to them.

Offshore fishing is done a couple of different ways. A favorite method involves anchoring near one of the artificial reefs in the area and chumming the fish up to the boat. If possible, lead them far enough away from the reef so that when a big fish takes he can't get back into it.

The other main technique? Cruise along the weed lines which form during the summer looking for fish. When you see some, cast to them!

Any time you see fish on top blasting bait (as jacks, Spanish, bluefish, little tunny, or even blackfin or yellowfin tuna all do) get over near them as quickly as possible, drift down onto them, and start flinging hackle at them!

Gordie Hinds says, "As you can tell, in most of our nearshore fishing the biggest challenge is to pick one line weight and one fly, because you literally never know what you will encounter next. At any given moment you might have shots at ladyfish, or jacks, or cobia, or tarpon, or whatever. You never have time to switch flies or rods. My number one fly is a #2 ALF pattern, mostly white with some very light gray, not a lot of flash. It works on the entire gamut of fish here. I even got a sailfish with the ALF once.

"Over the wrecks when chumming I use a chum fly that will match the chum. Sometimes we make 'soup', but frequently we chum with chunks or even whole small fish. The ALF works here, too.

"Popovics's Glass Minnow, the one with the silicone head, that one is dynamite too. It looks like a Surf Candy but it's real tiny. It looks just like a glass minnow. Use it on the beach and you can catch anything that's out there.

"I also tie white Polar Fiber minnows on red hooks. In the fall that's about all you can get the little tunny and the blackfins to eat."

Access
For Waders: as detailed above.
For Boaters: boat ramps can be found at the following locations-
-on the east side of Choctawhatchee bay, there are ramps at both ends of SR 331.
-on the west side of the bay there is a ramp on the north side of the SR 98 bridge across the Intracoastal Waterway.
-at the north end of Beach Drive in Destin there is a public ramp on Joe's Bayou.
-at the east end of Destin Harbor there is a ramp at Sandpiper Cove.
-there is a private ($) ramp at Destin Marina.
-there is a private ($) ramp at East Pass Marina on SR 98.
-Legion Park, SW Choctawhatchee Bay, Choctawhatchee Beach.
-Choctawhatchee Beach Wayside Park, SR 20 on Choctawhatchee Bay, Choctawhatchee Beach.
-Sandestin Resort, 9300 Hwy 98 W, Destin.
-Fort Rucker Recreation Area, off Hwy. 20 on Choctawhatchee Bay, Freeport.
-Gene's Marina, on Choctawhatchee Bay, Freeport.
-Wheeler Point Wayside Park, SR 83 on Choctawhatchee Bay, South of Freeport.
-Grayton Beach State Recreational Area, 357 Main Park Rd. on Western Lake/ Gulf of Mexico, Santa Rosa Beach.

Fly Shops
-Paul Darby owns Quality Reel Repair, at the Shalimar Yacht Basin off of SR 85 in Shalimar, 850.651.2991.
-Blue Bay Outfitters, 877.321.3474; www.bluebayoutfitters.com.
-There is a Bass Pro Shop in Destin, 850.269.6200.

Guides
-Capt. Gordie Hinds, 850.231.9997; www.house-of-art.com/fich.html.
-Captain Paul Darby, 850.651.2991.
-Capt. Pat Dineen, 850.609.0528; www.flyliner.com.

State Parks and Other Attractions
-Grayton Beach State Recreation Area is about 15 miles east of Destin, right on the Gulf of Mexico. Camping is available. 850.231.4210.
-Rocky Bayou State Recreation Area is at the north end of Rocky Bayou, about as north as you could get on Choctawhatchee Bay. Camping is available here. 850.897.3222
Information about all state parks can be found online at www.floridastateparks.org.

Accommodations
There are many motels in this area. The Emerald Coast Convention and Visitors Bureau can be reached at 850.651.7131 or 800.322.3319; www.destin-fwb.com.

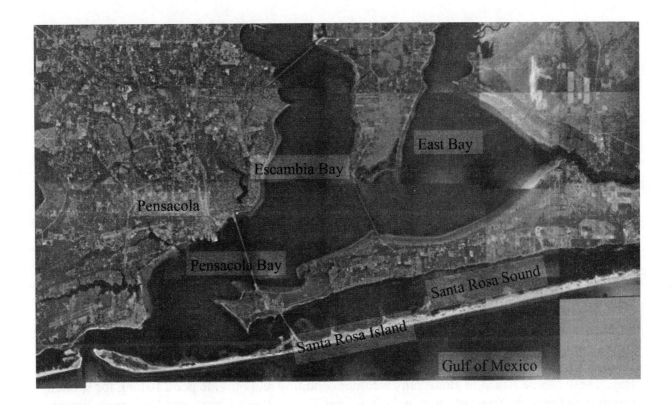

Pensacola

The last town in our survey of the Florida coast is Pensacola. Last, but certainly not least! With its laid back atmosphere, Pensacola fits most anglers like a comfortable old slipper. There's lots of room for the angler. Pensacola Bay and its branches, Santa Rosa Sound, and Big Lagoon taken together make up an extensive bay system with clear, clean water, healthy grass beds, and abundant fish- seatrout, reds, flounder, jack crevalle, Spanish mackerel, and other species. The Gulf of Mexico beckons those interested in the offshore species.

There's excellent access. A national seashore and two state parks mean that anglers without boats can easily reach the water.

Like the rest of Florida's panhandle, you'll find fishing best in the summer months. The cobia run starts off the season sometime in April, and fishing continues until October in most years, although sometimes if the weather holds good action can be had until Thanksgiving.

Captain Bob Gray supplied the information for this section in the first edition. Captain Hugh Smith supplied the updated information for this edition.

Opportunities for the Do It Yourself Fly Fisher
-Inshore Wading: Fly fishers can wade in thick grass beds and cast for seatrout, small grouper, Spanish mackerel, and sometimes redfish at Shoreline Park, in Gulf Breeze off SR 98 on the south side of the peninsula. The grass beds extend off of Deer Point to the south and east.

To the south across Santa Rosa Sound is a small island where the Environmental Protection Agency Laboratory is located, in the vicinity of Villa Sabine. Around this island some monster jacks to 30 pounds can be seen during the summer months, slamming into schools of mullet and other baitfish. Gaining access to this area goes only to those bold enough to ask private landowners for permission, and polite enough to have them say yes. I believe seeing a school of big ravenous jacks causing havoc on the surface would give me enough nerve to ask anyone for access!

Hugh Smith says that there are lots of good opportunities for waders, so many that asking landowners for permission to cross their property really isn't necessary. Some of the places with public access include Gulf Islands National Seashore, where anglers can fish either along the beach or on the miles of grass flats in Santa Rosa Sound, just across the road from the beach. The Big Sabine area is particularly good. At the west end of the national seashore by Fort Pickens is another excellent area. There's lots of access on both sides of the seashore, probably 50 miles worth.

-Hand Powered Boat: Anywhere you can get wading access is a place where a hand powered boat can be launched, allowing you to cover more water or reach fish you might not be able to on foot. Big Lagoon is another good place to fish, with trout and reds, Spanish mackerel, and jack crevalle available all summer. Bluefish will also invade the Big Lagoon.

On the east side of Pensacola Bay is East Bay, which extends farther east into the East River. Where this river enters the bay is an excellent area for hand powered craft.

At the mouths of the Yellow River and the Blackwater River, near the head of Blackwater Bay, is a labyrinth of channels and oyster bars. The mouth of the White River, at the head of Escambia Bay, is similar. There are lots of places for the paddling angler to find some fish.

-Inshore Boat: There are many bayous whose finger-like projections extend off of Escambia Bay. These can be fished in almost any weather condition and provide good fishing for spotted seatrout and redfish. Some of them include Bayou Texar, Bayou Chico, and Hoffman's Bayou. Many of these bayous have residential docks where fish gather, especially at night when the lights are turned on.

Anywhere you can get your motor skiff that was mentioned in the above section on hand powered boats will also produce fish for you. Big Lagoon, Escambia Bay, Blackwater Bay, and East Bay are all good areas for trout, redfish, and ladyfish. Mackerel, jacks, and bluefish will also be available sometimes.

Look diligently for surface action around the Pensacola Naval Air Station during the summer months, especially that area near the pass. Jacks, little tunny, Spanish mackerel, and sometimes even tarpon trap bait here and rip into it. On calm summer mornings this kind of activity is visible from a long way off, and provides extremely exciting angling.

This bay system is a big piece of water. Plan to spend some time poking around and exploring it.

-From the Beach: You'll find the same species along the beach here as elsewhere in the Panhandle- pompano, whiting, ladyfish, bluefish, jacks, and Spanish mackerel. Excellent beach access awaits on the east side of the pass in the Gulf Islands National Seashore. At the extreme west end of Santa Rosa Island in the National Seashore the Ft. Pickens Pier and the surrounding vicinity offers some superb angling opportunities. In addition to the typical beach species, king mackerel are sometimes caught from the beach here.

On the west side of the pass excellent beach fishing is available, but only to anglers with boats- there are no roads! But if you visit this thin spit of sand you can fish the beach side or the Big Lagoon side, or fish both sides within a few minutes of each other.

See the section above on inshore wading for more information.

-Nearshore: Nearshore fishing starts in March when the cobia run starts. Big schools of big fish move along the beach. Idle along in the boat looking for fish, then cast to them. Large white and/or pink flies are preferred, with tackle in the 10-11-12 weight range.

Days along the beach are a lot of fun. Ladyfish, jack crevalle, Spanish mackerel and little tunny are usually found by sighting them working on bait. It's usually best to motor upwind, then drift down on them. You will spook fewer fish this way. There are lots of fish, frequently non-stop action.

Redfish, big, bull redfish, load up in the pass during the fall months. Catching these reds at night is high excitement! Hugh Smith says a fast sinking shooting head and big flies are the way to catch these fish. The fly needs to be down 15 to 20 feet, fishing in the currents of the outgoing tide.

A series of artificial reefs is found two to three miles off the beach. Chumming over these reefs with ground chum or frozen minnows will pull the fish off the reef up to the boat, where they can be fished with flies. You can get king mackerel, big reds, little tunny, amberjack, cobia, sharks, and even red snapper this way. You never know what will show up in the chum line, and you can see all of the action.

Lastly, during summer big patches of sargassum weed sometimes blow in. Chicken dolphin are plentiful in these weeds. Cobia and tripletail like them too. Sometimes you'll find other species around, even sailfish or wahoo. Again, idle along the edge of the weed line looking for fish. When they are spotted, cast to them.

Flies and Techniques

Hugh Smith says that the Seminole Clouser, a garnet and gold creation, imitates the dark colored shrimp found locally. Hugh carries it in sizes 8 through 2/0. All you Gator fans will have to grin and bear it.

Smith also says that the standard chartreuse and white Clouser is another go to fly, especially along the beaches. Straight black Clousers are good for redfish.

Popping bugs work well early and late in the day (or at night) and are especially effective on ladyfish and crevalle.

Small white flies that imitate ghost shrimp are killers around lit docks at night.

Cobia's liking for big pink and white creations has already been noted elsewhere in this work. Flies for offshore usually are white with some other color like pink, chartreuse, green, or blue thrown in.

Bob Gray told me he thinks most fly fishers strip their flies too slowly. He likes a fast retrieve, sometimes even going to a two handed strip. He claims to consistently outfish the slow strip crowd this way, so give it a try.

Hugh agrees with this for the ladyfish and jacks.

Access

For waders- much of the access in the Pensacola area on the bay side has already been described. Most of Pensacola Beach is completely accessible to the surf fisherman.

For boaters- Public ramps can be found at the following places:

-both ends of the Three Mile Bridge (SR 98). Use these ramps with caution, as they are shallow.

-at Quietwater Beach, near the SR 319 Causeway that crosses Santa Rosa Sound.

-in Bayou Grande at Navy Point.

-in Bayou Texar.

-at the Rod and Reel Marina west of the pass off of Old Gulf Beach Highway, on the Intracoastal Waterway on Big Lagoon. ($)

-at Shoreline Park in Gulf Breeze. ($)

Fly Shops
The nearest fly shop is Blue Bay Outfitters in Destin; 877.321.3474,
www.bluebayoutfitters.com.

Boat Rentals
-Adventure Perdido, Inc., 850.492.9321, 888.492.9321; www.adventureperdido.com. Powerboat rentals.
-Key Sailing Pensacola Beach, 850.932.5520, 877.932.7272; www.keysailing.com. Powerboat
and kayak rentals.

Guides
Capt. Hugh Smith, 850.936.1867; www.bonescharters.com.

State Parks and Other Attractions
-Gulf Islands National Seashore, 1801 Gulf Breeze Parkway, Gulf Breeze 32561.
850.934.2600; www.nps.gov/guis. You can fish here, but no camping is allowed.
-Perdido Key State Recreation Area, c/o Big Lagoon State Recreation Area, 12302 Gulf Beach
Highway, Pensacola 32507. 850.492.1595. You can fish here, but no camping is available.
-Big Lagoon State Recreation Area, 12302 Gulf Beach Highway, Pensacola 32507.
850.492.1595. This park is located on Big Lagoon, and you can camp.
Information about all state parks can be found online at www.floridastateparks.org.

Accommodations
The phone number at the Pensacola Convention and Visitor's Bureau is 800.874.1234;
www.visitpensacola.com.

Section 3   Fly Selection for Florida Salt

The inexperienced fly fisher believes that there's a magic bullet, a fly that will work for any species, anywhere, anytime. Wouldn't that be nice?! Sorry fellas, it just doesn't exist.

The experienced fly fisher selects his flies using a combination of knowledge, intuition, and past experience. An examination of Lefty Kreh's book, Saltwater Fly Patterns, reveals that literally thousands of fly patterns have been devised, all with the same purpose- to entice a fish into striking a fraud made from fur, feathers, or other materials.

Do all these flies work? Most definitely. Does the Florida fly rodder need a barge to carry his fly boxes? Most definitely not. The best advice any fly fisher could give another is to choose those patterns which have proven themselves, ones which inspire confidence and which meet your needs.

What if it's your first visit to Florida? What if you don't have any experience fly fishing in saltwater?

Saltwater fly fishers need a selection of flies that cover the entire water column, from the surface to the bottom. You'll need some flies that float and make a commotion on the surface. Poppers, sliders, and divers fit the bill for this. The size depends on what you're chasing. The smallest surface flies would be about size 4, the largest could be as big as 5/0 for offshore fishes. Because this type of fly can be wind resistant and hard to cast, you need to choose them with care. Make sure they have sufficient hook gap!

Use surface flies when searching for fish, especially while wading. Poor visibility when wading (due to the low angle of the angler to the water) hampers sight fishing. So does wind, clouds, or dirty water. Try calling the fish by using a popping bug. Surface flies also work well early or late in the day, or in discolored water, for the same reason.

Needless to say when fish are crashing bait on top, a popper is a great choice! Poppers are constructed from deer hair, plastic foam, cork, and balsa wood. There's no need to carry all types. Just find the style you like best, and carry several in different sizes.

Many different minnow imitations exist. You could carry them all, but why? You need large ones and small ones, light colors and dark colors, slow sinkers and fast sinkers. If you have all of this, you have met 90 percent of your needs in Florida salt.

For fishing in deeper water or right on the bottom in shallower areas, the Clouser deep minnow is a must. The deep minnow has lead eyes which make it work somewhat like a jig. Carry Clousers with different weight eyes, to cover different fishing situations, in sizes #4 to #1, in brown and white, tan and white, and chartreuse and white. Lefty Kreh has caught over eighty different species of fish on Clouser minnows. Most of us will never equal his record, but don't go out without these flies.

Shallow grassy areas require a somewhat weedless fly. Bendbacks fill this need well.

Everyone knows Lefty's Deceiver as a minnow imitation, used for everything from freshwater trout to billfish. Some of the newer patterns tied entirely with synthetic materials work even better than Lefty's classic pattern. Regardless of the material that your minnow imitations are constructed from, carry them in sizes #4 to 3/0, or even larger if you fish offshore much. Carry various color combinations of light and dark colors so you can experiment when fish are being spooky or fussy.

Large fish often want a decent mouthful, so don't be afraid to tie one on. Although most saltwater fish aren't fussy often, some of them make a career out of fussiness. Tarpon, bonefish, permit, and to a lesser extent redfish, all come to mind. Most anglers prefer being prepared if the fish are being fussy, so have some tricks up your sleeve.

Another important minnow pattern is the Seaducer which has a heavily hackled body, giving it a very slow sink rate. It's great in shallow water, or when fish are suspended under overhanging structure. It can even be greased with dry fly floatant and used right on top. Some guides like to weight their seaducers with lead eyes. Take these in the same sizes and colors as the deceivers. Be sure that some have weedguards.

Another popular style of fly, especially for bigger species like tarpon and cobia, are the rabbit strip flies. Few materials suggest life like a strip of rabbit fur. There are small versions of these flies, too. The bonefish bunny comes to mind.

Many types of seagoing fish eat crabs at every opportunity. Redfish, permit, and bone-fish are three that jump to mind. Consider a good crab imitation a must when you observe fish eating these crustaceans.

Although crab imitations come in epoxy, deerhair, hot glue, and various other materials, the Merkin Crab is easy to tie and very effective. With a carapace made of wool strands and lead eyes for a fast sink rate, it takes only a few minutes to tie and crab eating fish like permit, bonefish, and redfish just love it. Again, it's not necessary to carry all the different styles of crab flies, just the one you prefer in a variety of sizes and colors.

One thing to keep in mind is that regardless of the style of fly, some of them must have weedguards. The fish live over grass, around oysters, under mangrove trees and docks, and many other locations where an unprotected hook point can foul. Instructions on how to tie a simple and effective weedguard follow.

Some fish have had special flies designed specifically with them in mind. Tarpon flies come to mind, as do barracuda. The classic tarpon fly is tied with the wing at the bend of the hook, to cut down on the fouling of the wing around the hook. Cuda flies are tied to imitate nee-dlefish. Bonefish flies tend to be on the small side, tied with a reverse wing, and often weighted to sink in deeper areas where mudding fish are seen.

With a basic selection of flies, anyone going after seatrout, snook, bonefish, tarpon, or any other of Florida's great saltwater gamefish should have the flies and the confidence to fish successfully. Those targeting specific species that have special needs should carry those flies as well. A variety of specialty patterns needed for specific species of fish.

Keep your hooks sharp. I always sharpen mine before I put the hook in the vise. While different folks sharpen hooks different ways, I do it as follows: use a four inch flat mill file. Luhr-Jensen markets the best one in my opinion. Place the file under the right side of the point at roughly a 45 degree angle to the top of the point and push it back toward the barb. Three or four strokes generally does the job. Then place the file under the left side of the point again at 45 degrees the other way and again push the file toward the barb. Then lay the file on top of the point and push it back toward the barb. This creates a triangular point. Test it to see if it digs onto your thumb nail. If it doesn't, work on it until it does. It really needs to be sticky sharp.

Florida Salt's Top Ten Flies List!

While I believe you should carry those flies that you know damn well are going to work for you, people like these kinds of lists. I get asked this sort of thing all the time. So as a service to my readers I hereby supply a "top ten flies to carry to Florida" list. Remember, you will always need some flies that are equipped with weedguards.

1) Popper/Slider/Diver. You need some surface flies, from subtle to obnoxious. Depending on where you're headed and what you're fishing for, these could range in size from #4 to 3/0. Most fish, with the exception of permit, bonefish, and black drum, will take flies off the surface at least some of the time.

2) Clouser Deep Minnow. You also need a fly that sinks fast so you can fish on or near the bottom. The Clouser minnow is the best fly for this. All kinds of colors work, with some of the more popular ones being black, brown, purple, tan, olive, chartreuse, and combinations of these over white. Sizes to be carried depend on the target species and the water depth, but #4-1/0 with eyes ranging from bead chain to 1/24th ounce will cover almost every situation. Also, there are all kinds of modifications you can make to the basic pattern.

3) Crab patterns. These prove invaluable sometimes. There are many different ways to make a crab fly, but the Merkin or more recently the Kwan are probably the easiest to make and the most versatile and durable. A selection of sizes from #4 to #1, again with different size eyes, is what you'll need.

4) Seaducer (Homer Rhodes Shrimp Fly). This classic pattern is another versatile pattern that depending on size and color will take a wide variety of fish. It can also be weighted with lead eyes to make it sink faster. My favorite color is plain grizzly, although I've enjoyed good success with many different colors of this fly. Sizes 4 through 3/0 can be useful, from unweighted to heavily weighted.

5) Rattle Minnow. Several different folks have been given credit for developing this pattern, which is basically an inverted-tied bucktail with a rattle tied in along the shank. It is very useful when the water is dirty, or the light levels are low, in sizes 2 and 1.

6) Spoon Fly. While I prefer using flies, this fly rod lure can be a day saver. Again, several different people have developed spoon flies. My own favorite is made by Jim Dupre.

7) Bunny Strip flies. This is a pretty generic description, but bunny flies can be as small as #4 or as large as 4/0. They can be tied weighted or unweighted. They get heavy and can be hard to cast, but they always look great in the water.

8) Blondes/Deceivers. Joe Brooks designed the Blonde, Lefty Kreh the Deceiver. Actually I prefer the Blonde since it works just as well and is a lot easier to tie (no feathers). These work in a variety of sizes and color combinations.

9) Modern Synthetic Minnows. These include my own Sexyflies, the flies by Puglisi, the PolarFiber minnows, and more. These flies are all synthetic and work incredibly well on a wide variety of fish. I carry them in sizes 2 to 4/0 in a variety of colors, and use them for any fish that eats other fish. They work particularly well on tarpon.

10) The Bendback. Sometimes an unweighted fly that rides hook up is the only thing that will work. These should be carried in sizes 4 through 1 in a variety of colors.

Of course you can catch fish on a wide variety of flies, but if you have everything listed here you are ready for anything Florida Salt has to offer, including tarpon, bonefish, redfish, sharks, billfish, the entire range of saltwater fish you're likely to encounter.

Tying the Flies

This section of the book gives directions for tying many of the flies mentioned else-where in the book. Some assumptions are made- that the reader knows how to perform basic fly tying techniques, such as starting the thread, attaching lead eyes, tying in hair, feathers, and other materials, and whip finishing. If you don't know how to do this, get a basic fly tying text. Better, have someone show you how.

Different tiers have differing philosophies on how flies should be tied, on what the end result should look like, on the entire zen of fly tying. My philosophy on fly tying, as in life, is keep it simple. We deal with enough complications every day without making things more diffi-cult for ourselves when we're supposed to be having fun.

As long as the fly holds together during use, as long as it does the job it's supposed to do- attracting fish and enticing them to strike- then it has done its job well. If you want to spend an hour tying a fly that could win an award at an art show, that's OK. If you want to tie six flies per hour that might be a little rough around the edges, that's fine too. The important thing is to enjoy it!

Basic materials needed for most flies listed on the previous page include the following:
-hooks, Mustad 3407 or equivalent, sizes 4 through 3/0;
-thread. Danville's flat waxed nylon is pretty standard among saltwater fly tiers;
-head cement. Clear Sally Hansen's Hard as Nails fingernail polish works as well as any head cement on the market, although many tiers are addicted to Whitlock's Flexament, Softex, or ep-oxy. Epoxy hides a lot of mistakes and makes an indestructible head;
-lead eyes, 1/100, 1/50, 1/36, and 1/24 ounce;
-a grizzly neck. Economy necks work fine, we're not tying dry flies;
-strung saddle hackle in various colors including white, yellow, red, and brown;
-bucktails in white, chartreuse, and brown;
-a nice piece of deer body hair, natural color;
-a calftail in brown or tan;
-grey and fox squirrel tails;
-bunny or other strips in your favorite colors;
-synthetic wing material (sexyfiber, EP fiber, PolarFiber, etc.);
-chenille, medium fly tier's, in brown or tan;
-Aunt Millie's rug yarn (for crabs);
-some kind of foam for popper bodies (I use the foam from boogie boards);
-some kind of flash (crystal flash, flashabou, firefly) in pearl, silver, and gold or copper;
-some plastic worm rattles. I like Woodie's Rattles; and
-medium mylar tubing, pearl color.

Lately I've been getting away from using feathers and have been using a lot of synthetic wing materials. There are some great ones on the market now, something that wasn't true when the first edition of this book was published.

Of course this list won't cover everything, but it is a good start. Other materials needed for specific fly patterns will be listed along with the directions for how to tie them.

Let's see how to tie up some patterns.

Author's Note– all of the flies in the following photographs were tied by the author unless otherwise noted.

Tying in a Double Mono Prong Weedguard

In Florida we have "weeds" in the water in some places. Oftentimes flies are cast against structure, like docks, oysters, or mangrove roots. Weedguards are a simple solution to having the fly fouled with grass, or hanging up all the time, and functionally one of the best types of weed guards for flies is the double mono prong. Further, it's pretty easy to add one to your fly as long as you leave sufficient room behind the eye of the hook.

Here's how I make a double mono prong weedguard:

1. Tie your fly, leaving a little more room than usual for finishing the head.
2. Take a piece of 15 pound test hard monofilament about three inches long, and bend it back on itself in the middle. If you have a small pair of pliers with flat jaws, crush this spot.
3. Place the mono over the hook just behind the eye such that the prongs extend well below the hook point. Wrap the mono with figure eights until it's secure, taking care that it lies properly. Then whip finish and cement the head.

Once the head dries, trim the prongs to the desired length. I like mine to extend past the hook point about a quarter or an eighth of an inch. Your weedless fly is now ready to fish.

Whether you prefer a hair bug, the Crease Fly (tied by Joe Blados) or the Floozy, you absolutely must carry some top water flies.

The Floozy Popper

I love surface lures, especially flyrod surface lures. The crushing strike of a big fish on a popper or slider in inches of water is something anyone who enjoys angling should experience.

I'm using the term "popper" generically here, but it includes sliders and divers.

Sometimes fish will follow a popper for several feet before making up their minds. They usually clobber it unless the hook has picked up some floating grass. Watching a huge wake following inches behind your lure will do things to your adrenaline that persons with weak hearts should avoid. Other times they will strike out of nowhere. Either way the excitement level is stratospheric.

Poppers and sliders are some of the best flies for big trout. You can use poppers to get baby tarpon. Although you get unbelievable, awesome strikes, sticking one of these babies when they come up for a bug is really difficult. I believe the pressure wave they push ahead of them moves the bug out of the way of their opening mouth, causing them to miss most of the time. Bring lots of patience.

Charlie Waterman has written reams of material about deerhair bugs in the Everglades' backcountry. Snook crush surface flies, and poppers are a popular choice for fly fishers trying to fool the linesiders.

Other fish take them with a vengeance as well. Ladyfish, jack crevalle, bluefish, even such odd catches as pinfish and hardhead catfish have been made by this writer with poppers. As long as the water is less than about three feet deep, they'll be effective on most gamefish.

The Floozy is an ugly but utilitarian fly that unfortunately lacks durability under the onslaught of sharp teeth. I like them because they're easy to make, easy to cast, and pop beautifully. You can trim them any way you want to make a popper, a slider, or even a shallow diver.

You'll need to make a plug tool out of a piece of quarter inch copper pipe, readily available at any hardware store. This tool should be about six inches long, with one end filed as sharp as you can make it.

Materials-

Hook- Mustad 34011 or equivalent, #2 or 1.
Tail- tier's choice. This is the only use for which I like Fishair.
Body- foam plug cut from a swimmer's noodle, color tier's choice. I recently discovered that the foam in a boogie board is firmer and more durable and works even better.
Glue- superglue works as well as anything else.

1) First off, get your noodle (or boogie board). Measure the length of the hook shank against it the long way, and use a sharp knife to slice off a slab of foam. It's like cutting a thick slice of salami. Then use your plug tool to punch plugs out of the slice. You should get seven or eight per slice. One swimmer's noodle will yield thousands of popper bodies.

2) Sharpen the hook, fix the hook in the vise, and start the tying thread. Wind it back to the bend of the hook.

3) Tie in the tail, using the materials of your choice. Extend the fibers up the hook shank most of the way to the eye to give the body something to grip.

4) Wrap thread around the fibers to give the foam body something to adhere to, then half hitch and cut the thread.

5) Take one of your foam plugs and use your dubbing needle to poke a hole through it lengthwise. Centered at one end (the front) and slightly off center at the other (the back) is best.

6) Coat the hook shank with superglue, then slide the plug over the eye of the hook into position. Rotate the plug to get maximum hook gap, remembering that you can always use a razor blade to trim it after it dries.

7) Barring any trim work needed, the fly is done as soon as the glue is dried.

Use a razor blade to cut the front of the plug to suit your needs. If you slant the face with the long side down you have a diver. If you taper it with the narrow end towards the front you have a slider.

If you want a weedguard, cut two one-inch long pieces of 15 pound mono. Use the needle to poke two holes into the plug such that when you insert the mono pieces they protect the hook point. Put a drop of superglue on the end of each piece of mono and insert them into the plug. Once the glue is dry cut the mono to the proper length.

Once the body is shot, put the fly aside until you get home, then tear the body off and glue a new one on. You can re-use the hook and tail several times by doing this.

The Clouser Deep Minnow (Bob Clouser)

Bob Clouser developed his deep minnow for Susquehanna River smallmouth bass. It was spectacularly successful. Time and experimentation has proved the deep minnow to be spectacularly successful on many other species of fish as well, in both fresh and salt water.

I've taken tarpon, snook, seatrout, redfish, black drum, bonefish, jacks, ladyfish, snapper, tripletail, moonfish, Spanish mackerel, landlocked salmon, brown trout, walleyes, largemouth and smallmouth bass, crappie, bluegills, and many other species with them. Lefty Kreh has taken over eighty different species of fish on Clouser minnows, including permit and king mackerel. It's a fly of choice for about 90 percent of the guides interviewed in this book, and belongs in every saltwater flyfisher's box.

In addition to its fish catching abilities, the deep minnow is easy to tie. This makes it an ideal fly for the beginning tier.

Materials-
Hook: Mustad 3407 or equivalent, size 4-1
Tail: none
Body: none
Wing: bucktail (or squirrel hair, or synthetics) tied inverted. Favorite color combinations include white and chartreuse, white and brown, and white and tan.
Eyes: lead eyes to match size of hook and desired sink rate.

1) After sharpening the hook, place hook in vise. Wrap the thread back about halfway down the shank, then wrap it forward again. Stop about 1/4 of the way back from the hook's eye.

2) Tie the lead eyes on top of the shank about 1/4 the distance back from the hook's eye. Coat the wraps with nail polish.

3) Cut a small (about half the diameter of a pencil) bunch of hair from the white bucktail. Pull out the short hairs, then tie the bunch in behind the lead eyes. Coat the wraps with nail polish.

4) Remove the hook from the vise and turn it over so the point is up.

5) Tie in twelve or so strands of flash over the white hair.

6) Cut a small bunch of hair from a dyed bucktail (color your choice). Tie this in over the crystal flash. Do not tie the fly too full (a common error)!

7) Taper the head and whip finish. Coat the head with one or two layers of cement.
   Versatility is what makes the Clouser minnow such a valuable fly. Its silhouette resembles many baitfish. It can be tied in small sizes for bonefish, large sizes for offshore fish like dolphin, or anything in between. By using small lead eyes and a floating line it can be used on shallow flats. Large lead eyes and sink tip lines or hi-D shooting heads can drop the fly to the twenty foot level, even in currents. It can be crawled along the bottom or ripped through the water. Fish like it. Try it. You will, too.

The Clouser Derivations

You can make all kinds of modifications to the basic Clouser, and lots of folks have. Listed below are a few of the more standardized Clouser derivations.

The Half and Half
Clouser Minnows are usually tied with bucktail. This choice of material limits the size of the fly you can tie. If you want a larger fly but want to stick to natural materials you can tie in some long, fat neck hackles (typically white ones) at the bend of the hook. If you do this you have built a Half and Half.

Half and Halfs are popular with those chasing blackfin tuna and little tunny, especially when fishing behind shrimp trawlers.

Hook- Mustad 3407 or equivalent, #1/0-3/0

Eyes- lead dumbells, 1/36th ounce or larger, depending on desired sink rate

Tail- three pairs of matched white neck hackles

Flash- Flashabou, Flashabou Accent, or other, tyer's choice

Wing- bucktail or synthetics, color tyer's choice

Some derivations of the Clouser Minnow, clockwise from left, the Mosquito Lagoon Special, Maxx's Mud Minnow, and the Son of Clouser. All three have been very good to the author.

Son of Clouser

The Son of Clouser is one of my own all time favorite patterns, in any water anywhere. I originally tied it for redfish in the Indian River Lagoon but have used it to catch landlocked salmon in Maine, brown trout in Utah, and walleyes and smallmouth bass in Minnesota. By using fox or grey squirrel you can make it a little darker or a little lighter in color.

Hook- Mustad 3407 or equivalent, #4.

Eyes- lead dumbbells, 1/100th or 1/50th ounce, depending on desired sink rate.

Wing- red or gray squirrel, topped by eight strands of gold or copper Flashabou Accent, topped by a tuft of brown marabou.

Head- medium brown or tan chenille, wrapped around the lead eye to form a fat head.

The Mosquito Lagoon Special (MLS)

The MLS was derived from the Son of Clouser. I wanted a small, easy to cast fly that sank reasonably fast, but had a fat silhouette that could be perceived as a crab, shrimp, or minnow. Like the Son of Clouser, it's deadly on redfish.

Hook- Mustad 3407 or equivalent, #4.

Eyes- 1/100th or 1/50th ounce lead dumbbell.

Wing- grey or fox squirrel topped with eight strands of gold or copper Flashabou Accent, longer than the hair.

Head- tuft of deer body hair tied in over the lead eye, flared and left untrimmed.

Maxx's Mud Minnow

We have in the Indian River Lagoon a lot of killifish, locally called mud minnows. Maxx came up with this derivation in a successful attempt to imitate them. He ties it in variety of colors.

Hook- Mustad 3407 or equivalent, #4, 2, or 1
Eyes- 1/100th, 1/50th, or 1/36th ounce lead dumbbell
Wing- Either white bucktail or grey squirrel tail, depending on the size of hook used. Top with 12 strands of pearl Flashabou Accent twice as long as the hair, then top with a clump of Arctic fox hair (color tyer's choice). The fox hair is tied in above the lead eye and is not tied in at the butts, but rather behind the butts allowing them to flare.

Maxx's Redfish Fly

My son Maxx came up with this one, tied especially for redfish. Of course other species will take it, too. While lots of saltwater fly patterns are flexible as to color of materials, this one is quite specific.

Hook- Mustad 3407 or equivalent, #4, 2, or 1
Eyes- 1/100th, 1/50th, or 1/36th ounce lead dumbbell
Wing- root beer colored bucktail, topped by 12 or so strands of gold Flashabou Accent, topped by eight or so strands of peacock herl.
Head- medium olive chenille wrapped around the dumbbell eyes.

There are undoubtedly dozens and dozens of other patterns that have evolved from the original Clouser Minnow, all useful, all effective. This piece was only designed to stimulate your thinking about all of the possible Clouser derivations.

The Merkin Crab

The Merkin (the legless Kumiski version) is the cute little feller in the upper right. The bigger one below is a Chernobyl Crab, tied by Tim Borski.

Carrying some type of crab fly is a necessity in the world of Florida Salt. There are lots of different ways to make a crab fly, and they all work. I came up with a pattern myself, the Furry Foam crab. While effective and easy to tie, it lacks durability.

The Merkin is effective and reasonably easy to tie, and it is as durable a fly as you can make. By varying the size, weight, and color, you can use them on every crab eating fish, from bonefish to tarpon.

Materials
-Hook: Mustad 3407 or equivalent #2 to 1/0.
-Thread: Danville flat waxed nylon, black or blue.
-Tail: Wide hackle tips. Try to match the tail to the body. I tie a small bunch of calf tail or squirrel tail hair in before adding the feathers.
-Body: Rug yarn in tan, brown, olive, gray.
-Legs: The original fly calls for white rubber legs with red tips. I usually don't bother with the legs (redfish don't care), but the Sili-Legs do look good.
Eyes: Lead eyes in various sizes. Try to match sink rate to anticipated conditions. I use 1/50th and 1/36th ounce eyes most of the time.

1. Start the thread and tie in the eyes. Make sure to leave enough room for the weed guard if you choose to use one. Weedguard use on this fly is highly recommended.
2. Wrap the thread back past the bend, completely covering the hook shank.
3. Begin the tail with a small clump of calf tail or squirrel tail. This hair should be tied in on the bend, pointing back and down.
4. Using one pair of hackles per side, tie them in now. Splay the hackles so that the feathers curve naturally outward.
5. Begin the body by cutting yarn into 2-inch lengths. The original Merkin has alternating bands of brown and tan yarn, but make it whatever color you need.
6. To make the body, tie in a piece of yarn at a right angle to the hook shank just in front of the tail. Secure the yarn in the middle with an "X" wrap. Tie in the next piece as close as possible and again secure with the "X". Continue doing this until you reach the eyes.
7. If you would like to install a week guard you can do that now.
8. Whip finish the head. I usually cement mine, but some permit fishermen frequently don't, believing that permit can smell the glue. It doesn't seem to bother redfish, though.
9. The fly now needs to be trimmed. Begin at the eye and trim backwards. Lefty Kreh insists the shape should be that of a Colorado Spinner blade, very narrow at the eye and progressively bigger towards the bend of the hook.
10. When you are happy with the shape, you can install the rubber legs if you choose to use them. Simply thread the leg through the body and tie it in with a single overhand knot. Tie in three or four legs.

The Seaducer (Homer Rhodes)

This very effective pattern was developed by Homer Rhodes back in the 1930's. My copy of J. Edson Leonard's Flies contains this quote by Homer Rhodes:

"My favorite all-year fly is my Shrimp Fly that I developed nineteen years ago after taking my first bonefish. These flies have a yellow, barred rock, and white stiff neck feather (rooster) in each wing with a heavy salt and pepper yellow and white hackle."

The color plate in the book shows a dressing identical to that of the fly now called the Seaducer. Leonard's book was published in 1950. It seems pretty obvious that the pattern has been around for awhile, by more than one name.

The Seaducer works best in shallow water. The hackles greatly slow its descent. As mentioned earlier, some guides like this pattern tied with lead eyes to give it a jigging action. Adding a weedguard is an excellent idea.

The fly will take all of Florida's saltwater gamefish, excepting perhaps permit. There are many good color combinations for this fly. Like most lures, every angler has his own favorite color or combination of colors. Experiment to see which ones you like best. Be sure to carry both light and dark flies in different sizes. Here is how to tie it.

Materials
Hook- Mustad 3407 or equivalent
Wing- three or four pairs of neck or saddle hackles, tied in at bend of hook. Accent with crystal flash or flashabou if desired.
Hackle- large neck hackles in complimentary or contrasting color wound Palmer from bend of hook to head of fly.

1) Sharpen hook, then affix in vise. Wrap thread to bend of hook.

2) Choose three or four pairs of matching hackles, color(s) your choice. Match them up with the concave sides facing each other, them tie them in. Tie in the flash now if you want it.

3) Take a pair of large, webby neck hackles, match them, trim the ends, and tie them in at right angles to the hook shank. Wrap them Palmer-style to near the eye of the hook. You may need several pairs of feathers depending on how bushy you like them and the size of the hook.

4) Finish and whip the head, then cement.

The Rattling Minnow

Although at first glance this fly looks like it's tied on a keel hook, it's actually an inverted tie on a 2X long shank hook. The design is clever. The fly incorporates a plastic rattle, adding the element of sound. It has become one of my favorite subsurface minnow imitations for situations with low light or dirty water. It can be tied weighted or unweighted.

When you tie these it's best to make several bodies and coat them with epoxy. Once they dry, then the wing is tied in.

216

With a plastic worm rattle installed, this fly is ready to call the fish to itself.

Materials

Hook– Mustad 34011 or equivalent, size 2

Body– hollow Mylar tubing with rattle inserted. This must be coated with five minute epoxy.

Wing– Bucktail or synthetics, color tier's choice.

Eyes (optional) 1/50th or 1/36th ounce lead eyes.

1) Place the hook in the vise and start the thread. Wind it back to the bend of the hook.

2) Take the mylar tubing and remove the core. Measure it to length against the hook shank, then cut off a little more than you think you'll need. Extend the mylar slightly behind where the thread stops and tie it in. The end of the tubing extending past the thread will unravel, making a sort of a tail.

3) Wrap the thread up the shank of the hook to a point about 1/3 inch behind the hook's eye. Let the bobbin hang there while you prepare the rattle.

4) I use the rattles manufactured by Woodies Rattlers (407.282.4001; www.luresonline.com/shopping/woodies_rattlers.html). These are plastic and can be trimmed and filed somewhat. I like to file the point and sharp angles off of them. I think it helps the fly's body last longer. After tapering it down a little, insert the rattle into the mylar tubing. Then tie off the open end of the tube with the thread. Coat the tube and hook shank with a coat of epoxy. Let the epoxy set until dry.

5) After the body dries take the fly out of the vise, turn it over, and put it back in. If you want a lead eye this is the time to tie it in. The wing is tied inverted, going up over the hook point. I usually tie in a small clump of white bucktail, then a small clump of crystal flash, then a small clump of chartreuse bucktail. Use whatever colors you like best. After the wing is tied in, whip finish and cement the head and the fly is ready to fish.

The Dupre Spoon Fly is on top, the CK Spoon Minnow (complete with chamois tail) below. Both are very effective fly rod lures.

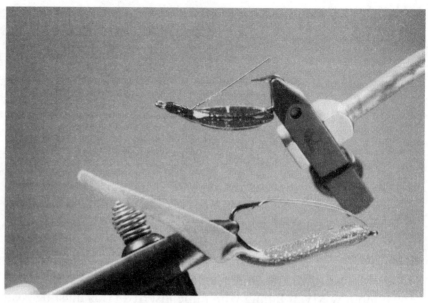

Spoon Flies

We have no instructions on how to tie any of the various types of spoon flies here. I don't enjoy working with epoxy, and would rather buy such spoon flies as I use.

Let's discuss briefly my feelings about these "flies." By no definition I could use are these baits flies. They cast easily with a fly rod though, and are usually extremely effective. I prefer using flies I made myself, but I always have a few of these in my box for use when sighting conditions are poor (they are superb attractor patterns), or when the fish have snubbed everything else I've tried. My own favorite is the Dupre Spoon Fly, closely followed by Chuck Kraft's CK Epoxy Minnow. Both of these spoon flies work perfectly every time.

If these spoon flies are not available at your local fly shop, you can buy them direct.
-Jim Dupre, 352.335.2254.
-Kreel Tackle Company, www.kreeltackle.com, or 434.385.0200.

For those of you who want to make your own spoon flies, construction instruction is available on-line. Some sites include:
-http://fly-rodding.net/flaypatt/epoxy_spoon.htm
-http://fly-rodding.net/flaypatt/lady_bug_spoon.htm
-http://www.flytyingworld.com/PagesK/kd-sf.htm

These ought to get you started.

Strip Flies

One of the most valuable tricks a fly tier can have in his repertoire is the strip. We're not talking about fishing here, we're talking about tying. Strip flies. Bunny strips, arctic fox strips, Finnish raccoon strips. Strip flies.

Strips are just that- narrow strips of skin with the hair still on that are cut from a prepared skin from the animal in question. Bunny strips are the best known, and have the shortest (one half to three quarter inch) hair. The hair on an arctic fox strip ranges to two inches in length, and on a Finnish raccoon strip to more than three inches. This difference in hair length allows the tier to use different types of strips for different applications.

Since strips are a natural product they come in a wide range of natural colors. Of course dyed strips are available in any color you might want.

Pictured here are two examples of strip flies. The upper fly is a Haystack, tied by Tim Borski. The lower is a Bunny Booger, a creation of the author.

Four features combine to make strip flies among my personal favorites: 1) they're a fast and easy tie; 2) they look fabulous in the water; 3) they're more durable than feather flies; and 4) they catch fish like crazy. What's to not like?

Strips do have two disadvantages. If the tail is too long they tend to foul, and when they get wet they get heavy. In my opinion the advantages greatly outweigh the disadvantages.

There are only two techniques, both extremely simple, used in tying the majority of strip patterns. One is to take a short (to about two inches) section of strip and tie it in as a tail at the bend of the hook. The shank of the hook can then be dressed any way you like.

The other is to tie in a longer (four to six inch) strip at right angles to the hook shank, also at the bend of the hook, and then wrap the strip around the hook Palmer style towards the eye of the hook, where the strip is tied off.

You can tie in a loop of 15 pound mono extending out past the bend of the hook to help prevent longer strip tails from fouling.

The three patterns below illustrate how to make effective flies with these materials.

Bunny Booger

This is one of my favorite patterns for redfish and black drum in the Indian River Lagoon system.

Hook- Mustad 3407 or equivalent, #4, 2, or 1.

Tail- about one inch of bunny zonker strip. My favorite colors include brown, black, purple, and "grizzly."

Body- Another bunny zonker strip wrapped around the hook shank, hair side out.

Eyes- lead eyes, 1/50th or 1/36th ounce, depending on desired sink rate.

1. Affix hook in vise, start the thread, and tie in the lead eyes.

2. Wrap the thread to bend of the hook. Tie in a one inch long zonker strip, fur side down. Cement it in place.

3. Tie in another zonker strip at right angles to the hook shank and pointing away from you, fur side up. Wrap the thread to the lead eyes, then wind the bunny strip around the hook Palmer style.

4. Tie off the strip, build up a bit of a head, add a weedguard if desired, whip finish and cement.

Cousin Itt

This fly can be tied weighted or unweighted and is effective of on a wide variety of fish including snook, seatrout, and redfish. When tied in larger sizes it's an excellent tarpon fly.

Hook- Mustad 3407 or equivalent, #1 through 4/0.

Tail- a few strands of Krystal Flash or Flashabou.

Body- arctic fox or Finnish raccoon zonker strip wrapped around the hook shank, hair side out.

1. Affix hook in vise, start the thread, and tie in the lead eyes if desired.

2. Wrap the thread to bend of the hook. Tie in a small clump of flash, one and a half to two times as long as the hook shank.

3. Tie in the zonker strip at right angles to the hook shank and pointing away from you, fur side up. Wrap the thread to close to the hook eye, then wind the strip around the hook Palmer style, leaving plenty of room to finish the head.

4. Tie off the strip, build up a bit of a head, add a weedguard if desired, whip finish and cement.

Tarpon Itt

Hook- Daiichi Circle Wide, #4/0, or Gamakatsu SC-15, 3/0

Tail- Krystal Flash, color to complement wing.

Body- Finnish raccoon strip, color tier's choice.

Wing- a "shell" of gray squirrel tail hair (optional, but makes a crabbier looking fly).

1. Affix hook in vise, start the thread.

2. Wrap the thread to bend of the hook. Tie in a clump of flash, one and a half to two times as long as the hook shank.

3. Tie in the Finnish raccoon strip right on top of the flash, hair side up. Wrap the thread to the front of the hook leaving enough space to tie in the squirrel tail wing and finish the head, about a quarter of the way back from the eye. Wrap the strip around the hook shank Palmer style to where the thread is. Tie off the strip and cut off the excess.

4. Cut a clump of squirrel tail hair from the tail, strip out the fluff, and take a couple of wraps of thread around the butts. Slide the hair around so it lightly covers the entire top half of the fly, then wrap it well.

5. Build up and whip finish the head. Then cement or epoxy.

None of these flies mimic anything specific in the water, but all three have incredible action even while motionless and certainly suggest something alive. Tie up a few strip flies and give them an honest try, and they will become some of your favorites.

The Return of the Blonde

Before Lefty, there was Joe Brooks. Before the Deceiver, there was the Blonde.

A few years ago I was tying Deceivers to be used for little tunny behind shrimp trawlers near Cape Lookout. I needed a lot of flies in a short period of time and matching the hackle feathers for the tail was driving me batty. The ghost of Joe Brooks watched me for a bit, and then whispered in my ear, "Why not make Blondes?"

It was a great idea.

Blondes, traditional and modern. The lower fly is the traditional Blonde, tied with bucktail. The upper fly was tied using a synthetic wing material (SexyFiber) and nearly identical technique (a throat was added), but gives a very different looking result.

Although in that instance I used bucktail, with today's synthetics you can make Blondes of any length for almost any application. Since you don't have to match the feathers you can crank them out literally twice as fast as Deceivers. A well tied Blonde looks great in the water, every bit as good as a Deceiver, and the fish take them just as readily.

The late, great Joe Brooks developed this pattern during the early 1950's. Brooks was one of the early pioneers of salt water flyrodding in general, and Florida salt water fly rodding in particular. The selection of fly patterns available for saltwater use back then was tiny. Patterns which worked on everything were what was needed. Joe Brooks' series of Blonde flies filled this need admirably.

Nowadays by using synthetics Blondes can be tied as small or as large as is necessary, even to billfish sizes. Use tiny ones to imitate small glass minnows or other small forage fish. Use larger Blondes when larger bait is around. Blondes have taken most saltwater species and work on many fresh water game fish as well. By using synthetics you can easily make six or eight inch long Blondes, excellent flies for northern pike.

Blondes are minnow imitations. They should be fished as such. Short strips will generally be better than long ones, but if one retrieve doesn't work feel free to experiment.

As is often the case with saltwater flies, the pattern describes a method of tying rather than a specific color combination. An adjective is often used before the word "Blonde" to describe its color. Some examples include the "Strawberry Blonde" (red), the "Platinum Blonde" (white), the "Lime Blonde" (lime green and white), and the "Mickey Blonde" (yellow and red).

Use your imagination and experience to develop your own favorite "Blondes".

Blondes are what I refer to as an "industrial strength" fly- easy to tie, durable, effective in a variety of different situations against a wide variety of fish. Here's how to tie both the traditional bucktail version, and the updated synthetic one.

Materials
Hook: Mustad 3407 or equivalent, size tyer's choice.
Body: traditionally wide, flat Mylar tinsel; now anything or nothing, as you wish.

221

Tail: bucktail or synthetic fibers, color tier's choice.
Wing: bucktail or synthetic fibers, color tier's choice. The wing can and should be accented with Flashabou or Flashabou Accent (not available in Brooks's day).

<u>Tying the Traditional Blonde</u>
1) Sharpen the hook and fix the hook in the vise. Tie on the thread and wrap it to the hook bend.
2) Get a small bunch of bucktail, about the thickness of a pencil lead or slightly more. The fibers should extend two or three times the hook length beyond the bend of the hook. Tie the bucktail in, being sure to have the butts extend forward to a point about one-third of the distance from the hook's eye. Wrap the thread forward to secure the butts. Coat with head cement.
3) Tie in the mylar at the point where the butts from the tail stopped. Wrap the mylar back to the bend of the hook and forward again. Tie it off, the coat again with clear nail polish. Give the stuff a few moments to dry.
4) Tie in the flash before tying in the rest of the wing.
5) Cut a piece from the bucktail about twice as thick as the tail piece to tie in for the wing. It is entirely possible to cut two thinner bunches of contrasting colors in order to get a stripe, as illustrated. Whip finish and cement the head, and the fly is finished.

<u>Tying the Modern Synthetic Blonde</u>
1) Sharpen the hook and fix the hook in the vise. Tie on the thread and wrap it to the hook bend.
2) Get a tuft of synthetic fibers (Kinky Fiber, Sexy Fiber, or Angel Hair work well for this) and tie it in at the bend of the hook. As with the traditional Blonde a smooth body requires you to extend the butts forward to where the wing will be tied in.
3) If a body is desired tie in the material and wrap it to where the wing will be tied in, then tie it off. In the photo on the previous page no body was used.
4) In the fly illustrated a throat has been added on the underside of the hook.
5) Tie in the wing fibers. As with the traditional Blonde you can mix colors for effect. In the illustration two colors were used, and the flash is tied in between them. Also, you can slide the fibers to get coverage around the hook, giving the fly a bulkier appearance.
6) Taper and whip finish the head, then cement.
7) Remove the hook from the vise and brush the fly out, then trim it to shape. Witchcraft 3-D holographic eyes can be added (use Zap-A-Dap-A-Goo 2 as the adhesive) to make a very attractive finished fly.

Lefty's Deceiver

Of all the flies developed for use in salt water before the advent of synthetic materials, this one more than any other is the universal baitfish imitation. Anyone examining any flyfisher's fly box will probably find this fly in various sizes and color combinations. We all use it!

The Deceiver may be tied as an imitator or an attractor fly. The length can be anything between two and fourteen inches. Color combinations could be anything from natural minnow colors to dayglow pink and green. The fly is not a specific pattern, but a method of tying.

When dressing this fly, remember that maintaining the minnow profile is important. For this, the wing must have enough bulk, usually six or eight saddle or neck hackles, and the collar must extend well past the bend of the hook.

Although the wing is normally tied with hackle feathers, marabou or synthetics could be

The master himself, Mr. Lefty Kreh, tied this particular fly.

substituted. Certainly by using synthetics a fly with a length in excess of twelve inches can be tied, making it useful even for large pelagic species like billfish.

Bucktail is normally used for the collar, often accented with flashabou or crystal flash. Marabou is also used as a substitute for bucktail in the collar. In addition to the collar, cheeks of various materials can be tied in, as can be herl as a topping. Don't make the dressing of the fly too full or it may not sink.

The fly I've described here is the "classic" Deceiver. Remember, feel free to substitute materials as suits your needs.

Materials
Hook- Mustad 3407 or equivalent,
Wing- three or four pairs of matched saddle or neck hackles tied in at bend of hook. Colors are tier's choice. The photo shows three pairs of white hackles.
Collar- Bucktail extending back well past the bend of the hook.
Body- optional. The fly shown here lacks a body.

1. Sharpen the hook and place it into the vise. Wind on the tying thread and wrap it to the bend of the hook.
2. Match three or four pairs of hackles (neck or saddle) and tie them in at the bend of the hook. Wetting the butts with saliva first will make tying them in easier. "Matching" in this case means by length, not by color. Colors may be freely mixed. Putting some cement on the wraps will insure the feathers remain in place.
3. Wind the thread to a point about one-third of the way behind the eye of the hook. Cut some bucktail of sufficient length to reach well past the bend of the hook and tie it in. I like to tie in three small bunches of bucktail- one on each side and one on top of the hook. Before tying in the final top bunch I tie in my flash.
4. If cheeks are desired, tie them in after the collar. A topping of peacock herl is another another nice touch. Whip finish and cement the head. If eyes are desired, wait for the cement to dry and paint them on. After the paint dries, cement the head again. The fly is now finished.

Synthetic Minnows

Two examples of Synthetic Minnows. The upper fly, tied by Rick DePaiva, was made with Sexy-Fiber. The lower fly is a commercially available tie from Enrico Puglisi.

Synthetic minnows include flies such as the Enrico Puglisi series, The Polar Fiber and Kinky Fiber Minnows, or my own SexyFlies. Although they're not all tied quite the same way, they are all variations of the hi-tie, using synthetics instead of bucktail. They make beautiful, effective minnow imitations and no Florida fly fisher should be caught without a selection.

This is a somewhat generic explanation of how to tie them, using what I call a Slender Minnow as an example. It actually closely resembles the synthetic Blonde discussed earlier.

Hook- Gamakatsu SC-15, size 1 through 4/0, or equivalent
Wing– Synthetic fiber such as SexyFiber, EP Fiber, or Polar Fiber, colors tier's choice. In this example we will use sexyfiber.
Flash– Use whatever flash material you prefer. Flashabou, Flashabou Accent, Fire Fly, and many others all work well.
Eyes– The eye problem is solved in several ways. I use Witchcraft 3-D eyes, sized to fit the fly, cemented into place with Zap-A-Dap-A-Goo 2.

1) Fix the hook in the vise. Start the tying thread. Wind the thread back to the bend of the hook.

2) Take a small clump of sexyfiber, about the thickness of a pencil lead. Lie it on top of the hook shank so that part of it extends out past the hook bend, about four times the length of the hook shank. Tie it in with about six wraps of thread.

3) Since a hank of sexyfiber is about 10 inches long, quite a bit of sexyfiberwill be extended out in front of the wraps. Bend it back on itself, over the sexyfiber that has already been tied in. Cut it so that it is a half inch shorter than the sexyfiber already tied in. Place the cut sexyfiber aside for future reference. Then hold the sexyfiber that's been bent back on itself in place, and tie it in with enough wraps so that the wraps taper smoothly.

224

4) Take another piece of sexyfiber (the cut piece from step 3) and prepare to tie it in. It will be tied in directly in front of the last clump. Its ends should be 1/2 inch shorter than the last piece tied in, since you are trying to taper the length of the wing. Once you get it arranged to your satisfaction, tie it in. Then bend it back on itself and tie it in again, making it shorter again, just like in step 3.

5) Time to add the flash. Take six to eight strands of flash (we use Krystal Flash on small flies, and Fire Fly on the larger ones) and tie them in at their center, such that the strands run the length of the wing on each side.

6) Time to tie in the cheek. Take a more or less two inch long (depending on fly size) clump of sexyfiber. Hold it next to the fly-in-progress such that half the length of the clump extends back along the hook shank on your side of the hook, hiding the wraps you have already made. It should extend from past the bend of the hook forward past the eye of the hook, with its mid-point about where you tied the flash in. Tie this clump in at its mid-point. Then bend the front of this clump over the hook, along the far side of the hook shank so that it hides the wraps on that side, too. Tie it in, and taper the wraps.

7) Take one last clump of sexyfiber and tie it in in front of where the cheeks are tied in. Bend it back on itself and try to spread it out a little so it sort of wraps around everything that's already there. Make a nice, tapered head, then whip finish.

8) Take the nearly finished fly out of the vise. Place it on a firm surface. Take a small brush and brush it out, starting at the head and working backwards. Flip it over and do the same thing. Then take your scissors, hold it over a trash can, and trim it to the desired shape.

9) Remove the correct size witchcraft eye from the paper and place them sticky side up somewhere on your tying bench. Take your bodkin or a toothpick and put a drop of zap-a-dap-a-goo 2 on its point. You don't need much! Apply the drop to the back of an eye and spread it evenly. Then place the eye where you want it. Do the same for the second eye.

10) Cement or epoxy the head, then let the goo and cement dry. You've just tied a very sexy fly!

Tie the SexyFlies Foxy Lady exactly the same way, with one important difference. In the SexyFlies Slender Minnow the fibers start long and get progressively shorter as you tie them in. With the SexyFlies Foxy Lady you start very short and make them longer as you work forward. The same technique combined with a different taper pattern makes for a very different silhouette, great for imitating deep bodied baits like menhaden.

The Modern Bendback

A modern bendback, tied with synthetic materials. This one was made with Sexy Fiber.

As tied conventionally, the bendback has a chenille (of one sort or another) body and a wing of flash, bucktail, hackle feathers, and/or marabou. The length of the bucktail and marabou fibers puts an upper limit on the size of fly you can tie. These ties are generally supposed to generically imitate a small fish, shrimp, or crab.

Tied with synthetics, you can build bendbacks on any size hook you need. Tied as per instructions below they will always be minnow imitations. Polar Fiber, Kinky Fiber, EP Fiber, or Sexy Fiber all work well. If you need a faster sink rate (for tarpon flies for instance) you can wrap the hook shank with fuse wire and cover it with tying thread, or you can carry a supply of DOA Pinch Weights with you and add as much lead as you need at that moment to the hook shank by pinching a section or two of the weight onto the shank.

One of the things I like best about these flies is that in spite of how beautiful they look and how well they work they are simple, easy, fast ties. With the exception of applying the eyes the building of one of these flies should take no more than five minutes.

The single most important consideration when tying them (aside from making that all critical bend) is to tie them fairly sparsely. It's very easy to overdress them. Avoid making that mistake.

You can tie these in any color combination you desire, so the recipe below defines a style rather than a pattern. Here's how to make the updated bendback.

Materials:
-Hook: Mustad 3407, Gamakatsu SC-15, or equivalent. Size tyer's choice.
-Thread: Danville Flat Waxed Nylon, color tyer's choice.
-Wing: color combination and synthetic material used are tyer's choice. The fly in the photo was tied using SexyFiber.
-Flash: This is also the tyer's choice. I'm partial to Flashabou Accent or Krystal Flash for smaller sizes, and Fire Fly for larger flies.
-Eyes: Witchcraft 3-D Stick-on eyes, sized to fit the fly, cemented into place with Zap-A-Dap-A-Goo 2. Eye color is tyer's choice.

226

You'll also need a small brush (a fingernail brush or similar) to brush out the nearly finished fly before trimming it.

1a. <u>Slightly</u> bend the hook, place it in the vise point up, and start the tying thread. If you don't intend to weight the fly wrap the thread half way back to the bend.

1b. If you will be adding fuse wire wrap the thread all the way to the bend. Tie the wire in at the bend and wrap it half way towards the eye. Wrap the thread over the wire sufficiently to hold it down or cover it, as you prefer. The fish won't care one way or the other. When you're done the thread should be half way between the eye and the bend.

2. Take a small (20 fibers or so, more for a larger and less for a smaller fly) clump of your light colored fibers and lay them on top of the hook such that at the tail end they extend about three times the length of the hook shank past the bend. Make five or six wraps around them with the thread to hold them in place.
    Take the fibers that are facing forward and bend them back. Then tie them into place as well. If these fibers extend too far back trim the excess and save it for your next fly.

3. Tie in the flash material of your choice in the color of your choice.

4. Take a small (20 fibers or so, more for a larger and less for a smaller fly) clump of your dark colored fibers and lay them on top of the hook such that at the tail end they extend about four times the length of the hook shank past the bend. Make five or six wraps around them with the thread to hold them in place.
Take the fibers that are facing forward and bend them back. Then tie them into place as well. If these fibers extend too far back trim the excess and save it for your next fly.

5. Make a neatly tapered head, then whip finish. You can use head cement on the smaller flies, but I recommend epoxy for the tarpon sized flies. They will sink faster and last longer.

6. Use the brush to brush the wing out. Then use your scissors to trim it to shape. The wing should be attractively tapered.

7. Peel a pair of Witchcraft eyes off the backing and put them down on a clean surface, sticky side up. Use a bodkin or a toothpick to spread a small drop of Zap-A-Dap-A-Goo 2 on the sticky sides. One at a time, carefully place the eyes where you want them on the front of the fly. The Zap-A-Dap-A-Goo 2 takes about 24 hours to dry completely. Once it has dried your fly is ready to fish.

Last Word

Well, you've made it to the end of the book. Thanks for reading it!

If you're a fisherman and not a member of the Coastal Conservation Association you really should join at your earliest opportunity (see the appendix for information). The organization isn't perfect, but it's one of only a few looking out for the interests of recreational anglers. You might not agree with everything they do, but when you disagree with something the government does do you leave the country? CCA has been a tremendous force in improving Florida's (and other states) coastal fisheries for the last 20 years or so.

The forces aligning against recreational angling are organized and well financed. As an individual you can't do much about Marine Protection Areas and other results of junk science, but as the member of an organization you have some political clout. It's sad that we have to think and act this way, but if we don't defend our own interests we can be sure no one else will do it for us.

If we don't care about fish, who will? Who are the advocates for fish, if not fly anglers? As a group we are the best educated, most affluent segment of the angling community (billfishermen excepted). We have the best connections, the most political clout. We need to be organized in order to use it, though.

I cannot begin to describe how much fun it is watching a youngster battle a fish like this.

Success! It's even more fun with a positive outcome. Jacks are superb fish for kids, since they're strong and aggressive.

In a related vein, who's going to take the torch for these types of battles in the future? Your kids are. The kids down the street. The kids across town, who you don't even know. You need (yes, <u>you</u>, dear reader) to take kids fishing, every chance you get.

I was once a school teacher. I can assure you that there are a lot of kids out there who would love to go fishing but never get a chance. You may know some- your kids, your nieces or nephews, your grandchildren, or neighborhood kids. If you belong to a fishing club you could organize a fishing day for kids, something I do every year with the help of the Backcountry Fly-fishing Association, the Kiwanis Club of East Orlando, and the Boys and Girls Clubs of Central Florida.

Share your knowledge with a local scout pack. They need to know, there's a fishing merit badge. You'll be doing them a service, and you'll feel better for doing it.

So please, take a kid fishing. A future with clean water and plenty of fish depends on it.

And, as a practical matter, when you get too old and feeble to go fishing by yourself anymore, hopefully those kids you took out so many years back will now take you!

Finally, please remember to use courtesy and etiquette while out on the water. Treat others the way you'd like to be treated. And good luck to you as you're flyrodding Florida salt.

Appendix

Florida Saltwater Fishing Licenses and Fishing Regulations

This information was current at the time this book went to press. For up to the minute information visit the Florida Fish and Wildlife Conservation Commission's website at http://marinefisheries.org/license.htm, the place where I got the following information. By the way, do you have a law degree?

You do not need a Recreational Saltwater Fishing License if you are:
-Any child under 16 years of age.
-Any resident who is a member of the United States Armed Forces and not stationed in this state, when home on leave for 30 days or less, upon submission of orders.
-Any resident fishing in saltwater from land or from a structure fixed to the land.
-Any person fishing from a for-hire vessel (guide, charter, party boat) that has a valid vessel license.
-Any person fishing from a vessel, the operator of which has a valid vessel license issued in the name of the operator of the vessel.
-Any person fishing for recreational purposes from a pier that has been issued a valid pier saltwater fishing license.
-Any resident fishing for a saltwater species in fresh water from land or from a structure fixed to land.
-Any resident fishing for mullet in fresh water who has a valid Florida freshwater fishing license.
-Any resident 65 years of age or older who has in her or his possession proof of age and residency. A no-cost license under this paragraph may be obtained from any tax collector's office upon proof of age and residency and must be in the possession of the resident during hunting, freshwater fishing, and saltwater fishing activities.

There are more. I edited it somewhat in the interests of space.

What this means in English is that if you're a Florida resident and wading or fishing from shore, as long as you did not use a boat to get wherever you are, you don't need a license. If you're fishing from the boat of anyone who does not have a vessel license, or if you used a boat to get to your wade or shore fishing spot, then you do need a license.

For example, if you drove to St. George Island and were wading from the state park there, you <u>wouldn't</u> need a license. But if you drove to St. George Island, dropped a canoe in the water, paddled over to Little St. George Island, and went wading there, then you <u>would</u> need a license. Are you confused yet?

Non-Florida residents have a picture that is much clearer. With only a few exceptions you need a license regardless of where you are. If you are fishing in a boat with a guide who has a vessel license, then you don't need one yourself. If you are fishing in a kayak by yourself then you do, even if you're with a guide. His vessel license is for his vessel, which you are not in. If you are fishing from a pier that you paid to use, then the pier has a license which covers all users. You wouldn't need one.

Personally, I feel strongly that everyone who fishes in saltwater (with only a couple of exceptions) ought to need a license.

Wait, there's more. If you want to take a legal sized snook home to eat during the open season, then in addition to your license you must also have a snook stamp. If you want to have a tarpon in your possession then you must be in possession of a tarpon tag.

Where can you purchase a Florida saltwater fishing license? Many fly shops and tackle shops carry them. You can get them at many Wal-Marts. The county tax collector's offices carry them. You can get them online at the web address listed on the previous page. But for sheer, unadulterated convenience you can get a license issued over the telephone if you have a credit card by calling 888.347.4356, any time, any day.

Now, you still have to obey the fisheries regulations. A friend who works in law enforcement for the FWC tells me the fisheries regulations are the dimensions of this book, only twice as thick. It's pretty easy to break some law without even realizing it.

The state of Florida issues a very informative, quarterly, eight page update to its fishing regulations, called (quite reasonably I think) "Florida Recreational Saltwater Fishing Regulations," which has as much succinct information on the rules as most fly fishers will ever need. This publication can be picked up at the county tax collector's offices, at some tackle shops, or can be viewed online at http://marinefisheries.org/Regulations/REC_Regs_Press.pdf.

Personally, I carry one of these documents in my boat at all times and refer to it fairly frequently. There's no way I could remember even this abridged version of all the rules.

Due to the complexity of the fisheries laws and the speed at which they change I will not make any attempt to list them here. My best advice to you is to obtain the most recent quarterly update and carry it with you if you intend to keep any fish for any reason.

On Joining the Coastal Conservation Association

Do yourself and every other saltwater fisherman a favor and join CCA. If you could afford this book you can afford a tax-deductible CCA membership. Call them, or join online.

<u>Do it! Right now!!</u>

Coastal Conservation Association
6919 Portwest, Suite 100
Houston, Texas 77024
713.626.4234
800.201.FISH
www.joincca.org

Don't forget to take some children fishing!

How to Buy SexyFiber

If you found this page you must a fly tier with some degree of curiosity about SexyFiber. It's a great material for saltwater flies. My sons and I have toyed with the idea of getting into the fly materials/fly business, getting contract tiers to tie flies for us, the whole ball of wax. Right now though, it's a tiny operation out of our home. When it comes to SexyFiber, we cut it, we bag it, we ship it. Chances are good my hands were all over your order. So if you do order some, you just may stimulate the Kumiski family into a whole new line of entrepreneurial enterprise!

Retail Price- $4.25 per package. We accept personal checks, money orders, Mastercard and Visa.

Available Colors

Midnight Black
Salt 'n' Pepper
Dark Chocolate
Milk Chocolate
Chocolate Raspberry
Strawberry Blonde
Fire Red
Burgundy
Hot Pink
Powder Pink
Kelly Green
Chartreuse
Ice Blue
Deep Blue
Lavender
Purple
Fuscia
Sexy Blonde
Orange
Yellow
Gold
White

-Shortages or non-receipt must be reported to us within 30 days of the order date.
-Florida residents add 7% sales tax.
-Shipping charge if $4.95 per order.

Orders should be sent to 284 Clearview Road, Chuluota, FL 32766, or email to spotted-tail@spottedtail.com. Telephone orders may be made by calling (407) 977-5207. If the office is empty leave a message and we will return your call as soon as possible.

Index

Index, con't.

The Resource Catalog: INFORMATION!
from Argonaut Publishing Company

Books

Flyrodding Florida Salt– How and Where to Catch Fish on Flies in the Sunshine State
By Capt. John A. Kumiski

Do you like fumbling around when fishing new areas, trying to fit all the pieces together so that you can find a few fish?

This book contains all the information you need to fly fish successfully almost anywhere on Florida's lengthy coastline. Featuring interviews with Florida's top fly anglers, the book solves the problem of "how-to" by explaining what tackle to use, which techniques to try, and what you can expect to catch.

It solves the "where-to" problem with interviews of Florida's premier fly fishing guides. In these interviews they reveal their favorite spots and how to fish them, including many of their most closely guarded secrets.

It solves the "with what" problem by telling you what flies you need in order to have success, and how to tie them or where to buy them.

"The best part of Flyrodding Florida Salt is the extensive where to go section that blankets the coast by area with not only tips on specific fishing spots, but areas for wading, hand powered boats, boat fishing, best flies and techniques, access, local fly shops, boat rentals, guides, and other attractions and accommodations. For any saltwater fly rodder living in Florida or going there sometime, this book is a must read." **-C. Boyd Pfeiffer**

Before <u>you</u> visit the Sunshine State, <u>get this book</u>!

Flyrodding Florida Salt, 8 1/2 x 11", 240 pp., paperback,…………………………..……$29.95

Fishing the Space Coast- An Angler's Guide (Ponce de Leon Inlet to Sebastian Inlet)
by Capt. John A. Kumiski

Do You Want to Catch Fish on Florida's Space Coast?
This stretch of the Florida's Atlantic Coast and the adjacent Indian River Lagoon system offers world class angling for redfish, black drum, spotted seatrout, tripletail, and more. In addition, snook, tarpon, cobia, Spanish and king mackerel, little tunny, jack crevalle, bluefish, barracuda, sharks, and many other species can be found in these waters at various times of the year. Do you know how to catch them?
This book will make you a better fisherman. You will learn:
*How-to choose rods, reels, lines, lures, baits, rigging, and techniques that work here.
*When to fish. The fishery changes with the seasons. This book will help you adjust your strategies.
*Where to fish. Aerial photographs pinpoint hot spots all along the Space Coast.

Many of the Space Coast's finest fishing guides shared secrets contained in this book, such well known anglers as Eric Davis, Kent Gibbens, Fred Hill, Mike Hakala, Terry Parsons, Rodney Smith, and several more.

Fishing the Space Coast, 8 1/2 x 11", 120 pp., paperback, $19.95

Flyfishing for Redfish- The Complete Guide to Catching Red Drum on Flies
by Capt. John A. Kumiski

Flyfishing for Redfish will easily teach you how to catch more redfish by sharing these secrets: -how the fish behave; which tackle and flies to use; how tides affect the fish; how to find and see the fish; how to present your fly so the fish will eat it; tactics for wading and for fishing from a boat; who and where the guides and fly shops are in every state where redfish are found, complete with phone numbers; what flies you need and how to tie them (or where to buy them); and MORE! If you want to catch redfish on fly tackle, then you need this book!

Flyfishing for Redfish, 5 1/2 x 8 1/2", 160 pp., paperback, $19.95

Sport Fish of Florida   by Vic Dunaway

Vic's long needed book identifies 231 species of Florida fishes, everything from billfish to bait-fish. All are illustrated in full color and include scientific and common names, distinguishing features, food value, average and record sizes, range throughout Florida, habitats, game qualities, and best fishing methods.

Sport Fish of Florida, 5 1/2 x 8 1/2", 256 pp., paperback, $16.95

Vic Dunaway's Complete Book of Bait, Rigs, and Tackle   by Vic Dunaway

This book covers everything that might be implied by the title-spin, plug, and fly tackle, hooks, sinkers, floats, lines, leaders, knots, fishing accessories, and rigging methods for both natural and artificial baits.

Vic Dunaway's Complete Book of Bait, Rigs, and Tackle, 5 1/2 x 8 1/2", 224 pp., paper-back, $16.95

The Florida Atlas and Gazetteer   from DeLorme Mapping

Are you tired of getting lost trying to find those out-of-the way fishing spots? The Florida Atlas and Gazetteer solves your problem! Containing detailed road maps of the entire state, this book is an invaluable resource when finding your way from point A to point B on Florida's highway system is your highest priority.

The Florida Atlas and Gazetteer, 15 1/2 x 11", 128 pp., paperback. $19.95

-Fishing Maps-

Pasadena Top Spot Fishing Maps pride themselves on making reliable, accurate, waterproof charts with well marked fishing areas. Important information such as the best times of year, types of fish available, artificial fish habitats, and underwater structure are all shown in an easy to read format.

-Homosassa area, N-201
-Tampa Bay area, N-202
-Charlotte Harbor area, N-203
-Ten Thousand Islands area, N-204
-Everglades Park area, N-206
-Florida Bay area, N-207
-Middle Keys area, N-208
-Lower Keys area, N-209
-Miami area, N-211
-Fort Lauderdale area, N-212
-Palm Beach area, N-213
-Jupiter to Stuart area, N-214
-Stuart to South Fort Pierce and St. Lucie area, N-215
-Fort Pierce to Vero Beach area, N-216
-Sebastian Inlet and Palm Bay area, N-217
-Cape Canaveral area, N-218
-Mosquito Lagoon area, N-219
-Daytona Beach to Jacksonville area, N-221
Port St. Joe to Apalachicola; Carabelle to Lighthouse Point, N-230
-Panacea to Apalachee Bay; Steinhatchee to Cedar Key North, N-231

Top Spot Maps, $15.95 each

-Special Reports-

Special Reports by Capt. John Kumiski provide the detailed how-to and where-to information you need to step into a new area or situation and fish confidently and successfully. The five page reports are updated constantly.

The Keys
-How to Find and Catch Bonefish on Long Key,   SR-LK
-How to Find and Catch Bonefish at Pennekamp State Park,   SR-KL
-Fishing Keys Bridges, SR-KB
-Fishing the Keys from a Houseboat, SR-KH
The Everglades
-How to Find and Catch Fish at Flamingo, Everglades National Park, SR-FF
-Day Trips for Canoeing Anglers from Flamingo, Everglades National Park, SR-CF
-How to Find and Catch Backcountry Snook from Flamingo, Everglades N. P., SR-FS
-Fishing The Cape Sable Area, Everglades National Park, SR-CS

Special Reports, con't.

-Fishing Chatham Bend, Everglades National Park, SR-CB
-Fishing Lostman's River, Everglades National Park, SR-LR
-Fishing and Canoe Camping the Everglades, SR-EC
-Fishing for Cape Sable Seatrout, SR-ES
-Fishing the Everglades from a Houseboat, SR-EH
-How to Find and Catch Fish in the10,000 Islands, Everglades National Park, SR-TI
-Everglades Tarpon, SR-ET

Jacksonville and Vicinity
-How to Find and Catch Redfish in Nassau Sound, SR-NS
-Fishing for Redfish in Jacksonville's Backcountry, SR-JR
-Fishing Opportunities in Cumberland Sound, SR-OC

East Central Florida
-How to Find and Catch Redfish at the Merritt Island National Wildlife Refuge, SR-M
-Fishing at Ponce Inlet and New Smyrna Beach, Canaveral National Seashore, SR-CN
-Fishing the Banana River Manatee Refuge, SR-MR
-Tactics for Sebastian River Tarpon, SR-SR
-Orlando as a Fishing Destination, SR-OF
-Fly Fishing for Bass and Bream in the Wekiva River, SR-WR
-How to Catch Summer Seatrout in the Mosquito Lagoon, SR-SS
-Floating Florida's Spring Creeks for Bass and Bream, SR-SC
-Fishing the Intracoastal Waterway at Daytona/New Smyrna, SR-DB
-Fishing Opportunities Along Cape Canaveral Beaches, SR-CC
-Fishing Opportunities Along the Jupiter Coast, SR-JF

Southwest Florida
-How to Find and Catch Fish in Bull Bay, Charlotte Harbor, SR-CH
-Fishing Captiva Pass and Redfish Pass, SR-CP
-How to Find and Catch Pine Island Redfish, SR-PI
-Fishing at Cayo Costa State Park, SR-CY
-Southwest Florida's Beach Tarpon Run, SR-BT
-Charlotte Harbor's Winter Snook, SR-WS

West Central Florida
-Fly Fishing for Homosassa Tarpon, SR-HT
-Fishing Opportunities at Cedar Key, SR-CK

Saltwater Fly Fishing
-How to Choose your Fishing Guide, SR-CG
-Constructing Saltwater Fly Rod Leader Systems, SR-LS
-Practical Fly Selection for Florida's Saltwater, SR-SF
-Getting Started in Saltwater Fly Fishing, SR-GS
-A Primer for Waders, SR-PW
-How to Increase Your Ability to See Fish, SR-HS
-How to Fight Big Fish Successfully with Light Tackle, SR-BF

Special Reports, con't.

-Fly Fishing for Jack Crevalle, SR-JC
-Getting Started in Tying Flies for Saltwater, SR-FT
-Tying and Using Crab Patterns, SR-UC
-A Guide to Fly Fishing from Canoes, SR-FC
Miscellaneous
-Improve Your Fishing Photography, SR-FP
-Practical Tips for Redfish on the Surface, SR-RT

Special Reports, $6.95 each, or three for $17.95

Videos and DVD's

Here at Argonaut Publishing Company we have to admit that we prefer books. However, some videos are of such extremely high quality, and can illustrate some topics so much better than can the written word, that we feel compelled to offer the following, with our highest recommendations.

The Art of Fly Casting with Chico Fernandez

Filmed in a specially constructed studio, this film shows the difference between a good cast and a bad cast and shows how best to execute the former. Chico has been fly casting for over 40 years, and this is the finest, most comprehensive video available on how to fly cast.

The Art of Fly Casting with Chico Fernandez, VHS, 37 minutes, $29.95

Borski Ties Flies, Volume 1, featuring Tim Borski

In the studio, innovative tier and artist Tim Borski shows how to tie five of his flies (the Green Zima, Haystack, laid up tarpon fly, Big Orange Shark Fly, and Chernobyl Crab) in an easy, step by step format. Then he goes out on the water to show how to fish them. The on-the-water footage, all shot on location in the Florida Keys, is simply spectacular.

Borski Ties Flies, Vol. 1, DVD, 62 minutes, $24.95

Shipping Information

If your order is between:	Standard shipping cost is:	Priority shipping cost is:
$1.00 to 30.00	$4.95	$6.95
$30.01 to 65.00	$7.95	$9.95
$65.01 to 100.00	$10.95	$14.95
Over $100.00	No charge	$25.00

See the order form on the next page!

Order Form

You can contact us by mail, email, telephone, fax (call first!), or <u>order from our online catalog</u>. If sending a check, please make payable to:

Argonaut Publishing Company, 284 Clearview Road, Chuluota, FL 32766
-407.977.5207 (phone and fax)
-email: spottedtail@spottedtail.com
-Website: www.spottedtail.com

If there is no one in the office when you call, please leave a message. Please- speak slowly!
1) Tell us who you are and where you want the order shipped.
2) Tell us what you want to order.
3) Tell how you would like to pay (if by credit card, please leave the number and expiration date).
4) Florida residents, be prepared to pay 7 percent sales tax.
5) Shipping costs depend on what you order and how you want it shipped (see chart on previous page.) Standard shipping is free on orders over $100.00. On in-stock items, orders usually ship the same day or the next day.

Thank you for your business!

Ship to:_____

Street_____

City_____ State_____ Zip_____

Phone_____

Quantity	Description (title and author)	Price	Total

Method of Payment: Credit Card Check Money Order	Merchandise Total	
Credit Card #_____	FL Delivery, add 7% sales tax	
Expiration Date _____	Shipping and Handling (see p. 239)	
Signature _____	**Amount Enclosed**	